worship

culture
and
theology

David N. **power**, OMI

The Pastoral Press

Washington, DC

ISBN: 0-912405-77-5

The Pastoral Press
225 Sheridan Street, N.W.
Washington, D.C. 20011
(202) 723-1254

The Pastoral Press is the publications division of the National
Association of Pastoral Musicians, a membership organization
of musicians and clergy dedicated to fostering the art of musical liturgy.

Printed in the United States of America

Acknowledgments

Acknowledgment is gratefully made to the publishers and others for granting permission to use again, sometimes in edited form, the following: "Cult to Culture: The Liturgical Foundation of Theology," *Worship* 54 (1980), pp. 482-495; "A Theological Perspective on the Persistence of Religion," *Concilium* 81 (1973), pp. 91-105; "Two Expressions of Faith: Worship and Theology," *Concilium* 82 (1973), pp. 95-103; "Cultural Encounter and Religious Expression," *Concilium* 102 (1975), pp. 102-112; "Liturgy in Search of Religion," *Philippine Studies* 28 (1980), pp. 344-353; "Liturgy and Culture," *East Asian Pastoral Review* 1984/4, pp. 348-360; "The Odyssey of Man in Christ," *Concilium* 112 (1978) pp. 100-111; "Households of Faith in the Coming Church," *Worship* 57 (1983), pp. 237-254; "Liturgical Praxis: A New Consciousness at the Eye of Worship," *Worship* 61 (1987), pp. 290-305; "Hope Is the Joy of Saying Yes," *Pastoral Music* 11 (1986), pp. 20-26; "On Blessing Things," *Concilium* 178 (1985), pp. 24-39; "The Sacramentalization of Penance," *The Heythrop Journal* XVI (1977), pp. 5-22; "Confession as Ongoing Conversion," *The Heythrop Journal* XVI (1977), pp. 180-190; "The Fate of Confession: Editorial Conclusions," *Concilium* 190 (1987), pp. 127-131; "Let the Sick Man Call," *The Heythrop Journal* XVII (1978), pp. 256-270; "The Funeral Rites for a Suicide and Liturgical Developments," *Concilium* 179 (1985), pp. 75-81; "Le Calendrier de l'église. Les Saints sont-ils négligés ou mal représentés?," *La Vie Spirituelle* 69 (1989), pp. 691-699; "People at Liturgy," *Concilium* 170 (1983), pp. 8-14.

Chapter 10, "When to Worship is to Lament," is previously unpublished.

Dedicated to

Archbishop Denis E. Hurley, O.M.I.,

Archbishop of Durban,

President of the International Commission for English in the Liturgy,

in whose ministry

thirst for justice and zeal for true worship

have met.

Contents

Preface

SOME TIME AGO, VIRGIL FUNK OF THE NATIONAL ASSOCIATION OF
Pastoral Musicians suggested to me that I make a collection of
past articles for publication in a single volume. I had put aside
the thought for further consideration until August 1989, when
I attended the congress of the Societas Liturgica at York, Eng-
land, on Liturgy and Inculturation. It occurred to me that over
a space of nearly twenty years I had in sundry ways addressed
that issue. Hence I offer here a number of articles chosen on
the basis of a connection between advancing true worship and
cultural sensitivity. In some cases I have combined more than
one article in revised form under one title, but by and large
the editing or revising has not been extensive. If any reader
wants to mark progress, it is possible to find the date for each
article in the list of acknowledgments.

My attention to cultural realities has been enhanced by
working with a community of international students of the
Oblates of Mary Immaculate in Rome during the seventies, by
participating in the work of the editorial board of the international theological journal *Concilium* from 1969 until the
present, by the influence of colleagues and students at The
Catholic University of America since 1977, by the challenge of
collaborative study in the North American Academy of Liturgy, and by visits to the African, Asian, Australian, and Latin
American continents. I like to think that the cultural richness
and pluralism of my native country, Ireland, sowed the seeds

of this interest, as it certainly bred an ear for the poetic and an awareness of the conflicts of impinging cultures, replete with their religious ambiguities.

Though the articles here collected were written at different times and for different reviews, there is an order in the way in which I now present them. The articles in the first section of the book work out some positions on theology's role in mediating cult to culture, on the basis of a working understanding of what constitutes culture and what constitutes religion. In the second section, this methodology is addressed to specific instances of the encounter between liturgy and culture. In the third section, I have placed some articles that describe what I see as a new consciousness emerging at the heart of worship within communities that are particularly sensitive to the tasks facing humanity globally in forging a future that confronts the deep wounds that the present has inherited from the past and tends to exacerbate. In the fourth grouping of articles, important forms of worship are examined in this new context, particularly those of remembering, story-telling, lamenting, praising, and blessing. In the fifth part of the book, I have placed articles that address penance, sickness, and death. These show how past developments in these rites have been tightly linked with cultural perceptions and forms, and suggest what development might take place in an age conscious at one and the same time of historicity, of global interaction and of cultural diversity. A final article serves as both retrospect and prospect.

Liturgy's pertinence to culture is not simply a matter of allowing liturgies to develop which are appropriate to the African, Asian, and Latin American continents. It is a matter of deep importance to the northern hemisphere in negotiating the perilous journey through the sea of cultural change that it is now undertaking, one that goes far beyond finding the right words for the right melody or adjudicating between organ and guitar, and between marble altars and wooden tables. It cuts deep into many of the supposed imperatives, as into the imagery used to represent God, the world, the church, and the human venture.

Historical fact and current issues both have an important

place in these articles. In taking a distinctively theological approach, however, to the relation between liturgy and culture, my concern has been to find the models which allow insight. The use of anthropological and hermeneutical approaches is therefore quite apparent, as is also the effort to grasp what was taking place in more communal and social terms at any given point in history. If one thing more than others has developed in my work over the period of twenty years, it is probably the way of relating liturgy to praxis. The question becomes much more clearly that of the world to which people give shape through worship and ritual, and of how they relate practical, social, and political concerns to the memory of Christ and the worship of God. There is here a realization that liturgy can actually impede the transformation which of its nature it intends, and that different persons bring different interests and hopes to liturgy, even when joined in the same assembly or social ritual. In keeping with these perceptions, I have begun to focus more on the liberative power of the memory of Christ's Pasch and on the ways in which this is brought to act. This also means discerning the present time's vital dilemmas, which have to be brought consciously to mind in worship, in a way that in a deepening of faith recognizes both cultural pluriformity and global solidarity.

In 1971, only three years after I had completed my doctorate, I was invited to join Adrian Hastings in giving a series of lectures on ministry in Southern Africa, where we spoke in Pretoria, Roma, Durban, East London, and Cape Town. When expressing thanks at the end of our stay in Durban, Archbishop Denis Hurley voiced the hope that in years to come I would remember that the church of Southern Africa helped to launch me on the way of theological inquiry and writing with a global perspective. That debt is acknowledged in the dedication of this volume, as is my respect for one who has so admirably combined universal service, the quest for justice, and a zeal for God's worship.

I cannot close these introductory words without expressing appreciation for the work done by Larry Johnson, director of The Pastoral Press, in bringing these articles together in a form suitable for publishing. His has been a labor without whose assistance I might have continued to procrastinate. Thanks are also due to the Oblates of Mary Immaculate of the Province of Our Lady of Hope, particularly to its successive provincials and to the community in Washington, who towards the end of the seventies welcomed me to their midst and have afforded me the opportunity to pursue teaching, theological inquiry, and writing.

David N. Power, O.M.I.

RELIGION, WORSHIP, THEOLOGY

1

Cult to Culture:
The Mediating Role
of Theology

IN ITS PUBLIC EXPRESSION OF FAITH, THE CHURCH HAS ALWAYS used different styles. In general it is possible to distinguish between liturgical language, the language of devotion, doctrinal statement, and theology. Ideally, these are complementary to one another. In practice they are neither clearly distinguishable nor always in harmony. In each kind of expression, one has to discern between cultural factors and that which is essential to the mediation of faith.

The central interest of this article is the role which theology plays in mediating cult to culture, in light of the pluralism of cultures in the tradition of the church and of the greater conscious attention to culture that marks the current period of liturgical change. In the current situation, Bernard Lonergan has described the role of theology as that of reflecting on the significance and value of a religion in a culture and writes of "a notion of theology that integrates a religion with the culture in which it functions."[1] By way of contrast with the past, he distinguishes this notion from that which sees theology as the science about God and about all things in relation to God. However, though it did so less consciously, it needs to be observed that theology always conjoined faith, religious expres-

3

sion, and culture in some way and that it operated within given cultural and religious contexts that were in fact either culturally pluralistic or in the process of cultural change. Religion is a complexity of beliefs, practices, institutions, and ethics that refer to the ultimate. It finds its place within a culture primarily through its forms of symbolic expression, for both culture and religion take their hold among a people through the symbolic. Indeed, it is at the juncture of the symbolic that religion either fits into a culture or is at odds with it.

For the church, liturgy is at the heart of religion.[2] It is the central form of symbolic expression, that in which the church as church worships God and enters into communion with the holy. It is not the sole form of symbolic expression, but the failure of its mediating role occurs precisely in its inability to offer a symbolic expression in which the majority of people in a culture can dwell. It is then that masses of people resort to other forms of devotion, or accommodate liturgical symbolism to more popular forms of expression and a more popular sense of the holy, in ways not originally intended in the formation of the liturgical rites. Hence it may be asked how theology, given its role of relating religion and culture, serves the integration of Christian worship into a culture.

The question is asked against the background of the inadequate distinction between liturgy, devotion, and theology. All three are words that relate humanity to God, within the Christian faith. Consequently, they are not meant to be independent of each other and will of necessity intersect at times, even in the forms of expression. In broad terms, liturgy is the symbolic expression of the mystery of the pasch that stands at the heart of Christian life. Devotion is used here as a specific way to designate the affective. It is found within liturgy as elsewhere, but the more cult is extraneous to culture the more devotion overflows into other forms of expression. Theology is by definition cognitive and explanatory, but it will not subsist as an ecclesial service if it is not in harmony with the affective, and indeed if it does not include its own specific ways of expression that appeal to the affective. How theology can serve the interaction and harmony of the liturgical and the devotional within a culture, is the question of this article.

It will be shown first of all how theology endeavored to perform this function in earlier periods. First, it employed the method of typology in an age that saw created reality as a participation in the divine mystery. Then it worked through metaphysical theory in the great cultural upheavals of the High Middle Ages. By way of contrast, it will then be shown how in today's situation, where people are more culturally conscious, it has to employ the elements of cognitional theory, or more broadly all that comes into conscious retrieval with the sciences of the human subject and of human expression.

TYPOLOGY

Typology[3] played a great part in aiding the transition from Covenant worship to Christian sacrament, and in mediating this sacrament to a culture engrossed by mystery. Christ and the church were seen both as realizations of historical figures or types, and as earthly manifestations of a divine mystery and a heavenly liturgy. The large number of liturgical families, rooted in the primacy of the local church, are evidence of considerable cultural diversity in early centuries. Cultural adaptation was the rule of the day. It touches on such things as language, space, ritual, ministry, practices of initiation and penance, and the imagery of the eucharistic prayer. Across cultures, Christian writers employed a typology that served to mediate worship to culture as a participation in divine mystery and in the mystery of Christ's pasch. This was related to a neoplatonist kind of world-view that appears to have been intercultural, allowing for some diversity within it.

Human life in particular was elevated by the sense that it partook of a divine energy and was an image of a divine nature. All creation, however, though often beset by the diabolical, could be elevated to share in this mystery and, blessed by God's word, could speak in figurative and typological forms of divine mysteries. Ritual action, the spoken word, music, the visual, the configuration of space, were all apt media for expressing the great Christian mystery, but they did this in a variety of forms from one cultural milieu to another. The basilicas of Rome, Syria, Byzantium, and Ravenna are all fit places for divine worship, but their inner plan and their visual form are quite different.

Three questions can be asked about the success of this typological method as theological mediation. First, did it eventually accentuate the visual to the detriment of the word and in that way ultimately allow for the language barrier that developed between clergy and people? Second, did it mean that the devotional was often satisfied outside official worship? Third, did it neglect the exigencies of popular religious feeling, and contribute to the concomitance of two kinds of religious expression, one more popular and the other more clerical? The increase in importance in devotion to the martyrs, pilgrimage to their tombs and the appeal to their intercession, the subsequent rise of interest in the holy person and in hagiography, the interest in a variety of blessings and relics, were never quite fully integrated into liturgy, whatever the attempts, and increasingly constituted a world of devotion that existed alongside it, rather than as one with it. The episcopal stational liturgy at Rome was a splendid liturgy of inclusion, spreading out over the city and all the places graced by martyrs' tombs, but it was a courtly rather than a popular worship.

In the last centuries of the first millenium, the Carolingians used the model of the Roman liturgy, both its texts and its inclusiveness, as a way of mediating one worship to one empire, in a world view that conjoined the temporal and the holy as one magnificent divine creation.[4] The populace, however, on the whole did not appreciate the typological. Their piety was fed by an allegory that stirred emotion and appealed to the dramatic. The courtly liturgy gave rise to a sense of two worlds, the clerical and the lay, or the monastic and the lay, the holy and the ordinary, in which latter worlds blessings and saintly protection were needed to combat diabolical intrusions. The image employed by ecclesiastical writers of the Body of Christ composed of two sides, the one clerical and the other lay, was one way of trying to unite the two worlds, and it endured into the twelfth century.[5] However, it could not overcome the split, and the world around the church was changing in ways that required the vision of faith to accommodate a new temporal order. How could faith and worship allow for the sense of the individual person as one not totally immersed into a social order, and how could the independence of the temporal from the spiritual be expressed within a vision that was still that of the universe as a divine creation?

MEDIEVAL THEOLOGY, DEVOTION, WORSHIP

Though people may not have talked about it that way, the world of the twelfth and thirteenth centuries was a world of great cultural upheaval.[6] New economic forces were at work. There were new forms of social belonging and social division. There was a new sense of time in the perception of history as a long-term process, one which began to replace the simple contrast between human time and eternity. There was a new scientific and philosophical interest in things themselves, rather than simply in their participation in a higher reality. There was a new sense of the human as person and in the cognitive and affective operations of the person, which gave one independent movement and action and free choice, allowing greater independence from social and external determinations. In such a situation, though the religious universe was one in which eternal verities were expressed, it was not totally comprehensive, and how particulars related to the universal was a new question. Another new question was the relation between truth and the symbolic, between truth and the affective.

In this context monastic theology and the new scholastic theology often seemed to be at odds with one another. The monks feared a discourse which would turn out to be wholly human, a dialectic and a theorizing which would subject the word of God to the tools of human artifice and the reasoning of the human mind, but which would lose contact with the God who spoke through that word. The monks wanted wisdom, not grammar and philosophy. They sought prayer and contemplation, which would unite with God, not an analysis of human concepts about God. Whether at Cluny or at Citeaux, they believed in the mediation of the symbolic in worship, in Scripture, and in visual forms. Theology was to be a commentary upon and an invitation to these.

Scholasticism, on the other hand, faced the cultural realities more squarely. It could not be content with allegorism, which could give way either to errant piety or to scepticism. Along with its attention to the letter in explaining Scripture, as foundation to the other senses, it sought modes of argument and a theory which could foster a clearer relation of the Christian faith to the emerging culture and the new human interests.

The great achievement of Saint Thomas Aquinas was to find in the metaphysics of Aristotle, who had become known through the Arab commentators, that which complemented the Platonic vision of God, the universe, and humankind.[7]

It would be a great misunderstanding of Scholasticism, however, to miss how deeply grounded it was in the devotional. These devotional forms, however, themselves emerged within the newly emerging cultural world. The achievements of scholastic theology, on the one hand, were made possible by the new philosophy of nature and of the human. On the other hand, they were largely fed by a devotion that took root at the popular level. Evangelical movements claimed the Gospel and the ideals of Christian fellowship for the people. They fostered a new sense of the common Christian vocation, a popular interest in the word of God, and an ideal of Christian communion in which all had an egalitarian part. The mendicant orders, the home of scholastic theologians, fostered devotions that appealed to this religious sense. These included popular preaching of the Gospel, its presentation in graphic forms such as the crib and the way of the cross, practices of contemplation for all, forms of the divine office or of devotions (e.g., the rosary) that were accessible to all believers, and devotion to Christ present in the eucharist that appealed to the visual rather than to the word which could not be understood.

In mediating cult to culture, the dilemma of scholasticism was in great part that liturgy as such did not change. Hence the devotion which fostered popular piety, a new sense of the lay Christian, and the spirituality of the mendicant orders themselves, remained largely outside the sphere of official worship. A second dilemma was that the prevailing vision of the world remained that of an ordered universe, one hierarchically structured in the plan of creation and in the Christian economy, and hence one that allowed for degrees of both natural and spiritual perfection.

Within this compass, we can nonetheless see how the appeal to metaphysical theory was employed to mediate worship to culture. The analysis of human act that philosophy made possible could be integrated into a theology of faith and charity, so that one could see the place that faith played as a human act in sacrament. This opened the way to clarifying the role of the individual person and of personal devotion. The structures of the cognitional, relating sense experience to intelligence, had also been clarified, with the result that it was possible to give proper place to sign and signification in explaining sacrament and its sanctifying power.[8] Even the affective had to some extent been allowed for in the distinction between *voluntas ut natura* and the human act of willing. Within what remained a hierarchical vision of the church, owing much to the influence of Pseudo-Dionysius, Thomas Aquinas took over the image of the sacramental character.[9] He located it as a power in the intellect and developed it so that both priest and faithful could be seen to have their part in Christ's priesthood by embracing the world of meaning that Christ's redemption had inaugurated. While thoroughly and emphatically underlining the gratuity of faith, Aquinas was able to link participation in the sacraments and the gift of grace through them with sign and signification. On the one hand, this meant that they were appreciated as human acts and that God's economy was appreciated as a mediation through the humanity, first of Jesus Christ and then of the church. On the other hand, it meant that the economy itself was given its own intrinsic intelligibility, its *rationes convenientiae* or *necessitas*, and that partaking in the sacrament enabled people to participate in a godly order in a way that suited and perfected human nature, directed by a faith that allowed for understanding and consent.

The intelligibility of the sacrament to the culture, the possibility of grasping what it signified and of embracing this in faith, was largely opened up by analogies. Some of these Aquinas took from philosophy, so that they were open to the apprehension of the erudite. Others were more clearly rooted in the immediacy of experience and in the order of things that all could perceive around them

The most fundamental analogy of all, that which allowed Aquinas to wed signification with causality in explaining the sacraments, was the analogy of being. It is the very difficulty of this analogy which made it hard to present in popular form and gave rise to a rather mechanistic explanation of causality in later theology and catechetical instruction. On the one hand, it allows us to see the total dependence in being on God as cause and the total gratuity of created being. On the other hand, with what was kept of Platonism, it allows us to see sacramental grace as participation in the mystery of the Incarnate Word and in the divine nature itself. When Aquinas included human acts in the order of sacramental causality, he did not attribute an agent role to faith. Rather, he placed it on the side of receptivity, as that without which the grace of the sacrament could not be received. He made an interesting distinction between the acts of the subject in the sacrament of penance and the acts of the subject in baptism.[10] In the latter, the subject's contrition and confession constituted the matter of the sacrament. Their conjunction with the act of the priest constituted the sacramental sign, and hence the cause. In baptism, no such conjunction was allowed, although faith is necessary to sanctification. This is because faith is totally gratuitous. Like being itself, it cannot be said in any way to be the result of human agency. The total gratuity and dependency of being that grounds the relation of the created to the creator is carried over into sacrament and embraces the role of faith that underlies all human participation in the sacramental order.

A similarly erudite use of analogy occurred in the explanation of the presence of Christ in the sacrament, allowing for the differentiation between it and physical presence, without reducing it to a sign that appealed only to subjective response.[11] The analogy here was with the Aristotelian notion of substance and substantial change, canonized in Catholic theology by the use of the word "transubstantiation." This proved useful to Aquinas even when dealing with some of the phenomena of popular piety, such as bleeding hosts and ostensory visions,[12] though it was hardly very accessible to the imagination and minds of those who saw such things. What it does show, however, is that Aquinas knew the need to keep his theology tied to the practice of faith and devotion.

Other analogies, of more common impact, appealed to people's experience of life, both personal and social. Thus the root analogy to explain the sevenfold sacramental economy was taken from what people knew about the gift and the development of life itself.[13] Birth, increase of strength, nourishment, remedy, and the social order that fosters and protects human life, offered an image and intelligibility to the entire sacramental system. The analogy of sacrifice, destined to play such a role in Catholic theology, is incomprehensible outside the social order of the day and outside the changes in the penitential system that provided the context of much devotion.

When Anselm offered the analogy of satisfaction to explain the worth of Christ's redemptive death, he had a twofold grounding for it in the world around him.[14] For one thing, the society to which he belonged was concerned with the proper demands of justice. However much beneficence was a part of the social order, no order could exist without meeting the demands of a just and equitable system. Where order was disturbed, justice required that it be restored by procedures of satisfaction for injury, that included both restitution and punishment. Solidarity allowed that what the individual owed could in some measure, if not totally, be met by others, but what was due to the order could not be neglected. For another thing, the church's penitential system had adapted to this sense of a just order, inclusive of its notions of solidarity. This included the practice of confession of sin, the imposition of penances, the transmutation of penances into prayer in an appeal to the merits of Christ and the saints, or into other salutary acts such as pilgrimage, as well as the appeal to the prayer of the priest and of the monk. There was an immediacy to their experience which helped people to understand what it meant to say that Christ in his passion had satisfied for sin and that this satisfaction was operative in the sacramental system, especially penance and the Mass.

Aquinas, as we know, amended Anselm's soteriology by introducing the concept of sacrifice.[15] This is a highly cultic image, one that abounds in biblical and patristic writing and that is invoked in Christian celebration. He was able to balance off the concepts of love, offering, and vicarious satisfaction in describing an order which weds love and justice in a divine harmony. This image of sacrifice affected his eucharistic theology in two ways, not perfectly in harmony with each other, but both related to liturgical practice. In his article on the sacrifice of Christ, Saint Thomas took over Augustine's definition in Book 10, chapter 6, of the *City of God*. There sacrifice is explained as the perfect act of mercy which seeks the communion (*societas*) of all in God, and this is how Thomas explains the nature and efficacy of Christ's sacrifice, allying it with the notion of a vicarious satisfaction performed in an excess of love and an excess of suffering. Since Augustine gives his definition in a context where he invokes the eucharist as the sacrifice of the whole body, head and members, its pertinence to eucharistic and sacramental communion is clear. Hence, Aquinas could say that the eucharist operates as both sacrifice and sacrament, because it represents the sacrifice of Christ, the benefits of which are received in communion, sacrament of charity and ecclesial unity.[16] Aquinas, however, was also familiar with the practice of having priests offer the eucharist for the living and the dead, as this had grown through the spread of the stipendiary system. As an offering, this too had to be worked into his theology. He distinguished the efficacy of this offering from the efficacy of the sacrament, first by simply saying that it was possible to make the distinction, and secondly by measuring the sacrificial efficacy by the devotion of those who made the offering, joining this prayer to the prayer of Christ.[17] Later, what loomed largest in the integration of his theology into the life of the church was the sacrificial efficacy of the priestly offering, rather than the sacramental efficacy of communion that joined the people in holy communion with the sacrifice of Christ. This, no doubt, was greatly due to the infrequency of sacramental communion and to increased reliance on Mass-offerings, for the living and the dead. The result shows the weakness of an analogy, whatever its intent, that is not closely allied to ritual practice, as well as the tendency of what is the practice to take over and mutate the original theological analogy.

Analogy's function is to serve the right use of symbolic language in worship and the doxology of the church. If that purpose is to be served, appeal to it has to be rooted in the word of faith as it is operative in liturgy. In the immediacy of faith experience, the symbolic is first order language and precedes the second order language of theology. It is a comprehensive language in its appeal to the sensory as well as to the mind, and in its affective appeal and bonding. Theological language and explanation may serve as an explanation of what is symbolically expressed, or it may serve as a corrective of the turns that the symbolic takes. If it loses connection with the practice and the symbols that in effect involve the faithful, it ceases to perform its ancillary function. When it ceases to mediate the tradition to the culture, there emerge two worlds. The first is that which remains embedded as tradition in the texts. The second is the performative symbolic world of priests and people, with its new accumulation of sacramental and devotional practices.

CONTEMPORARY MEDIATION

The need for a fresh kind of theological mediation is clear from the rather ambiguous results of liturgical change and revision, which in fact are too varied to be comprehensively grasped. In fostering liturgical renewal and revision, the Second Vatican Council appealed to the scholastic stress on signification and augured a liturgy that in its words, signs, and ritual would be comprehensible to the faithful, so that their participation might be enhanced.[18] In the midst of the liturgical renewal's real acceptance, other things also occurred. There were those who found this translated liturgy uninteresting. Others, some with their foot in a passing culture and some with their foot in a newly emerging one, found much in the liturgy that was culturally alienating. Others simply stuck to the old pieties, accommodating themselves more or less willingly to what the priests were asking of them.

What is now required is a theological mediation that is more explicitly attentive to the human subject and to the functionings of the symbolic. It needs to share modernity's turn to the subject and at the same time to negotiate post-modernity's apprehensions of, and about, the power and expressivity of language. It has to be universal in the sense that it can account for the diversity of cultures, even while offering insight into the compositeness and performativity of culture in mediating reality.

Today, Christian praxis and the transformation of experience are won through critical reflection upon symbols, which gives a second naiveté or a second immediacy. The power of symbols to express the transcendent, their capacity so to construe human experience as to reconstruct it, are attained through a process of demythologization and critical reflection, which opens the mind and the heart to a fresh and liberating hearing of the word of God. The remembrance of Jesus Christ can be received in this way as gift, and simultaneously as challenge to our inner selves and to our public conduct.

Theological Imagination

The recognition of theology's relation to cult can be linked up with the current interest of theological method in the role of imagination. The standard epistemologies that have been put to work in Catholic theology are not quite at home with the imagination and its artifacts. This criticism has even been made of transcendental Thomism, for all its acknowledged virtues. While it has restored the subject to theology, and in this way shown the importance of hermeneutics, it is queried whether or not it has taken enough account of the imaginative dimension of contemporary heremeneutics. On this score, it is sometimes dubbed neoconservative, since it is generally unwilling to indulge in a revisionist interpretation of traditional symbols, inclusive of acts of cult, but instead seeks to open up the standing interpretation to new explanations. In doing this, it may fail to take sufficient account of the archeological subject, or of the naive tendency to over-objectify, or of the rationalist tendency to overexplain. Taking these factors into account requires a thorough investigation of the role of the imagination, and a critical assessment of what it in fact expresses.

Replacing the language of revelation in the context of worship gives the context within which to perform the tasks of validation, demythologization, and arbitration of this language, which is essentially symbolic.[19] Worship expresses the teleology of the Spirit within which the archeology of the subject can be assimilated.

The validation of symbolic language means explaining its appropriateness to that sphere in which salvation is received as an offer, and in which the human spirit is brought into communion with the divine. Indeed, it means showing that no other kind of language is adequate to this task. But because of the multiple root of symbol in desire and in the cosmic, false interpretation and false hearing is possible. A whole tradition can for a while objectify and rationalize certain elements in the symbolism. False consciousness can arise through yielding to the appeal which the symbols make to certain desires, for example, security, sanction, univocity of meaning. Demythologization is a necessity, so that false interpretations may be eliminated and the true meaning of the symbolic uncovered. The dialectic of the use and interpretation of the symbols through Christian history can contribute to this process of demythologization, since it puts us in contact with living responses to the Gospel. The archeology of the subject and the etiology of the symbol can be examined together, for one can see how certain symbols, rites, and myths arose in fact, and at the same time to what part of the human subject's experience and desire they made and make appeal.

One then comes to the arbitration of the symbol to a culture. This is the task of presenting it, free from false interpretation and at the same time replete with the added force which it has acquired through history, as kerygma, as symbol through which human history can be read. On one level, this is true in a general way for all human history, but on another level it can have application to the history of a particular people. Talk of history implies teleology. Worship expresses the orientation which the Christian kerygma offers to the human story. It is not teleology in the sense that it explains what the end will be. It is teleology in the sense that it looks for truth in a communion of the Spirit.

Theology, then, requires a hermeneutics which respects the fact that Christian language is both imaginative and primordially cultic. The implications of this for a transcendental methodology may be illustrated by a comparison between Karl Rahner and Paul Ricoeur on original sin.[20] Rahner sets out to interpret the dogma of original sin, with all due consciousness of the historical factors involved in the dogma and with the intention of finding new categories into which to translate it. Ricoeur is interested in how Christian tradition ever came to such a concept, and in the retrieval of the Adamic story, in all its complexity, from which the concept is derived. He asks what is the process through which human minds came to express the truth of the story in such a way, and then he asks what is the meaning and intent of the story itself. He places hermeneutics at the service of the kerygma, or the deployment of the salvific potential inherent in the symbolic telling of the Adamic story.

Rahner, of course, eschews the naive and obviously mythical elements of stain and transmission, so that in this sense he does perform a demythologization. The process of demythologization, however, in which he engages seems to be that of a purification of the concept. He expands the concept by an appeal to the existential situation of human freedom and its limits. Indeed, he acknowledges that original sin may not be the best or the most important concept in which this part of revelation is being expressed, but simply one of the concepts that belong within the history of dogmatic teaching, one that for particular reasons was given special sanction. His own explanation, however, which consists in an examination of the existential situation of freedom, its limits, and guilt, is not won by returning to the story. It is an appeal to the fundamental categories in which he has chosen to present the Christian truth. This means, first of all, that he does not examine very closely why the concept of original sin was used as a means of expressing the response to the biblical story. Second, it means that he does not return very clearly to any fresh hearing of the story, granted that this is in some respects present inasmuch as he takes current exegesis into account. However, it is difficult to escape the impression that Rahner deals with imaginative language simply as a more primitive language, which needs to be translated into more abstract and philosophical terms. His lengthy elaborations on symbol have never dealt with the issue of imaginative language as such.

Ricoeur, on the other hand, is interested in the conceptualization which leads to the idea of original sin. Rather than taking it simply as an example of a true but limited expression of the faith, one has to look at it as an example of the whole human subject's response to the kerygma. The truthfulness of the response is inseparable from the elements of false consciousness inherent in it. Conceptualization has origins other than simply those of the mind. Psychological tendencies and the inability to deal with narrative forms both have their part to play in coming to this particular expression. At the same time, Ricoeur does examine the factors of a genuine teleological re-

sponse which are present in the Augustinian conceptualization, within the dialectic with other formulations.

Most important for him is the return to the story, as it can
be listened to anew. He asks what kind of human experience is
imaged in the stories and symbols which deal with sin and
with its forgiveness. Rahner has no firm place for the juridical
element of the story or concept in his explanation, since that
would seem to postulate a juridical body and a historical
Adam, and such elements of truth could not be traced back
from the present existential situation to the story.[21] Because for
his part, he takes the juridical as a paradigm, an imaginative
expression, an image of something rather than an explanation,
Ricoeur leaves the juridical figure intact. To experience life
and the absurdities of life, the violence and the wrongdoing,
as a punishment that has been inflicted, or as something
which merits punishment, is connatural to the human subject.
It is put before us in the biblical story, as something that eats
into the roots of consciousness, engenders the dread of death
and gnaws away at the hope of life. The biblical story about
sin's origins indicates how the human person and the human
community feel before God, when their religious consciousness awakens and they become sensitive to the failure of the
good. The blight on humanity's fortune derives not only from
wrongdoing but also from the urge to be responsible for the
world. Failure in responsibility means guilt before God and
deserves punishment from the one supreme judge. It is an impasse from which there seems to be no delivery. It is the intri-
cate and bizarre situation from which humanity cries out for
deliverance. As the story unfolds through the events and narratives of the Bible, it appears however that this way of conjur-
ing up the sin of the world falsifies the image of God. Balanc-
ing the sense of sin with its failure in the order of justice, or
overbalancing it, is the proclamation of the superabundance of
Christ, the destruction of the Law, the elimination of the Judge
from the story of the elect. The redress of what is signified by
the story of sin and punishment comes through the stories of
mercy, the promise of the superabundant grace of Jesus
Christ. Yet humanity is left with that on its conscience which
can be called the remembrance of guilt, punishment, judgment. It is inherent to the sinful condition of humanity that be-

fore Christ it lived under the Law, and that it is ever prone to have resort to it. Only in the memory of Christ is the memory of the guilt and judgment overcome. Only in recourse to the Father of love and mercy is the Judge of the world of human consciousness compensated. In other words, the God who has been cast as Judge is revealed in Christ the reconciler. Out of the depths which this proclamation evokes, one can hear it as the word of God, freed from the overlay of rational explanation, as well as from the first naiveté of mythical thought.

A revisionist theology attends to this dialogical and dialectical situation not simply as conflict between modes of thought but as a living reality which is present in worship, or in which God and the human community are present to one another. Demythologization for such a theology is not merely a matter of getting rid of factors which cannot be philosophically retained in the ultimate explanation of the truth. It is a process which explains what these mythical elements have to do in expressing the kind of ways in which humanity encounters God, and God humanity. It is not purely destruction of this kind of language, but validation of it, and the validation brings to the fore aspects of the matter which pertain to the reality into which theology inquires.

A Practical Theology

The difficulties which the transcendental method has with responding to the imaginative, can be linked with difficulties which it likewise experiences with praxis. One of the comments made about it is that it has little enough to say to social and political questions. This failure in the order of the practical may derive from a lack of imagination. Because of a lack of affinity with the imaginative, theologians may find themselves unable to "envisage" the situation of humanity, to put a face on it. They may thus be unable to "apprehend" the evil of the economic, the political, the oppressive, and consequently be weak in their discourse about redemption. This is not a matter of the theologian's private sympathies, but of his or her public self. Nor do I intend a writing which pulls at the heartstrings, but rather I refer to a capacity to gain insight into, express a grasp, and project hope for that complex field which is the social and political. The power of evil and the redemptive power of the weak, both require strong imaginative expression, powerful symbols that call upon us to explore the entire range of their forcefulness and impact. Precise and clear-sighted programs of recovery are indeed necessary, as well as a good sociological analysis of every situation. But theology has to explain why apocalyptic, satanic, or healing images are needed if the human story is to be told as a story of good and evil, of sin and of redemption. Ethical discernment and decision are best rooted in a community which does not fear to evoke these images and symbols and to use them in prayer before the Lord.

The Ritual Matrix

Anthropology and philosophy look into the nature of the relation between rite and myth, between the symbolic action and the word, between the story remembered and its sacrament. It is not a question of deciding which chronologically comes first, for often this cannot be known. What is of interest is the nature of their interdependence. Rites are often mimetic, a kind of acting out of the story. On the other hand, the flow of the story can be influenced by the rite in which it is enacted. The body will not permit the mind to gainsay the feeling of reality which it possesses in its bones, so that when the mind weaves its myths and its metaphors it has to obey the instincts which the body expresses in its ritual actions.

In explaining a culture, due attention has to be given to its ritual matrix. Cultural paradigms and cultural creations are checked against the most basic ritual behavior of the people. The identity, the cohesiveness, the values, the goals, the meanings, the experiential roots, of a people, while expressed in many ways, cannot finally be apprehended without insight into the most common or most fundamental rituals. Indeed, cultural crisis is decipherable to the extent that it is possible to discover why certain, or all, basic rituals cease to have social meaning.

In mediating cult to culture, theology will want to examine historically the ritual paradigms of the Christian tradition. There is in fact an interesting coincidence between anthropological studies of culture and biblical exegesis, inasmuch as

some recent exegesis points to the part that rite played both in
the origins of Judaism and in the origins of the Christian community. Of the first it is sufficient to note that the rites of the
new moon and of sacrifice are a necessary foundation to the
biblical narrative of the exodus and Covenant. More attention
can here be given to the place of rite in the early history of the
Christian community and of the formation of the Gospel.

One of the trends in New Testament exegesis is to note the
role which the community rite of common meal played in the
development of faith in Jesus and in the narrative of the passion.[22] The community meal, as is known, had its antecedents
in the Jewish practice of ritual meals. The first way in which
the disciples could express their belief that indeed the kingdom had come in Jesus was to continue the table fellowship
which they had experienced with him, following the customs
and rituals of Israel. This belief in the coming of the kingdom
turns readily into the feeling that the community's own identity is to be identified with Jesus.

Of the synoptic Gospels, it has been said that they are a passion narrative, with a prologue and an epilogue.[23] Perhaps its
origin can in part be located in the community meal and its ritual. When the disciples unfolded their own story, as the Jews
had unfolded theirs in the course of their sacred table gatherings, the suffering and death of Jesus would have been narrated and interpreted.

Largely due to the influence of Odo Casel, recent theology
has discussed the relation between the eucharist and the passion in terms of the relation between rite and myth. This has
given prominence to the idea of a reenactment of the passion
in the eucharist. The exegesis which I have mentioned adds a
nuance and a twist to this relationship. Instead of saying that
the eucharist was instituted as a way of commemorating the
passion, the position is reversed. That is to say, the rite which
proclaimed the kingdom, and in which the disciples found
their sense of communion with Jesus, could have been the context within which the salvific understanding of the passion
was elaborated, and thus was the rite kept as its commemoration. The narrative form and the blessings of the meal provide
the suitable context within which to develop the passion story
as that of a salvific event.

One of the implications of this for theology is that Christology starts with the Lord's Supper, celebrated by the community of the Lord's disciples. The communion expressed in the rite of the eucharist is a first, radical, and foundational expression of the belief about Jesus, and a criterion whereby to judge all else that is said about him. In this we see the inseparability of ecclesiology and Christology from the theology of sacrament and worship. It has to be asked whether the theology of Christ and church remains coherent with what is signified in the basic ritual, wherein the identity of the community and the presence of the kingdom are expressed.

CONCLUSION

It goes without saying that theology needs to establish the relation between Christian cult and the prevalent western culture. This task has taken on new proportions in the western world with the recognition that it now has entered into a post-Christian culture, with the result that the basic goals and meanings of western peoples are more difficult to ascertain than in a dominantly Christian age.

There is no people without a set of rituals, and no people without its mythologies, however secularized or sophisticated these may seem to be. One of the major problems facing American theologians in the last couple of decades has been that of the relation between Christianity and American secularism. It is interesting to note how much of the writing on this score has investigated symbol and metaphorical language. Theological writers, with the help of the human sciences, investigate the symbols of the culture and look for the disclosure factor in these symbols. When this avenue is pursued, it often happens that an affinity between Christian symbol and cultural symbol can be found, or at least some intersecting of the two, even when Christian beliefs and morals are held in question or in abeyance. When it is pursued with the aid of a philosophy of the subject and a contemporary hermeneutics, then the question of interiority and its relation to the transcendent becomes a key factor.

It mediating cult to culture, theology could start with the

concordant discord of symbol systems and rituals. It can investigate the clash of rituals, as well as the teleological questions which are raised by the respective systems. It can pursue the dialectic between traditional Christian rituals and contemporary secular rituals. This does not mean trying to harmonize or blend the two. On the contrary, it means that the Christian kerygma and rituals can emerge as a challenge to the dominant culture.

Liturgy is not just another discipline in religious studies. It is in its way foundational to theology, and so recurs as a point of reference for every topic that is considered. Indeed, theology's role can be described as that of mediating cult to culture. This means that an examination of the dialectic of cult is part of a method of dialectical inquiry. It means that rite and sacrament provide a basis for such disciplines as Christology, ecclesiology, and God-talk. It means that theology has to appreciate and interpret the language of the imagination, and find a critical means whereby to generate the second immediacy which makes a faith both critical and reverent. It means finally that the intersection of cultic ritual and cultural ritual is an area of continual inquiry.

Notes

1. Bernard Lonergan, *Philosophy of God and Theology* (London: Darton, Longman & Todd Ltd., 1973) 33-34.

2. Constitution on the Sacred Liturgy no. 10.

3. On the use of typology in mystagogical catechesis, see Enrico Mazza, *Mystagogy. A Theology of Liturgy in the Patristic Age*, trans., Matthew O'Connell (New York: Pueblo Publishing Co., 1989).

4. See Angelus Haussling, *Mönchskonvent und Eucharistiefeier. Eine Studie über die Messe in der abendländische Klosterliturgie des frühen Mittelalters und zur Geschichte der Messhäufigkeit* (Münster: Aschendorf, 1973). The historical details are summarized in Theodor Klauser, *A Short History of the Western Liturgy*, 2d ed., trans., John Halliburton (New York: Oxford University Press, 1979) 45-93.

5. This was a regular theme in ecclesiology in the eleventh and twelfth centuries. See Yves Congar, "Les Laics et l'écclésiologie des 'ordines' chez les théologiens des XIe et XIIe siècles," in *Etudes d'écclésiologie médiévale* (London: Variorum Reprints, 1983) 83-117.

6. On the background to the new developments in theology, see Marie-Dominique Chenu, *Nature, Man and Society in the Twelfth Century. Essays on New Theological Perspectives in the Latin West*, selected, edited and translated by Jerome Taylor and Lester K. Little (Chicago: The University of Chicago Press, 1968).

7. Very important in this regard is Marie-Dominique Chenu, *Toward Understanding St. Thomas*, trans., A. Landry and D. Hughes (Chicago: University of Chicago Press, 1964).

8. Thomas Aquinas places the sacraments *in genere signi*, and only then discusses the causal efficacy of the Christian sacraments. See *Summa Theologiae* 3, qq. 60-62.

9. See *S.Th.* 3, q. 63, especially art. 4.

10. See *S.Th.* 3, q. 90, art. 1.

11. On substantial change and presence, see *S.Th.* 3, qq. 75, 76.

12. On visions in the blessed sacrament, see *S.Th.* 3, q. 76, art. 8.

13. On the reason for seven sacraments, see *S.Th.* 3, q. 65, art. 1.

14. On Anselm, see G.H. Williams, "The Sacramental Presuppositions of Anselm's Cur Deus Homo," *Church History* 26 (1957) 245-274.

15. On the sacrifice of Christ, see *S.Th.* 3, q. 48, art. 3, where Aquinas adopts the definition of Augustine.

16. See *S.Th.* 3, q. 83, art. 1.

17. See *S.Th.* 3, q. 79, art. 7.

18. Constitution on the Sacred Liturgy no. 59.

19. See Paul Ricoeur, "The Language of Faith," in C.E. Reagan and D. Stewart, eds., *The Philosophy of Paul Ricoeur: An Anthology of His Work* (Boston: Beacon Press, 1978) 223-238.

20. For a summary of Karl Rahner's position, see *Foundations of Christian Faith* (New York: Crossroad, 1978) 106-115. For Paul Ricoeur, see "Original Sin? A Study in Meaning" in *The Conflict of Interpretations*, ed. and trans., Don Ihde (Evanston: Northwestern University Press, 1974) 269-286.

21. See Karl Rahner, *Foundations of Christian Faith* 114: "Everything which cannot be arrived at by [this] aetiological inference from the present situation to its origin belongs to the mode of representation and the mode of expression, but not to the content of the assertion."

22. For a discussion of this trend and for the relation of the passion narrative to preaching and worship in general, see J.R. Donahue, "From Passion Traditions to Passion Narrative," in W.H. Kelber, ed., *The Passion in Mark: Studies on Mark 14-16* (Philadelphia: Fortress Press, 1976) 1-20. See the discussion of "meal Christology" in the early church by V.K. Robbins, "Last Meal: Preparation, Betrayal, and Absence," in Kelber, *The Passion* 21-40.

23. The remark is that of M. Kahler, *The So-Called Historical Jesus and the Historic, Biblical Christ*, trans., C. Braaten (Philadelphia: Fortress Press, 1964) 80. The remark has been termed both "insightful" and "misleading" by other exegetes.

2

Christianity As Religion

WHEN CHRISTIAN THEOLOGY CONSIDERS THE PHENOMENON OF RELI-
gion and religious practice in the world, it takes its factual information and some theories from other sciences, such as comparative religion, anthropology, sociology, and religious
psychology. At the same time, it acts upon its own presuppositions in assessing this phenomenon and in relating questions
about the persistence of religion to questions about Christianity itself.

As a working description, it may be accepted that religion is
in its many different forms a complexity of beliefs and practices which expresses the meaning of life and the order of existence in terms of relationship to the sacred. It is not just a question of acknowledging the existence of the sacred, but one of
establishing a relationship to it in practices and rites and of accepting a consequent ethic. Religion is as varied in its beliefs,
practices, and ethics as the notion of the sacred. Determining
the meaning of the sacred and the alternation of the sacred
and the secular depends on how one deals with the question
of human transcendence and of divine presence in the world—
where divine presence is not necessarily taken to refer to a personal God. Depending on how one sees these issues, the sacred is conceived either as a separate sphere of human existence in which the requirements of the sacred world are
satisfied or as a distinctive dimension of the whole of reality.

Even within Christianity itself, there are different approaches to the question of the sacred and the alternation of the sacred and the secular. At the same time, Christianity will presuppose that "genuine religion always involves worship of what is genuinely ultimate. Religion, worship and ultimate reality are thus indissolubly related."[1]

Christian theology will also make some distinction between faith and religion. It is not one which is easy to delineate, since the distinction is not between two wholly separate realities but necessarily allows for a relationship between the two. In general, faith can be understood as the interiorization of a meaning, the inner response to an expressed meaning, presented by another. It involves a personal relationship and a commitment to the other person. Religion is the mediation of faith, as well as its expression and its support, in teaching, ritual, institution, and behavior. The greatest difficulty here is to distinguish between those expressions which are essential to faith in religion, and those which are variable because they are subject to different cultural influences. This variability in religious expression is necessary to the mediation of faith, since it is presented to people who belong to different cultural backgrounds and environments.

WHAT THEOLOGY ASKS ABOUT RELIGION

A reflective Christian theology can ask four questions about its relation to religion:

1. What does Christian revelation itself have to say about the nature of the God-human relationship which points to the necessity and permanence of religion?

2. What are the criteria by which religious authenticity may be judged?

3. Why does religion often take on imperfect and at times even debased forms and survive in these forms?

4. What are the conditions that authentic religious expression may endure?

These questions follow one another in a logical sequence, as we shall now show. The Christian symbol-system, in its kerygmatic proclamation, its mythical[2] presentation and interpretations (as contained in the Scriptures), its community order, its sacramental celebration and its ethical demands, points to the fact that faith and beliefs[3] cannot be imparted and cannot survive without religion. This total symbolic complexity is necessary that the God-human relationship may be possible and that faith may act as a force in human lives. None of these elements can be explained simply as the consequence of a positive divine law, laying down the conditions of Christian obedience, and which could just as easily have been otherwise. Whether we take the form of the presentation of the message in the Scriptures, or the sacramental system, or the community order, or the conduct required of those who believe in Christ, each has its own intrinsic intelligibility and its own inner structure, which allows it to serve as an appropriate medium for the communication and expression of faith. The cultural elements which finally determine these factors have to be taken into account, and are not always that easily discernible, but without some similar symbolic system we know that faith would be rendered humanly impossible. The inner core and basic adherence to meaning of any religious system requires a similar complexity of factors to mediate it and keep it alive.

On the other hand, Christian revelation speaks to us of the love of a personal God for the world, of Christ as the focal point and transformation of history and the beginning of a new creation, of the presence of the Spirit in the world as the operative force of faith and salvation, and of the transcendence of human nature and God-given finality. Faith in such a triune reality of God's self-communication is impossible without religion, and so the knowledge itself of God's love makes us certain that religion will endure as the necessary medium of faith and love. The knowledge of this love also explains why religion undergoes periodic reform and revival, and enables us to accept the work of propheticism in bringing about such reform as the action of God's Spirit. Pushed far enough, confidence in the presence of Christ and the Spirit in the church may have at one time given rise in theology to an optimism about the spread of Christianity and a severe attitude toward other religions. But theology is bound to reflect upon facts, as well as upon the sources of tradition. In face of the comparative provincialism of the Christian religion, theologians in more recent times have begun to ask whether the loving God may not use the medium of other religions for communion with humankind. In other words, they have begun to inquire into the possible salvific value and into the significance of non-Christian religions.

Since religion also exists in imperfect or even debased forms, to look for God's action through religious forms makes it necessary to work out criteria whereby we can assess the authenticity of religious beliefs, practices, and systems, namely, the real value which they may have in permitting people to commune with the transcendent and loving God, and to worship that which is genuinely ultimate. But since religion sometimes takes on forms which are degrading, or since it can exclude the existence of a personal God, one does not explain the endurance of religion simply by saying that God's presence in the world by the Spirit assures this. Besides setting the criteria whereby we can judge religion's authenticity, is it possible to explain why it survives even when it can hardly be said to serve as a medium of communication with God?

Some basis for this is found in the fact that religion deals with the problems of life and death, and with the anxieties of a person's relations to community and to the powers which one cannot control. This is true even of religions, which combine an answer to these problems with the worship of a personal God. When it loses its vision of a loving God, religion may still exist as a way of dealing with these anxieties, particularly anxiety about the presence of the sacred in life, about human suffering or failure, and above all about death. In such cases, the element of faith is missing from religion, but the meaning offered resides in such things as the placation of spirits, hope for preternatural help, the search for some action or some area of human life, such as sexual love, in which the essential core of meaning is posited. Whether it turns out to be a tranquilizer or a challenge in face of these problems, is one good criterion for distinguishing a genuine from an imperfect religion, since a religion which takes account of a personal, loving, and saving God places demands upon the believer to take issue with questions of ultimate meaning and to commit oneself to an ethic that takes the religious affirmation seriously. Sometimes the concern with one's own human problems, or the community's problems, is dominant in religious practice so that it survives principally as a way of allaying anxiety, and the real challenge is avoided. If this remains the uppermost concern, then it is bound to take on many superstitious and debased forms. On the other hand, by focusing on the problem of human living, it may awaken the need for ultimate concern and meaning, and thus be a means of opening up to the perspective of faith. The Christian symbol system incorporates these problems into its kerygma and sacramental universe. It has its own way of answering them, but we cannot be surprised that even when the Christian answer is discarded, or any answer which takes in faith a loving and saving God, religion survives as a way of dealing with these problems.

The biggest problem facing Christianity in the western world today is that of remaining viable in a changing cultural environment and of dealing with the crisis of faith which necessarily ensues when the whole manner of its expression is subjected to flux.[4] This means that in surveying the conditions under which Christianity may take on suitable religious forms in and for this new situation we are talking about conditions under which any religion may persist in an authentic way. To appreciate the difficulties which Christianity faces in keeping its faith vital in the course of a cultural transition is by the same token a help towards understanding why it has largely remained a western phenomenon. The failure to meet the cultural challenge involved in taking on the aspects of non-European civilizations can be accounted to a deficiency inherent in the Christian religion itself.[5]

CONDITIONS FOR A CHRISTIAN RELIGION WHICH MEDIATES FAITH

These conditions can be listed and explained as follows.

1. An authentic Christian expression treats of life and death, evil, sin, personal worth and community belonging, of reconciliation and human communion. The fear of death, the clinging to and guilt of sin, the anxiety about personal worth and the disruption of human community, with their opposites, the hope of life, the desire for grace and pardon, the desire to be

loved and to be able to love, the search for communion, and
the awe of the holy which somehow influences the doings of
this world, constitute the fundamental human experience in
which religion is grounded. This is what it transforms into a
meaningful reality, in which these fears are conquered and
these hopes fulfilled. Even though it may possess an apparent
nobility, a religion which has nothing to say about these factors of human existence will eventually be ignored.

It is also possible that a religion may choose to isolate some
one factor and, by concentrating on it and putting all human
hopes in it, blind its adherents to more fundamental questions.
This happened in some ancient religions, which relied too
much on sexual experience, and even on ritual sex, as an answer to the need for life and happiness. Ancient religions
which betrayed this interest in sex nonetheless retained or developed their mythologies about the gods. Some modern sexual behavior has its own ritual aspect, and one can find such
things as celebrations and rituals of love in which the stress is
on sexual expression, and in which such love, without any reference to a world of the gods, is taken to be the answer to human woes.

Christian religion on its part has often erred in the opposite
extreme with regard to sexual love and treated it as something
to be feared or looked down upon. Its betrayal of its followers
can consist in the isolation of other elements of the Christian
message or undue attention to some one particular human
problem, with the consequent loss of a total vision. This happens, for example, if in practice Christianity encourages resignation to sorrow without its counterpart of courage and hope,
if it denies personal worth by subordinating the individual to
communality or religious system, or if on the other extreme it
turns religion into a purely individualistic affair. It can also
adopt one or other of the extremes of Pelagianism or Puritan-
ism in face of sin, or falsify the nature of death and the hope of
the resurrection by too material a concern with the life of the
new creature who emerges from the transforming power of
death in Christ. A genuine Christian practice keeps the balance between the hope in the resurrection and the way of the
folly of the cross.

2. Authentic Christianity, it follows, keeps the personal ele-

ment of religion in the foreground. The unique element of the Christian faith is the revelation of the personal God who is Father, the cosmic lover who asks for the response of love and thus promises union. This is falsified whenever Christian practice loses the sense of response, if it becomes too centered on human development and forgets that "God first loved us" and that all we do is the glorification of God, if it makes God into a lawgiver instead of a savior and father, if it does not foster the interiorization of the word and the law and the love of God in Christ through the Spirit, if it becomes a superstition to deal with the troubles of life on the basis of a false notion of providence instead of developing a way of living which is response to God's love.

3. To be truly integrated into the life of any people or civilization, Christian faith needs to receive a poetic and symbolic expression which is indigenous to the culture, not foreign to it. This applies to ritual, celebrations of every sort, devotions, art in its different forms, or in other words to every expression of the faith which appeals to the affective and seeks to make it a living force which involves the totality of the human person and to develop the intersubjective relationships of the community on a basis of Christian vision and mission.

The language of kerygma, of catechesis, of mystagogy, of worship, in short all the symbols of a religion, are very much charged with cultural elements, because they are the ways in which religion presents its message as an answer to and a transformation of the human experience of a given people or culture. What an authentic religion tries to do is to transform, not to contradict, human experience and its various expressions. Faith must seek through these religious symbols, and a people develops and grows in its faith, and discovers all the consequences and further meaning of its faith, through them.

Credal expression itself takes in cultural elements and uses symbolic language. It is not a purely objective expression which presents the articles of faith to be accepted by all. In facing cultural transition, one of the difficulties of the messenger of the faith is to discern the objective content which has to be kept intact, as well as the expressions which are conditioned by a culture, or by a particular problematic which belongs to a given time or place.

Elements of revelation and faith can somehow be present in a non-Christian or in a profane culture. When discovered, these are respected and may serve as media of a fuller faith commitment. Old Testament and Christian revelation was not in the first place a matter of introducing entirely extraneous elements into the lives and practices of the Semitic or Hellenistic peoples. Revelation was often the inner light which allowed a people to perceive the full implication and potential of an event or of given beliefs and practices. It gave a people the possibility to pass through and transcend a given stage in their religious experience and to come to a greater awareness of God and of God's love for the people

In presenting Jesus Christ in new cultural conditions, the question is how far we can present him as God's answer to the aspirations of, and the already existent awareness of the sacred present in that culture. Jesus said of himself that he had come to fulfill, not to abolish, the Law and the prophets. The fulfillment was not just an addition to what they already said. It was a perfecting of the faith-experience of God which the people, who had interiorized the Law and the prophets, already possessed. Granted the singular nature of Jewish religious history and of its special relation to Christ, something analogous could be said about the faith-experience of a transcendent power which any people has attained through its religious expression, or even through its fidelity to its profane commitments when these involve communion and respect for the potentialities of life.

To use the poetic, symbolic, and ritual expressions of a culture to mediate Christian faith requires dialogue, in which several questions are involved. How does a people give voice to its feelings and aspirations when these concern the religious problems of which we have already spoken? What is its reaction to traditional Christian symbols, and how far can these be used to transform human experience in this new setting? How far can an authentic Christian faith be expressed in symbols taken from a new culture? Or how can a developing culture express its faith in new symbols? Involved in this inquiry is the question of the existence of universal symbols that can find resonance in any cultural setting and the extent to which some of the basic Christian symbols, such as the water-symbolism of baptism or the eucharistic meal, belong in this category.

One point worthy of particular note is the approach to a culture's cosmology, or in other words its vision of the universe. Many cultures and religions see the world peopled by spirits of various sorts, or by dynamic forces. This is their symbolic way of expressing their relation to the universe, its mysteriousness, and their own limitations and possibilities in entering into communion with it. It also expresses their sense of the sacred or of the divine which is present in the universe and of its part in human affairs as far as these involve some attempt to control one's surrounding and one's own life as it depends for development upon the environment in which one lives. When faced with such a vision of things, which leaves room for the symbolism of spirits, Christian preaching can either contradict it or turn it into a theophany. The Semitic peoples who were called to be the people of the one true God lived in a world peopled with spirits. This persuasion sometimes led them into idolatry, but on the other hand it formed the basis for the angelology of the Old Testament. In later times, Christianity often misunderstood this angelology and gave too literal an interpretation to the talk about the angels, whereas in Old Testament times and in some Eastern Christian rites (where, for example, Christ and the Holy Spirit are called angels, or where the angels are invoked to conjure up the reverence due to God's majesty) angels were a kind of divine revelation, a way of expressing God's own mysterious nearness to the people. It was a way of coupling a sense of awe before the transcendence of God with a sense of a gracious nearness in love. The approach to other peoples who symbolize their relations with the cosmos and the sacred in the figures of spirits can surely learn something from this.

In its present phase of cultural development, the western world is increasingly convinced of the independence of ths secular and finds it hard to cope with stories of miracles, saints, or special divine interventions. At the same time, it has its own need of the sacred and its own need of evincing its awe of the universe—even though it is now possible to travel to the moon and contact other planets. To persist in a symbolic and devotional expression which makes miracles and special interventions of God and the saints necessary would spell the ruin of Christian religion, even if such language were still attractive to some people. Some would reject a religion which postulated such beliefs, but even those who accepted them would inevitably experience an inner tension and conflict between their theories and technical knowledge of the universe and its forces on the one hand, and their symbolic expression of their relation to it on the other. Philosophy and theology have already responded to this new awareness by developing a theory of the sacred and the secular which emphasizes the sacred and the transcendent as a dimension of reality rather than as a separate sphere of existence, and speaks of fidelity to the profane as an opening out to the sacred. What is still lacking is a new symbolism, which allows humankind to encounter God simultaneously with a grasp of the universe and the particulars in it, a ritual and a prayer expression which is a discernment of the divine presence in human life and history and a challenge to a response in faith, which channels all human drives, affective as well as intelligent.

4. Without a witness of life on the part of its disciples, a religion cannot succeed. This constitutes the spiritual and living experience which is communicated through religious practices, and is the ultimate factor which makes religion credible. The Christian Gospels always insisted on this sign of credibility and on the existence of the community of charity into which new members are incorporated. Faith is interpreted and presented in word and symbol, but by that same token the word and symbol are an interpretation of the works in which faith shows its vitality. What is shared with others is faith in God as the Father of the Lord Jesus Christ, the charity which unites, the personal relation to God and Christ, the sense of the Spirit, the experience of what this means for the problems of good and evil, life and death, meaningful involvement in the world coupled with the hope of the future. It is also prayer, in its religious ritual and its ultimate quality of contemplation. Today, what is needed more than anything is the witness of involvement in the needs of the world and in the transformation of society, without any loss of faith in God and without any devaluation of contemplation as the truest end which humans can pursue in this life.

5. Besides its witness and its symbolic expression, religion also needs its institutions, namely, its forms of government and organization, and its law which regulates relations among its followers and adherents. The institutional element of Christianity is still the subject of controversy between churches, and among members within single churches. It is an important question in a stage of cultural transition, because the view taken of these structures makes all the difference between attempts at adaptation and a more radical reform, in the strong sense of that word. There seems to be a growing realization that the institutional factor in Christianity is less a matter of the institutions formed by Jesus Christ or the apostles as a necessary means for the communication of his word and grace, than a question of the forms most apt to express the community's self-awareness in a given time and place, in continuity with a past Christian tradition. The nature of the church is that of a community which is one with Jesus Christ through faith and charity, the body which through his Spirit is identified with him and is his sacramental presence in the world. Not only are the spiritual values primary in the sense that they are the most important, but also in the sense that they precede the institutions. The role which the institutions play is to support the spiritual values, of which they are in the first instance the expression. They depend for their credibility and permanence, or at least for their efficaciousness, on the continuing relationship with these values. A divorce can and often has occurred between the institution and the value of which it was originally the expression, and yet the institution has lived on in its historical form, simply because it was there to begin with, and there is an innate conservatism in any community which promotes past structures. This divorce occurs either because the community's self-awareness in faith changes or modifies the sense of values, or because there is a corruption within the institution and it maintains the form without the spirit. In either case, the result is that the institution is no longer supported by the spirit of the community and is not an apt instrument whereby to promote the expression of faith in any of its religious practices or in its works.[6]

There is need today for institutional reforms, in both non-western and western countries, and the same changes cannot hold good for every part of the world. To take only the example of the western crisis, an authoritarian institution, which is sometimes also unevangelical in its style of life, cannot support the values of a Christian community which has come to a greater awareness of the co-responsibility of its members in the mission of Christ. The forms of government, priesthood, and law need to be configured to the sense of mission. This sense of mission is the product of Christian faith in a cultural environment which encourages participation. It would be naive to simply state that the Christian faith which comes to us from the New Testament indicates a community which through the working and charism of the Spirit accepts the responsibility of all its members for the life and mission of the church, and thus claim that in fostering co-responsibility we are returning to a purer Christian ideal. Such an explanation fails to take account of other cultural influences, and of the ultimate fact that faith as a response to God in Christ works within a community which is subject to the influences of a given culture, causing this community to find its own response to God in Christ within that culturally determined situation. It is indeed true that in New Testament times there was a strong sense of the presence of the Spirit, as the inner anointing which every Christian received to interiorize the word of Christ, and that this led to a respect for the distinctive contribution of different charisms. It is also true that a loss of this sense of the Spirit was one of the factors which led to a growing separation between clergy and faithful. None the less, we cannot either forget that today in the western world faith commands a response from Christian communities in which the cultural influence urges people to a greater sense of sharing and participation, and in which this contribution is possible because of standards of education and pluriformity in skills which prevail in our society. This of itself demands new forms of law, institution, and obedience. The ultimate Christian obedience is to the forms of expression which this word takes, but they must be forms apt to communicate. This holds for laws and institutions, as well as for other ways of expression.

6. Without historical consciousness, none of these changes in religious expression is possible, whether it be a change in symbolic expression, in creed, in ritual, in devotion, in institu-

tions, or in life-style. Historical consciousness[7] is aware of the creativity of faith and of the cultural differences within which this creativity takes place. It knows that faith is not a formulation which has to be couched in certain terms, but a constantly growing response of the believing community to the Christ-event, an event whose intelligibility and potentiality can never be exhausted. Faith then creates its own religious expression, but according to the needs and the cultural sense of the believer. Historical consciousness does not deny the continuity which comes from Christian tradition or from the common nature which all people possess, but it avoids too many *a priori* answers in setting the boundaries of continuity.

7. Finally, a systematic reflection is a guide to every religion, and for Christianity this means a reflective theology. An indigenous theology, be it western or otherwise, is based on a knowledge and explanation of the world of interiority of a people and its culture. This comprises the values, the modes of communication and self-expression, the ways of thought proper to a culture. To come to know it, it is necessary to develop a philosophical anthropology which comes from a reflection upon experience, both internal and external, both personal and dialogal. This enables a people to meet the demands of theory in grounding and explaining the faith-experience, and assures that there is no hiatus between the symbolic, devotional, and institutional on the one hand, and the quest for truth on the other, but rather grants them internal coherence in the mind of the community and its individual members. Scholasticism sought such a theology for the newly emerging western culture. The same needs to be done for non-European cultures.

CONCLUSION

Christian religion is the constant process of creativity which needs to meet the conditions explained here. To endure it must so pursue ultimate reality that it does not exclude or render impossible faith in a personal God. It also needs the credible witness of its adherents and respect for its religious tradition, as well as the cultural expression of faith in a symbol system, an institution, and a reflection. This cultural expression, as it is renewed or newly formed, itself adds to the religious tradition, but it remains continuous with earlier tradition because of the original sources, because of respect for history, and because of the common humanity which has the same universal needs and tendencies.

The Christian is conscious that not all religious expression is authentic and that the Christian religion must undergo constant purification and development. In a sense, the religious response in which faith is embodied is always a response to a call similar to that which God made to Abraham: "Go from your country and your kindred and your father's house to the land that I will show you." (Gn 12:1)

Notes

1. Carl G. Vaught, "Two Concepts of God," *Religious Studies* 6 (1970) 221.
2. Mythical does not mean untrue, but refers to the literary form in which the message is expressed.
3. Beliefs are not as fundamental as faith and do not affect the core of meaning found in a religion. Thus the existence of angels may constitute a belief for some Christians, but is not an essential part of the faith.
4. On the changing conditions of religious expression, see Bernard Lonergan, "Theology in Its New Context," in L.K. Shook, ed., *Theology of Renewal*, vol. 1 (New York, 1969) 34-46.
5. One may here distinguish between the Christian religion and the truth of the Christian kerygma. Religion is the whole complex by which faith is expressed, grows, and is mediated, and so it is much influenced by diverse cultural elements.
6. For several examples of this, see Yves Congar, "Renewal of the Spirit and Reform of the Institution," *Concilium* 73 (March 1972) 39-49.
7. On the nature and relevancy of historical consciousness, see J.W. O'Malley, "Reform, Historical Consciousness, and Vatican II's Aggiornamento," *Theological Studies* 32 (1971) 573-601.

3

Cultural Encounter
and
Religious Expression

APART FROM THE TIME OF ITS BEGINNINGS IN ISRAEL, CHRISTIANITY has always been a faith which came from outside the cultural setting of the place where it was preached. It has always arrived in an alien dress, and so has always been faced with the problem of a fusion of cultures. How far evangelization needs to affect the cultural modes of the evangelized is an ever-recurring question. In this chapter we intend to examine the implications of this problem, in the interest of new developments. Can we discern, in its most basic forms, the influence which faith has on cultural expression? On the other hand, can we see how faith may be stifled by the failure to meet the cultural problem?

CULTURE

Definitions and descriptions of culture are often based on the image of a self-contained society. There is harmony, organic unity, unified vision. A person does not have to look too far to find personal values. They are given in the rites, institutions, traditions, and myths of one's people. Life partakes of a cosmic force: along with one's tribe, a person is at the center of the universe and the still turning-point of time.

Like Augustine on time, we know what culture is but cannot accurately define it. Loosely speaking, we can say that it includes economic, political, and religious systems. It is whatever is expressed in traditions, beliefs, customs, institutions, art and artifacts, symbols, myths and rites. Its core is the values and the meaning on which human life, individual and collective, is based. The idyllic picture of culture is that it represents a unified whole. Of religion within such a pattern, it would be said that it harmonizes with all else, is interwoven with it, and somehow indicates that life is sacred.

Whatever the truth of such a description, there is hardly a single example in the world today of a society and a culture which has not entered into contact and conflict with other cultures. Patterns have been unwoven, so that there are no holy centers from which a group derives undisputed value and meaning. Meeting the economic and political crises of the day may mean discounting religion as a vital factor in the harmonious development of society. People are trying to live peacefully together, despite rather fundamental differences on questions of life and death. Nonetheless, those who live by faith remain convinced that to them at least it should be the source and focal point of meaning in life. Moreover, societies which have been religious in their foundations do not expel all semblance thereof too lightly from their fabric, and some religious practice can remain side by side with very secular attitudes.

EXAMPLES

Messianism in Africa

Observers do not all agree on the significance and force of messianism in African countries and churches.[1] It is some blending of beliefs and traditions taken from traditional religions and from an imported Christianity: imported, that is, in the garb it acquired through long centuries of dwelling in Europe. Messianism is the expression and creation of (or for) the less sophisticated members of peoples whose life-structures have been fragmented by the intrusion on their continent of white races, bringing with them new economics, new politics, new family customs, and new religions. Often enough, the religion was initially accepted along with the rest, but like the rest did not meet its promises of betterment. Neither the wholesale return to traditional religions, nor the wholesale adherence to western forms of Christianity, can remedy a rather disappointing situation. Messianism in its various shapes endeavors to integrate elements from the clashing cultures into a religious practice which spells hope. It is not a homogeneous phenomenon; its message of hope is not the same in all places and in all the emerging "Churches," but its common point of interest is its attempt to give unity, wholeness, and promise.

At this juncture in history, African messianism has an apocalyptic sound. As is the wont of apocalyptic, it can draw people towards vision of millenium. It can be the promise of good things not to be sought for in politics and economics (where people cannot cope anyway), but which will be given by some saving hand to those whose resignation in face of hardships will bear its reward, or to those who practice the virtues of thrift and hard work, avoiding the vices born of despair and displacement. On the other hand, it can be a more positive force, which engenders an effort to achieve self-determination. Since it is apocalyptic, it will belittle the apparent might of invading forces and systems. It will teach that these are not necessary for salvation and improvement. It can convey a spirit which impels a people to do all that it can to shape out its own place on the earth. The more it draws on the people's own past and mythologies, the more it can convince them that out of their own heritage they can build up a future, not relying on a return to the past ways but in a truly creative spirit.

Whether this messianism is syncretistic or not, depends on how it weds the elements taken from different cultures, and on what kind of hope it gives. If its main purpose is to make daily life more bearable, it will probably be syncretistic in the worst sense of the term, for it will take from either religion whatever seem the best practices to satisfy particular needs. A Christian saint and an African charm may be a good combination in time of sickness. A miracle story from the Gospels and some of the titles of Christ can go well with local legends to build up an ideal messianic figure, whose help is expected in times of hardship and in giving some immediate happiness in festivities, or in promising social position to the thrifty and abstemious.

The more, however, that it seeks to foster trust in the spirit that is within, the more likely it is to achieve a unified vision and expression. It can go beyond the stages of syncretism and forge a new mentality. The creative blending of past and future exacts this, whereas a limited concern with the daily present will be content with lesser gains, and prone to invoke whatever power is deemed attendant on the day's calamities. The unity which is achieved beyond syncretism is not one that emerges from a piecing together of cultural contents. It derives from attention to the dynamic thrust of symbols, and from a learning of the processes of storytelling and symbol-making. The people that can tell stories of their own death and rebirth can also live in hope, and in that hope create elements of a new order.

Religious Practice of Romans

From data collected in 1969-1970, a sociologist was led to express the opinion that while some ninety percent of Rome's populace at some stage in their lives practiced the rites of the Catholic Church, only five percent are authentically Catholic.[2] Whereas one may justifiably quibble over his interpretation of the data (sociologists not being infallible), it remains a fact that in Rome there is a religious practice which does not seem to express what the rites themselves intend, if they are taken in their historical purity. It is another case of the average person's religion (one may be a millionaire industrialist as easily as a *barracche* dweller). In this case, however, it is not the result of a meeting between cultures. Rather, it is linked with a cultural development of changing values and visions, attendant on technological and social process. The traditional rites of the Catholic religion do not seem to fit, and for many they matter little enough. Yet the practices continue, giving rise to a series of questions about the religious sense they express.

From these two examples something emerges about the pattern of religious practice in the present time. In times past, religion was all-pervasive and at the heart of the matter. Sacred and profane were not separable, except in the sense that the profane was the unintegrated. A society's religion was at one with its cultural values and meanings. If you did not share them, you were a sect (as was the case of Christianity in imperial Rome) and that meant living outside the social pale. All that has changed, and with the diversification of cultures has come a disruption of religious belief and practice. In this new state of affairs, the position of religion is variable. It may be rather on the fringe of what is happening. It may be put to use to reconcile people to the fact that development has passed them by, without giving them a share in its benefits. It may, however, also seek new forms which allow it to insert its presence at the heart of where things are going. It must then be asked whether there are criteria available to permit a critique of what occurs.

A CHRISTIAN'S CRITIQUE OF RELIGIOUS EXPRESSION

The key question in this critique is the following: is the core of Christianity content and form, or is it a particular dynamics of religious experience? In other words, is it doctrine and ritual, or is it a dynamics of faith which structures the human experience of the transcendent?

If the answer to this query favors content and form, then the task of evangelization is that of adaptation and acculturation (or incarnation). To use the second of these terms is considered more progressive than to use the former, because it more readily allows for internal growth, and reduces in number the tenets of doctrine and the forms of ritual considered essential. It makes more place for dialogue with other religious traditions. However, its implications have hardly been worked out as yet, particularly in regard to the relation between content and dynamics.[3]

If the view taken of Christianity is that it is a dynamics of religious meaning, then we must have principles of action to guide its expression and its relation to other religions and cultures.

A first principle is that religion is consummated in faith,

and that faith grounds religion when it is authentic.[4] As Bernard Lonergan says, faith is the knowledge which is born of love, of being in love in an unrestricted fashion. It is a dynamic state of being, a movement toward self-transcendence and toward communion in spirit. In more biblical terms, it is the Spirit of God within us, the Spirit speaking to our spirit, seeking to create a communion in love, transcending divisions, and finding ultimate oneness in the mystery which abides in all things. "Religious experience spontaneously manifests itself in changed attitudes, in the harvest of the Spirit that is love, joy, peace, kindness, goodness, fidelity, gentleness, and self-control. But it is also concerned with its basis and focus in the *mysterium fascinans et tremendum*."[5] It will not develop unless given expression, and the expression will be culturally manifold. It may also be stultifying, to the extent that it arises from inauthentic experience, and one of the most stultifying factors is to allow preoccupation with content and form outride dynamics and inner consciousness.

In Christian terms, what is to be lived is the father-son relationship, for which Christ is paradigmatic. It is a relationship which exists only in the Spirit, and finds its fulfillment in the Spirit. As Paul Ricoeur comments:

> Far from being easy to address God as Father, by looking into an archaic past, such address is rare, difficult and audacious, because it is prophetic. It is turned to the future and to accomplishment, rather than to beginnings. It does not look backward to a greater ancestor, but forward in the direction of a new intimacy, modelled on the knowledge of the son. In Paul's exegesis, it is because the Spirit testifies to our sonship (Rom 8.16) that we can cry, Abba, Father. Far then from being a hostile and distant transcendence, the religion of the father is a fatherhood which exists because there is sonship, and there is sonship because there is communion in the spirit.[6]

This dynamics is not maintained without inner freedom. The spirit of servitude tempts us to adopt ossifying formulations, with which to rest content and secure, keeping the distance between God and us. To religious expression, Christian faith can contribute the necessary freedom.

When it is emphasized that faith is a dynamics, the second important principle to be kept in mind is what might be called "the intention of truth" in symbolic expression.[7] In symbols and their variant use, people express their quest for meaning. They indicate how we experience life and what sense we make of it.

This is a field in which the meaning of terms is not fixed. To avoid confusion, let us try to make some matters clear on how reality is perceived and truth appropriated.

For some, whose world is only that of feelings, reality is identified with images and sense perceptions. It is in that world that they live and move and have their being. To be responsible, to truly love, to know the mystery of life, they must need go beyond such a world, recognize the need to transcend the world of sense, to conform feeling to reality and not vice versa. The artist and the philosopher are thought to have an important part in culture, because they can break the world of feelings and challenge to new perceptions of reality.

The "sophisticated" westerner tries to come to grips with these different worlds by making distinctions. There is the primitive world, in which people live completely by feeling, identify the worldly and the other-worldly with their myths. Then there is the more advanced world, in which the artists have their part, since with literary and other skills they challenge perception and invite to new projects. Then there is the world of the philosopher, who makes clear the distinction between sense and thought, feelings and love, subjective and objective, experienced and unexperienced, immediate and mediated.

In effect, cultures which are built on mythologies, symbols, customs, traditions, rituals, may be more differentiated than the western observer is inclined to think. They may have (in some cases certainly do have) their own ways to shock and challenge reality sense. Consciousness of the "known unknown" and of the need to transcend the self to enter into it, is awakened by the interplay of myths, symbols, parables, metaphors, narratives, images, and rites. There are more ways than the philosophical to invite to interiority. Indeed, as we have come to acknowledge, the interplay of symbols is necessary for this, since feelings must be shocked and invited if thought and decision are to be set free. Language studies show more and more how this is done. Some application is made to the study of the Bible, particularly in regard to myth, narrative, and parable.[8] In the work of evangelization and faith-insertion in other cultures, their own language devices have to be put to use.

Paul Ricoeur gives us some paradigms for a "discernment of myths."[9] In his study of the myths of evil, his stance was not that of a substitution of one myth for the rest, but an appropriation of all myths within the perspective and dynamic of one, which is allowed to dominate because it offers greater freedom to the human creative spirit, and greater hope in the pursuit of good.

> By putting all other myths into a perspective with relation to a dominant myth (i.e., the Adamic), we bring into light a circularity among myths and we make possible the substitution of a dynamics for a statics of the myths; in place of a static view of myths regarded as having equal rights, the dynamic view makes manifest the struggle among the myths. The appropriation of the struggle among the myths is itself a struggle for appropriation.[10]

The crucial question for Christianity's religious expression is whence it derives its power to free the spirit that is at work in us. If this dynamics can be discovered, then it can be introduced into any culture or religion. Of its very nature, it allows for creative development of language, a dynamics of symbols, within culture.

Perhaps Italo Mancini has found a happy expression of the dynamics of Christian faith, when he says that Christianity always preaches *kairos*, *doxa*, and *eschaton*, and that it necessarily lives a spiral whereby it takes form, contests all forms, and prefigures new forms.[11] The cycle, or spiral, of forms inevitably follows within a vision of the time of salvation which allows for the praise of God and gives rise to hope for the future.

The proclamation of *kairos* turns every moment into the "still turning-point of time," makes of it a moment in eternity in which the God of love is encountered. The sense of *kairos* is well expressed by David Tracy, when he says that "the proclamatory sayings of Jesus do not provide us time-plans for the kingdom as future, as past, or as present. Rather . . . these sayings actually bestow on us the event of an authentic time: time as the e-vent, the happening, for the disclosure of God's gracious and trustworthy action to happen now."[12]

This sense of salvific time leads to a particular way of viewing and narrating history. The Christian witness combats any particularism which selects one people in preference to another. It announces God as a God whose saving Spirit blows where it wills. Its witness is to this Spirit, this love of God, at work in all time, in all history, and in any particular history. The past of a people is to be symbolically interpreted in keeping with this vision. The effort must be to give this interpretation not from without, but from within, its own memory and symbolic traditions. Without such a memory of the past, which automatically coincides with a hope for the future, the present will always appear as a moment to be survived, instead of as a point of God's promise and covenant.

Awareness of "God's gracious and trustworthy action" fosters an attitude of praise. Praise is the antidote to the magical tendencies inherent in any religious system, and it is the only adequate way in which God may be invoked as Father. Too facile a tendency to call God "Father" has been the bane of Christianity and one of the major obstacles to true evangelization. The missionary church is tempted to pick out points in non-Christian traditions whereby to illustrate, or allegorize, a fatherhood which is related to creation, origin, and beneficence. In effect, this encourages a superstitious and inert dependence, and a magical approach to rite. The paternity we proclaim of God is more truly related to alliance, promise, and choice. It exacts a fidelity similar to that between spouses, and one which promises freedom to the adopted children. An impoverishment and self-emptying is required if God's power is to be known. This is an attitude in face of the mysteriousness of God's love, such as is found in Job, or in the just of wisdom literature who in suffering and though reviled by humans keeps trust in God. The enigma of this relationship "makes sense" only in Jesus' invocation of God as his "Abba." This invocation could not be made if there were no recognition that God has given the Spirit to the Son, and that the son-father relationship is grounded in this alliance in the Spirit.[13]

An appropriation of the trajectory of the Judeo-Christian

revelation may well serve as a preparation for the one who seeks ways in which to express the Christian *doxa* in non-Semitic and non-Mediterranean cultures. Ricoeur's studies of symbol and myth show how far the "dilemma of God" or the "enigma of the transcendent" were inherited by the Jewish people from non-Jewish mythologies and traditions. It is in encounter with the prophetic announcement of *kairos* that religious traditions are purified and develop, and eventually come to a point where God can be invoked and praised as Father, by that or some other term that captures the faith-relationship.

Christian evangelization has often been too preoccupied with Christianity's institutional elements. This is an obstacles to a liturgy of praise and a ritual which can find a place in other cultures. Whatever about flexibility in word and catechesis, the church has shown very little flexibility in recent centuries in sacramental worship, least of all in the eucharist. Even today, the Roman Curia feels obliged to authenticate the translation of the words of consecration into Xhosa and Tagalog. But how do we know that such a translation conveys anything of the dynamics of the relationship between God and Christ, or between Christ and those whom he loved on the Father's account, even to the shedding of his blood?

The creed and the eucharistic prayer proclaim and praise, in the first place, the God of creation. This has little to do with the *ex nihilo sui et subiecti* of scholastic theology. It has much to do with the cosmogonies taken up by the prophetic tradition in ages past, and interpreted and appropriated from the stance of the Adamic or Pentateuchal variation of these myths. The creed and eucharistic prayer proclaim that Jesus Christ gave his life in sacrifice for the many. This has little to do with the reverence to God's honor about which the Tridentine Fathers were so preoccupied. It has much to do with the covenant treaties that Abraham found necessary in portioning out the land for his flocks and for those of his rival herdsmen, with the human sacrifices whereby Israel and her neighbors sought to enter into the cycle of time, with the blood wherewith fearful humanity sought to wash away sins and guilt—and with the love which traced a path through the labyrinth of fear, guilt, jealousy, and scandal.

Whoever wishes to proclaim God's praise among a people must take on the ways in which it has sought to wrestle with the harshness of the earth, the enigma of life, the fear of death and oblivion, the constant struggle for power and possession which destroys community. How can the people be freed? How can their stories be told and retold, so as to weave a path of freedom and hope through the maze of agony, fear, and superstition? How can the truth that is in these stories and customs be liberated and set into the light of day? How may God be praised in authentic words, rather than in the babblings of the enslaving language of another culture's institutional preoccupations?

The time of salvation and praise is a future-filled, hopeful anticipation of life. Persuaded of the life in the Spirit, a people can live in hope. It can work towards that hope, for the "Spirit speaks to our spirit," and is the ground of liberation.

The critique of forms, the taking-on of new forms, a critique of these same when they in turn begin to ossify, a constant prefiguring and pretasting of new forms, is a necessary part of the spiral of saving presence, praise, and hope. It is the work of free spirits. The tendency of a religious system, and this is no less true of Christianity than of other religions, can be to suppress the creative spirit.

It is one of the theses of Joseph Campbell in his work *The Masks of God* and especially in the volume *Creative Mythology*[14] that in the western world the creative spirit works only outside organized Christendom. Campbell points to a path going from the legends of the Grail and similar literature to recent writers such as Joyce and Mann. Along this path, creative individuals have travelled in a desire to be free from the "anticipated death" of traditional mythologies and established formulas. His criticism may be exaggerated, but has undoubtedly its moment of truth. All too often, in the story of Christendom, individuals, on the pain of death or excommunication, have been required to submit to the mass or to the structure. But the true "mythology" of Christian faith offers solidarity in the paradox of the lonely quest of the individual, in the wilderness experience of a taking-on of Christ's relation to God. There has to be a dissociation from much that is established, if truth is to be pursued.

There is a Christian ideal which says that the ecclesial community is a fellowship of free spirits—free, that is, in the Spirit. The desire to allow for a Christianity that is of the masses works against this, for expression begins to succumb to the formalism which satisfies masses unprovoked to thought or awakened consciousness. However, the symbol of the small remnant within the cultural tradition is part of the dynamic of Judeo-Christian faith. Paradoxically, it is not a small remnant which seeks to isolate itself. Like Christ, it seeks to be "for the many." It knows the tendency to formalism and ritualism, but does not despair, because it has the Spirit. It is patient enough to know that salvation is a history, and that a dialectic of forms is necessary. It is senseless to talk of a dialectic, unless allowance is made for the words which people use to express their actual selves. People must be allowed to sing the songs they wish to sing, and the small remnant does not balk at that. But it will make its own contribution by way of prophetic song, a song which frees and holds out future promise, which provokes and challenges, even if it risks also angering and disturbing.

SUMMARY AND CONCLUSION

Behind much of the malaise over prevailing forms of popular religiosity is the failure to resolve questions of faith-expression when cultures meet. On the one hand, the Christian from a foreign culture fails to perceive the intention of truth in the strivings of other religions or traditions. On the other hand, any religious expression, including that of Christianity, is constantly subject to the temptation to identify reality and faith with conceptual content and linguistic form. Either mistake blocks the development of new ways of saying, and leaves a strange mingling of bodies, foreign to one another.

Few myths, customs, or rites need be rejected out of hand, without more ado. Faith allows a Christian to be free in regard to one's own culture, and to invite partners in dialogue to be similarly free in their habitat. Myths and histories and rites can be played with in creative freedom, so that their feeling for human life and its meaning is unearthed and their enslaving demon expelled, giving rebirth to the hope of which they bear the seed and the promise.

Today, culture and religion are in foment, the component "religion" apparently less relevant. The answer is not purely a secular mentality, a concentration on the human realm to the exclusion of the gods. If we secularize human problems and meanings completely, "God need no longer be counted upon to solve problems in the world; the problems—at the level at which divine intervention would avail—have been dissolved."[15] If Christian proclamation and prayer "attends first, foremost and exclusively to what the given is given *to*, it winds up with nothing *given* to. More especially, it does not allow the given to identify the world and its decisive strifes, to interrogate the world and the world's self-analysis, and to establish that world in which man is to be housed in fulfillment."[16]

Enslaved to the present, in disjunction from past and future, tied down to forms of prayer and rite intended to obtain divine beneficence, assuring only the future of afterlife to undo the hardships of the present, religion is both enslaved and enslaving. Suffuse it with the Christian Gospel of *kairos*, *doxa*, and *eschaton*, and it becomes a fomenting presence in any culture, one which sets free in the power of the Spirit, so that we may house the world with our own peace and to the glory of God.

Notes

1. See David B. Barrett, *Schism and Renewal in Africa* (Oxford: Oxford University Press, 1968); Louis-Vincent Thomas and René Luneau, *La Terre Africaine et ses religions* (Paris: Larousse, 1975) 322-327.

2. Emile Pin, *La Religiosità dei Romani* (Bologna, 1975).

3. Since this chapter originally appeared in article form, much has been written on this topic. For the terminology of church documents, see Nicolas Standaert, "L'Histoire d'un néologisme. Le term 'inculturation' dans les documents romains," *Nouvelle revue théologique* 110 (1988) 555-570. On the question of liturgy, see Anscar J. Chupungco, "A Definition of Liturgical Inculturation," *Ecclesia Orans* 5 (1988) 11-23.

4. See Bernard Lonergan, *Method in Theology* (London: Darton,

Longmann & Todd, 1972) 101-119.

5. Ibid. 108.

6. Paul Ricoeur, "Fatherhood: From Phantasm to Symbol," in *The Conflict of Interpretations*, ed. and trans., Don Ihde (Evanston: Northwestern University Press, 1974) 491.

7. See Garrett Barden, "The Intention of Truth in Mythic Consciousness," in P. McShane, ed., *Language, Truth and Meaning* (Dublin: Gill, 1972) 4-32.

8. For a summary and bibliography of such attempts, see David Tracy, *Blessed Rage for Order* (New York: Crossroad, 1975) 120-145.

9. Paul Ricoeur, *The Symbolism of Evil*, trans., Emerson Buchanan (Boston: Beacon, 1967) 306-341.

10. Ibid. 309.

11. I. Mancini, "Cultura cristiana: specificità e senso," in *Christianesimo e Cultura: Atti del XLVI corso di aggiornamento culturale dell'università cattolica: Loreto, 21-26 settembre 1975* (Milan, 1975) 36-57.

12. Tracy, *Blessed Rage* 134.

13. Ricoeur, "Fatherhood" 491.

14. Joseph Campbell, *The Masks of God: Creative Mythology* (New York: Viking, 1968).

15. Ray L. Hart, *Unfinished Man and the Imagination* (New York: Herder & Herder, 1968) 39.

16. Ibid.

LITURGY MEETS CULTURE

4

Liturgy in Search of Religion

THE LITURGICAL MOVEMENT REACHED ITS PEAK AT THE SECOND VAT-
ican Council insofar as liturgical principles of active participation and adaptation are concerned. The Constitution on the
Liturgy centered the church's life around the traditional image
of the paschal mystery of Christ. It showed the relationship between worship and the realities of the life of faith, between
cult and community in love. It presented the ideal of a liturgy
which could no longer be called the work of the priest, but
rather the community's celebration. Accordingly, it fostered
the conscious and active participation of all the faithful, as
well as a diversification of ministries in the assembly. This
dream has continued to be pursued in the revision of the liturgical books, which do indeed place an immense treasure in the
hands of Christian communities.

AFTER VATICAN II

The book, however, is not the sacrament. From the council
onwards, those who have endeavored to follow its guidelines
have also experienced how difficult it is in practice to realize
that perfect worship, in which all present act out of a keen
knowledge of the Christian faith, a keen sense of Christian
community, and a keen appreciation of the liturgical books'

measured forms. Over the past years, several questions have arisen from attempts to realize in practice what Vatican II set down in theory. These questions do not merely pose problems for pastors and educators. They have also been taken up by theologians of the liturgy, who realize that they have to be taken into account at the level of understanding, if the discipline of the liturgy is to serve the community of faith.

One of the first things to strike promoters of a more perfect and pure liturgy was that what was considered an ideal did not always hit a responsive chord among the people. Certainly, there was a good amount of enthusiasm about a vernacular liturgy and about hymns tuned to contemporary melodies (however artistically appalling!), and it took a surprisingly short time to increase the number receiving communion at Sunday Mass. But people cling a long time to such things as the bells in the middle of the eucharistic prayer, and it does not take too keen an eye to see how restless a congregation becomes during some of the scriptural readings, which might as well be read in Hebrew or Greek for all the impact they have on a congregation.

Another thing which struck home quite early in the reform was the truism that gathering a number of people into one building for an act of worship does not turn them into a community. Looking beyond the immediate and practical problem of how to get people to participate in a Sunday Mass or an infant baptism, it became obvious in many instances that the reality whereby the liturgy is defined did not exist. In the absence of both the human and the faith dimension of community, liturgy descends to ritual of rather doubtful meaning.

If it were only a question of developing a greater sense of community, the matter would be relatively simple. Since theologians often live in cities, it was perhaps too easy for them to draw a connection between liturgical problems and the anonymous life of the modern metropolis. A look, however, at the barrios around cities or at rural populations gives a different perspective. In such areas people still possess and express fellow-feeling, on the basis of long-standing customs and values, as well as of human sympathy. It is not, however, in the forms suggested by the liturgical books that their customs and values are expressed, or their fellow-feeling encouraged. The fiesta draws people into a sense of oneness far more effectively than a well-ordered sacrament.

The gap between liturgy and those devotions which draw and touch people is perhaps most obvious at a time such as Holy Week. On the one hand, the liturgical ceremonies give an improved representation of the paschal mystery. On the other, the crowds are more numerous and involved in such manifestations as the stations of the cross, the procession of the dead Christ, or the "encuentro" between the Risen Jesus and his Mother, which for some peoples is the real climax to this week.

Not that it is necessary to wait until Holy Week to observe this gap. On any Sunday morning in the Quiapo church in Manila, it is possible to take note of the abyss that separates the priest in the sanctuary celebrating Mass from the line of people doing reverence to the Black Nazarene at the rear of the church. They feel closer to the Lord in kissing his suffering feet than they do at the moment of the eucharistic memorial.

Another observation made in practice was that the times at which ideally Christians are drawn together into one as God's people are paradoxically the times at which a local population splits up into smaller units of family and kin. Having a child baptized is a worry to parents and grandparents, and the occasion to provide it with sponsors or patrons more socially powerful than themselves. Who dares to make of a wedding in the family an occasion for a parish celebration? In a word, the great events of the church's worship, the sacraments, are either private matters or the concern of a closely knit kinship. The desire and request for sacrament expressed by many people simply do not correspond to what an official presentation would make of them.

EVANGELIZATION AND SACRAMENT: A PROGRAM

In face of these observations, the reaction was to stress the need to ground piety more firmly in the knowledge of the Gospels and of Christian teaching. The negative side of popular devotion was stressed, a side described in Paul VI's exhortation on evangelization as follows:

> Popular religiosity is often subject to penetration by many distortions of religion and even superstitions. It frequently remains at the level of forms of worship not involving a true acceptance by faith. It can even lead to the creation of sects and endanger the true ecclesial community.[1]

Hence pastoral theologians and episcopal conferences throughout the world began to suggest programs of evangelization among baptized Christians, which would lead to better sacramental practice.[2] The main ingredients in such programs were a better education in the knowledge of the Scriptures, teaching people how to pray such forms as the Lord's Prayer and the Creed, the development of a true sense of Christian service and Christian witness, better instruction in the meaning of liturgical symbols and ceremonies. Sacramental seminars, however, based on these elements often turned out to be abortive. And, of course, there was always the problem of what to do when people did not wish, or were not able, to follow the prescribed courses prior to reception of the sacraments, yet persevered in their request to be admitted to them, and continued to turn up faithfully for fiestas and novenas.

An element was apparently missing in the efforts to renew liturgical life. Pastors and educators were addressing people without knowing them properly, and theologians were writing only about ideal forms. People were being corrected on their forms of piety, but nobody had bothered very much to inquire into the significance of these forms. What was lacking was a real grasp of the nature, roots, and meanings of popular religion.

PEOPLE'S RELIGION

Popular religion is an expression of piety which needs understanding. It has strong foundations in history and in the conditions of life under which many people live.[3] Perhaps it needs to be educated, its potential drawn forth, but it cannot be banished. On the other hand, liturgy itself cannot be seen as the celebration of ideal forms of worship. Its own renewal has only to gain from being more closely in tune with some of the practices of popular piety.

holds out future promise. By focusing on the memory of Jesus Christ the Christian imagination offers other ways to explore the meaning of these moments. It suggests to us that it is because in these moments we are put in touch with the weakest and most vulnerable part of ourselves that they are so rich in the promise of life. Remembering the way in which Christ encountered human weakness, his own and that of others, reveals to us that in this very vulnerability is their power. He neither denied nor manipulated weakness. He "passed through it." By this memory we are called to an awareness of our own simultaneous temporality and immortality. For anybody who arrives at that center of consciousness, the present is full of possibilities. The trials, the questions, the problems, and the suffering are not dismissed, but they can be faced in a new way.

This is vital to the question of Christian rites for the moments of the life-cycle. How we deal with new life and its reproduction, with sexuality, with death is of immense importance for the future. Every society has its projects and its hopes for the future, and often enough they center around these realities. Christians can in many cases concur with the symbols and institutions in which these hopes are expressed, or at least they are ready to discuss them in open forum. At the same time, through faith in Christ they see that all future possibility depends on the *hodie* of God and humankind in covenant. This can be of great consequence for a Christian's contribution to the secular, or any other cultural, project.

LIFE-CYCLE RITUAL AND SACRAMENTS

At the outset of this chapter, it was said that the traditional seven sacraments may not be used to answer the needs of life-cycle ritual. At the same time, it would be wrong to give the impression that there are two ritual systems possible in the church, the one that of the sacraments and the other that of the life-cycle. The latter have to be related to the former, and the nature of the relation lies in the *call* to personal conversion experienced at moments of the life-cycle and expressed in terms of Christian belief in these rites.

An answer to the meaning of human life can be given at birth through the Christian symbols of the holy and of redemption. This necessarily raises the question of initiation in the faith and of membership in the Christian community. Pastors and theologians today often suggest that birth or infancy is not the appropriate moment for baptism. Instead, they indicate the possibility of a rite of welcome and inscription, which envisages the eventual initiation and personal faith of the child. This could well be associated with the Christian symbols of birth, important to the parents in commencing the education of their child in the Christian faith, and in the fullness of the life which is God's gift. The moment of personal initiation would then be decided in later years by the child's own personal choice, while at the same time it is prepared within the community from the child's birth. On the other hand, if children are baptized at birth, as cultural forces may well demand, this is done not so much to take them out of an original sin that taints life, as it is to express the community's acceptance of new life, and to express the welcome of the child into a community of faith and hope, in a world disrupted by evil.

The question of conversion and Christian belonging is raised for the growing person at many critical moments, and chiefly in adolescence. Any rites related to growth serve to raise the issue of personal initiation, and can be steps whereby through a personal integration of the factors involved in the growth process a young person moves toward faith in Christ.

In the case of marriage, it seems a great mistake to make a valid (and genuinely human) marriage and sacramental marriage coincide in time. The rites occurring at the beginning of marriage call for a personal evaluation of its meaning, but they may not in effect signify as yet a deep personal faith on the part of the marriage partners. The marriage becomes truly sacramental when it can be said that through personal faith it is lived by both partners in the Lord. It may be hard to express an exact moment at which this is the case, but it is more in the eucharist than in a marriage ritual postulated at the inception of marriage that the sealing in faith often takes place. If the church were to maintain a marriage sacrament (i.e., rite) truly signifying the personal choice to be married in Christ, this would have to be dissociated from the beginning of marriage and allowed for at a moment chosen in faith by the partners, within the compass of their experience of marriage. A marriage ceremony at the inception of marriage is more in the nature of a call to faith and to live marriage in faith.

CONCLUSION

I began this chapter by recalling the place of life-cycle rites in diverse cultures, and the position of these rites in traditionally Christian countries. I then said that the problems which this raises today cannot be answered by an appeal to the sevenfold sacramental system, nor on the direct evidence of the Scriptures. Through the example of marriage, I then showed how human meaning can be integrated into the Christian. After a brief word about the current secular experience of passages, I indicated that the traditional Christian symbols relevant to these moments can include secular values, while respecting their own intrinsic validity. The next step was to examine the implications of ritual, and to suggest that the ritual used in moments of passage when celebrated in the memory of Christ can be an open and transcending experience, revealing the *hodie* of salvation and the presence of God's Spirit in human persons.

We may then conclude that Christian rituals might well express the meaning of life-cycle events, without suppressing either authentic secularity or authentic Christian faith. On the other hand, the prevalent use of some of the sacraments does not constitute an adequate ritual, but rather does disservice to these sacraments. A recovery of the meaning of some traditional symbols may result in attempts to bring fresh understanding to explorations in ritual. The end result of this is hard to tell. We can agree with L. Bertsch, as he is quoted in the article by K. Richter, already mentioned: "Neither the repetition of doctrinal formulas nor the rational planification of new rites will bring the solution, but only the road which leads towards a faith ever on the increase, and on the basis of which new ritual forms of comportment and ecclesial life can be found."[20]

Notes

1. See "Problèmes sacramentaires. Dialogue interdisciplinaire," *La Maison-Dieu* 119 (1973) 51-73.

2. E.g., Langdon Gilkey, *Catholicism Confronts Modernity* (New York: Crossroad, 1975) 198f.; Raimundo Panikkar, *Worship and Secular Man* (London: Darton, Longmann & Todd, 1973) 59.

3. Klemens Richter, "Rites and Symbols in an Industrial Context as Illustrated by Their Use in a Socialist Context," *Concilium* 102 (1977) 72-82.

4. On this process for the sacraments of initiation, see Nathan D. Mitchell, "Dissolution of the Rites of Christian Initiation," in *Made, Not Born*, edited by the Murphy Center for Liturgical Research (Notre Dame: University of Notre Dame Press, 1976) 50-82.

5. Aquinas' synthesis, S.Th. III, q. 65, art. 1, is based on an analogy with the natural life-cycle, but does not relate the sacramental rituals to any of these moments.

6. Daniel B. Stevick, "Christian Initiation: Post-Reformation to the Present Era," in *Made, Not Born* 116.

7. Whether at the age of five or fifteen, there is no justification for presenting the traditional rite of confirmation or chrismation as a personal ratification of one's baptism. Any separation of baptism and confirmation goes counter to early tradition.

8. See Louis-Marie Chauvet, "Le Mariage, un sacrement pas comme les autres," *La Maison-Dieu* 127 (1976) 64-105.

9. See Stevick, "Christian Initiation" 114.

10. The question is whether one is prepared to make a wager that the Christian symbols can interpret being in the world, as experienced in these moments.

11. See Langdon Gilkey, *Naming the Whirlwind: The Renewal of God-Language* (Indianapolis: Bobbs-Merrill, 1967) 305-414.

12. See William Lynch, *Christ and Promotheus: A New Image of the Secular* (Notre Dame: University of Notre Dame Press, 1972) 123-142.

13. Ernest Becker, *The Denial of Death* (New York: Collier Macmillan, 1973).

14. L.C. Mohlberg, ed., *Sacramentarium Veronense* (Rome: Herder, 1956) 1110.

15. Ibid. 1104.

16. See Paul K. Jewett, *Man as Male and Female* (Grand Rapids: Eerdmans, 1975).

17. See Walter Von Arx, "The Churching of Women After Childbirth," *Concilium* 112 (1979) 62-72.

18. See Mary Douglas, *Purity and Danger* (London: Routledge & Kegan Paul, 1966).

19. Lynch, *Christ and Promotheus* 72. This is not to negate the importance of the cosmic, noted elsewhere in this volume, but to address the relation between the human and the cosmic.

20. Richter, "Rites and Symbols" 112f.

AN EMERGING
CONSCIOUSNESS

7

Households of Faith in the Coming Church

WHILE THERE ARE THOSE WHO PURSUE THE MODEL OF PARISH REOR-
ganization and revitalization as the way whereby to renew
church life and foster Christian community, the emergence of
informal groups of believers and of small communities which
have little to do with ecclesiastical and even confessional
boundaries is of indisputable significance for present and future. Whether some of these will in time replace current official groupings and structures, or whether they will be but a
significant phenomenon in a larger church, is not necessary to
determine at this stage. Suffice to say that in talking of households of faith in the coming church, it is of such groups that I
speak.

The church has always had its plenty of small, informal, and
often spontaneous groups, associations, and communities.
One cannot write the history of the church without taking note
of them, of their appearance, of their motivations, of their accommodation within a larger church, of their eventual survival or disappearance. They have, however, never been as
much studied and analyzed as in today's church, due in part
to the insights provided by sociology and psychology, which
greatly assist us in grasping their origins, qualities, motivations, and significance. Some of these insights make us acutely

aware of how ambiguous a cultural, social, and religious phenomenon is this current trend to smaller church or religious
groupings. It is not possible to canonize the movement and all
its various manifestations without ado.

The challenge to be addressed here is threefold. First, is it
possible to isolate and outline the issues at stake? In other
words, what are the cultural and social factors that perhaps lie
beneath the movement and that are generally verified, no matter how diverse the groups or communities may be. Here, it is
necessary to rely largely on the data and insights provided by
sociology. Second, can a theologian draw on tradition and systematic reflection in offering some Christian or faith assessment of this movement, as well as some suggestions about
what it could mean in the future? Third, can a liturgist look to
liturgical history to explain some of the emergent prayer-
forms and to assess how they may belong in a liturgy which
serves the transformation of these groups into ecclesial bodies
that testify to Christ's power and presence, and prophetically
serve the reign of justice and peace promised in Christ's death
and resurrection?

GROUPS AND THEIR SIGNIFICANCE

As already indicated, it needs to be made clear from the outset that in addressing the theme of households of faith I am
making the choice of considering groups that belong outside
formal structures, such as the parish, and cannot simply therefore be seen as ways of "building community" in a parish,
such as the creation of block groups and the occasional hold-
ing of Mass in homes throughout the parish. Such innovations
have their purpose and may even have affinities with what I
am addressing. However, I believe that the cause of serious reflection and healthy critique is better served by taking account
of communities wherein disenchantment with the established
order and with canonically recognized forms of community
organization, ministry, and leadership is more obvious. A
creative critique of the established ecclesiastical order, supported by a living proposal of alternative models, is needed.

Some groups do indeed seem to be based on fear and the

need for mobilization, and respond to highly ambiguous forms of charismatic and autocratic leadership. Others, however, display a strong sense of theocentric freedom, a freedom received as gift of the Spirit. This then becomes a source of energy and of charisms of service, as well as of free decision and choice, dominated by the persuasion of the gift of God's love and mercy. Where communities possess such freedom, structures develop which are more participatory than in the established order. Needless to say, there are communities which betray elements of both these extremes. This is not surprising if both are seen as responses to the same dilemmas of contemporary life and religious belonging. It can also be noted at this point that some groups form around a concentration of interest in the religious well-being of their members, whereas others have a more distinct sense of wanting to expend their energies in transforming society.

The whole movement, comprehensive of its varied forms, has to be related to the social and cultural pressures of our age. A basic question, explaining why the forms of community can be so diverse, seems to be whether it is possible to find reality and an authentic sense of self within contemporary society, or whether one discovers these despite it. Thus, to a crisis of authority in all its forms, there is linked a crisis of values. To a crisis of the interpersonal, there is linked a crisis of personal autonomy. To a crisis of identity, there is linked a crisis of intimacy. To a crisis of religious belonging, there is linked a crisis of mission.

THEOLOGICAL REFLECTION

Intimacy, identity, the interpersonal, authority, mission, and the degree of participation in the life of a body, are all issues important to the church's nature and its presence in society. We cannot fully recognize the significance of new households and their possible future, unless it is seen that they carry within themselves the search for a response to what can only be described as a breakdown in church life, which has in fact over centuries become largely nonparticipatory. This can be ascribed to various factors, such as sacralization, the split between clergy and the laity, or the domination of bourgeois values. A more fundamental description would be that there has been a distortion of Christian symbols, central to the distortion of communications within the church, which has prevented fuller participation of all baptized members in its life, while also impeding the mission of the church in serving society, particularly its lesser members. New groups in one way or another respond to this distortion, in terms which can be described as facing the crisis of the religious imagination. One need only think here of how the symbols of the presence of Christ have been distorted in meaning, by being treated and used as representative images, to the suffocation of the fuller human and spiritual reality with which this presence is involved. This of course very much affects the question of church leadership, ministry, and liturgy. Reductionism obstructs communication, as when bread and wine come to represent only the physical body and blood of Christ, and cease to symbolize the community participating in his life and mystery, as one in him, the new creation in Jesus Christ.

One of the greatest problems in this regard is that the Catholic Church in legitimating its own identity is "organization blind."[1] That is to say, because it adopts certain social structures as essential to its very identity as the church of Christ, it has no real eye for the weaknesses of the organization and little flexibility in allowing for more participatory structures, which however is the direction taken by "household churches." As has been said, "it is not destruction, but growing complexity and diversity, of ecclesiastical organization, a deliberate mixing of formal and informal structural elements, which seems to offer the greatest hopes for the future of the Church as a religious organization."[2]

While attention to this issue of structures cannot be avoided, one has to look to the fundamental reality of community in Christ to assess what is currently coming to pass among us. It is, therefore, to evangelical poverty, to concern for the poor, and to a search for the living meaning of poverty in Christ, that I would like to make appeal as a key to the future possibilities of households of the faith. By way of insight into this, a parallel is suggested with the twelfth and thirteenth centuries, one made as far back as 1959 by Marie-Dominique Chenu, when he wrote of what was then a very problematic issue, namely, worker-priests and their communities: "Taking a vow of poverty meant, in the thirteenth century, refusing categorically, institutionally, economically, the feudal regime of the Church, the 'benefices', the collection of tithes, even when sweetened by charitable and apostolic purposes . . . The mendicant friars rejected feudalism just as today the *Mission de France* has broken its solidarity with capitalism: the same evangelical, not ideological, violence. It is the return to the gospel which requires the break with the collective superstructures, as well as with personal disorders."[3]

It seems to me that it is true of every renewal movement in the history of the church that, in a way peculiar to its own time and in face of the second temptation, to wit an accommodation with the prevalent temporal power, it has had at its core a renewed awareness of the exigencies of evangelical poverty. This awareness combines the ideal of the Jerusalem community, as described by Luke (Acts 2:42), with the ideal of the community of Jesus with his disciples, both of which ideals are seen as a participation in Christ's mystery in the form of radical experience and overturning of human poverty. Michel Mollat in his studies on ecclesial poverty ascribes an originality to Francis of Assisi, which is in a way the originality of all renewal movements: "The originality of Francis consists less in an intellectual conception of poverty than in the manner in which he took up the challenges of his time to poverty. It would be too simple to say that he did not expect the poor man to come to apply to him, too simple to affirm that he went towards him. The real innovation is to have placed himself side by side with the poor man and to have sought to rehabilitate him in his own eyes, by bringing him a message against poverty in the name of a victory over poverty. It was to proclaim the dignity of the poor man for himself, not only as an image of Jesus Christ but because Jesus loved him for himself. This explains the episode of the 'kissing of the leper'."[4]

In all of this, there is not only an affinity with the poverty of Jesus in his self-emptying and a quest for community without barriers, divisions, and discriminations, but there is also a response to the deviations of society in its uses of power and wealth, a response based on a certain intimacy with the marginal and debased. Indeed, no response is possible without this intimacy, since it is the poor who provide the diagnosis of a society's ills.

A grassroots lay movement, a search for new forms of common evangelical life, attuned to the times, attentiveness to the lot of the poor, and new forms of popular devotion, these seem to have been the characteristics of the religious renewal movement of the twelfth and thirteenth centuries, of which the principal reminder today are the mendicant orders. A group typical of that age are those known as the *Humiliati*, or Humble Ones, of whom Lester Little notes: "The Humiliati of those early days were mostly laymen, some married who continued to live at home with their families, or else unmarried or formerly married who chose to live a common life in the religious manner . . . in addition to the personal reformation of their inner lives, the Humiliati sought to reach out into society to oppose actively the enemies of the Christian faith. The Humiliati not only claimed to follow the model of apostolic simplicity in their lives, but with uncommon audacity engaged in the apostolic act of preaching the Christian faith publicly."[5]

By 1201, when they received official recognition from Innocent III,[6] they had "evolved into an officially sanctioned order of the church, with three variant forms of life—canonical, monastic and lay—for both men and women."[7] Important here is to note the continuation of the third order for people who, because of conjugal and familial ties, could not adopt the fuller forms of common life, but kept the basic aspirations: "The particular piety of these laymen," writes Little, "consisted in their fasting two days a week, saying the Lord's Prayer before and after dinner, and reciting the seven canonical hours. They were to wear simple clothing, and should any of their number become ill or face some other kind of hardship, the others were to come to his aid; in case of death, to the aid of the departed person's soul and family."[8]

Those who were not literate did not recite the canonical hours, but recited the Lord's Prayer a certain number of times a day instead. All extended their charity in a particular way to embrace the poor and downtrodden, with special attention to lepers, and sought to live by the work of their own hands.

Mollat, Chenu, and Little have all shown how movements

of this sort constituted a Christian response to the changing social and economic scene, as Europe moved out of a feudal to a merchant economy, and adopted more communal power structures for the government of society. At the same time, they have pointed out that the scholars associated with the movement, represented particularly by the friars, did not address themselves only to the members of the orders or fraternities, but sought to evolve a moral teaching and a spirituality suited to all Christians, granted that this had its grounding in the vision and way of life of the renewal movement.[9]

One of course cannot talk of this age without recognizing its violence, the social, political, economic, and religious violence, as well as the heresies and the exaggerations in forms of piety. That is, however, one of the features that makes it a distant mirror to our times. Society was in upheaval on all fronts, all were struggling to come to terms with it, but in the midst of this struggle there were those who, resisting the deviations, found a new evangelical way of life and new forms of piety. There were indeed the exaggerations leading to heresy, and the valid insights unjustly dismissed as unorthodox, as well as the antisemitism, too easily tolerated or even promoted by church leaders. There was popular violence, and there were many forms of institutional violence. It is only by putting together the renewal movements and the deviations that one understands the age. Change is met in many ways, and one looks to the age to see both the failings and the deep evangelical insights.

One may also see how church authority accommodated itself to the scene. The reactions of pontiffs such as Innocent III are often applauded by church historians because they took advantage of the evangelical movement and through it fostered a strong church unity, under the increasing power of the papacy. They are, however, also criticized because they maintained and even strengthened the hierarchical and clerical domination of the church.[10] In particular, there was a failure on the part of liturgists and church authority to allow room in official worship for the new forms of piety and devotion, for a popular expression of faith, so that there remained and increased a gap between liturgy and popular piety, marked by much strong faith on the part of the people but also by extravagances. Some of the worst extravagances, of course, such as the endowment of chantries, multiplication of Masses and absolute ordination, were the result of an accommodation of the clergy to the needs of the rich, and clerical manipulation of popular piety.

Today, the call for the church to be the church of the poor has been sounded, and many forms of evangelical lifestyle are being tried. It is in the lives of those who live a way of life in contrast with some of our more public aspirations, who are in touch with the experience of the suffering and resurrection of Jesus Christ, that many of the world's ills are brought to light. They are remarkably like those of the twelfth and thirteenth centuries: violence, censure of outcasts, a search for a share in new forms of power, the sophistication of special kinds of knowledge. It is the contrast between certain styles of life and the violence of the times that shows the link between evangelical poverty and emancipatory praxis, since those who capture our attention are those who, while seeking community and simplicity of life for themselves, are also anxious to find ways whereby to release from bondage those who are the victims of the century's greatness. As we know, this interest has been taken up by some of the leading scholars of the day, especially in the theology of Jesus Christ. For them, Christology is a praxis, because it is a memory, couched in narrative form, and inclusive of the memory of all suffering and poverty.[11]

Hence one may summarily say of households of faith that respond most fully to the Gospel: (1) the form of life will be that of evangelical poverty; (2) the key to their relation to society will be emancipatory praxis, the desire and the struggle to come to the release of those who suffer bondage in the midst of progress, a resistance to the many forms of violence whereby the poor are oppressed; (3) their liturgies will be forceful commemorations of the suffering and resurrection of Jesus Christ, into which will be gathered a memory of all suffering and of all the forgotten and unnamed of past and present; (4) because their members possess a strong sense of the freedom that comes with the gift of the Spirit, they will develop community structures that are participatory and respectful of a variety and multiplicity of gifts.

LITURGY

Sociological investigations should make us very cautious about ascribing reasons for decrease in church membership and in worship participation, or for increase in the membership of some churches. One thing, however, that does seem to emerge is that the role of ritual or sacrament in maintaining commitments, or in influencing departures, is not clearly focused. If it is not really at the heart of things, this fact may be more symptom than cause. Yet a theologian or liturgist might make bold to say that without good and convincing celebration, ecclesial life as participation in Christ's mystery does not survive, whatever other functions an ecclesiastical organization or group experience may serve.

The liturgical expression of households of faith, where the interpersonal is put in evidence, is not a straightforward implementation of the new rites that have received official approval. Indeed, their very appreciation of the ways in which the revisions are based on tradition means that they are put into practice with considerable flexibility and with no little creativity on the part of individual communities. In writing of the right of a community to a priest, which is in effect its right to the eucharist, Edward Schillebeeckx not only highlights the contrast of grass-roots communities with more formal structures, and the emancipatory nature of their apostolic sense, but he also points out the contrast of their liturgies, which are more participatory and simple than what one often finds in older traditions. These liturgies are more flexible, allow more room for adaptation, and raise the issue of liturgical ministries in new ways.[12]

The difficulties experienced in the renewal of liturgy and sacrament in mainstream churches might well be described in this quotation from Richard Fenn: "The apparently minor role of ritual in [some recent sociological studies on churches] may reflect the gap between the church's myths and its current reality. The myth of a Christian community is difficult to sustain when the community has scattered, leaving only families and individuals, just as the myth of the people of God is difficult to sustain when the clergy are part executive, part professional, and only partly charismatic at best. The myth of a spiritual body is difficult to sustain when the church has itself become an hierarchical organization with control increasingly centralized in bureaucratic offices. Under these conditions the context of a ritual may provide very poor acoustics for the music of the soul. Conversely, when churches write and impose new liturgies on their members, it may be difficult for the laity to put their heart and soul into the new lines for at least one generation, regardless of the scholastic merits of the new versions, and some would argue that a bureaucratized church can hardly be expected to provide new rites that enable the spirit to soar."[13]

Elsewhere in the review, the same author describes an attitude to worship which may be central to the dislocation of liturgy: "Worship no longer *constitutes* the church, but the church engages in many activities of which some might be called worship. If worship is uneventful, then its time and place must be moved, some suggest, so that the church's celebrations can catch the eventfulness of secular occasions . . . The key notion . . . is of the congregation as an 'audience' . . ."[14]

In looking into the mirror of the twelfth and thirteenth centuries once more, one can note the forms of piety and devotion which held the populace and the fraternities, but which were not properly (if at all) integrated into official liturgies. There was the importance given to the recitation of the Lord's Prayer, then completed by the Hail Mary, giving us eventually the rosary, in recent times highly promoted by sovereign pontiffs, but dubbed "devotion" and "non-liturgical." Indeed, through the centuries this form of prayer was allowed to develop almost in opposition to liturgy, quite unintegrated into the liturgical cycle, even though it has profoundly biblical and popular roots. In short, the issue of how such prayer, with its immense popular appeal and simplicity, could be integrated into liturgy, never seems to have been faced.

There was also at the time of which we are speaking a great increase in pilgrimages and processions, public and cultural expressions of unity and strength, where the little people of the time could experience their solidarity and express their devotion. The emphasis of these devotions on the humanity of Christ contrasted with the then current sacramental emphasis on his divinity.

If the people largely played the role of audience and recipient in the Mass and sacramental worship, they did have other ministries and devotions which took the person as subject seriously and which sought to promote and enhance personal conversion and commitment. Preaching, confession, and works of penance seem to have gone hand in hand in this regard, since their joint purpose was the conversion and spiritual growth of the human person.

As Little notes in his study, the reform movements showed a deep appreciation of the spiritual worth of the laity generally, and of women in particular.[15] They wanted to break down the perception of society's religious function as the responsibility and domain of the few. Preaching, confession, and penance were important instruments in proposing and implementing personal piety and an apostolic way of life among the laity. It was in accordance with their aim, that some provision was made for lay preaching and for confession to lay persons. Such practices were not set up in opposition to the role of ordained preachers and confessors, but the extension of these functions to lay persons was justified by an appeal to the importance of the act involved. Current discussion of these matters makes us painfully aware that the alternate argument, stressing the status of the minister, in time prevailed over the possibilities of more active lay involvement. Precisely because of current needs, it seems helpful to note that the question went hand in hand with the development of an evangelical way of life and with a basically New Testament image of Christian fellowship.

Some of the most interesting things liturgically occurred within reform groups that are unfortunately known to history only as heretical, though now it would appear that it was extremes in these groups rather than their mainstream that entered into a collision course with ecclesiastical authority or subscribed to christianly untenable beliefs.[16] The Catharist Church, for example, practiced a ceremony called the *consolamentum*, described as follows: "The formal ceremonies of the Catharist Church . . . were markedly simple, being oriented about a view of what the early church must have been like . . . In the most important of Catharist ceremonies, the consolamentum, a ceremony of spiritual baptism, the believer gained forgiveness for all his sins, and the perfected ones, those who had been through the same ceremony, administered baptism to the believer by placing their right hands upon him. They did so as 'true Christians, instructed by the primitive church.' In one of the surviving descriptions of this ritual, the reader is urged not to look down upon his earlier baptism in the Roman Church, but to receive his Catharist baptism ('the holy consecration of Christ') as a supplement to that which was insufficient for his salvation. An abbreviated and simplified form of the consolamentum was made available for the sick and dying."[17]

Of similar interest is the *fractio panis* practiced by the Waldensians. This was a simple way of celebrating the Lord's Supper, based on the model of the Last Supper narrative in the New Testament, wherein the simplicity of style and accessibility to the faithful were the major concerns. Again, it is important to note that opposition to church authority or subscription to doctrines at odds with official intentions were not at the base of this development, but that this kind of opposition only came with time, when a harmonious integration of views and practices seemed to become impossible.[18]

From the few examples given, one can see a trend in liturgy towards simplicity of style, lay participation, personal faith, devotion to God's word, devotion to the humanity of Jesus, all gathered together under the umbrella of the desire to return to Gospel models of Christian life and Christian worship. For all the obvious differences between that age and ours, we can sense readily enough similar desires in contemporary households of faith, as well as similar hazards of nonintegration with the established order. How successful can the dialectic be today?

The development of good liturgy, expressive of what the church is, rather than an act which it does, will likewise be rooted in community experience in households of faith for the coming church. Similarly important are the quest for evangelical and apostolic community, the existence of fellowships of the baptized intent on a baptismal rather than on a clerical spirituality, the desire for simplicity in style, the bias against any form of discrimination, the search for contemporary forms of piety, and a christological focus which has been given keen systematic articulation in what are called "christologies from below," highlighting the solidarity of Jesus with the human condition, in particular with those who suffer and are cancelled out from the pages of history.

GOOD WORSHIP

Some of the characteristics and forms of liturgical expression appropriate to households of faith in the coming church might well appear from what has been said about participatory structures, about Christian freedom in the Spirit, about evangelical poverty, and about the trends of piety in the twelfth and thirteenth centuries that were not well integrated into official worship.

First of all, good worship is based on an aesthetic appreciation of the sacramentality of life and gives it authentic, albeit simple, expression, even while allowing it to be challenged and transformed by the memory of Jesus Christ. It is a worship rooted in the experience of home and family, of communities that are able to transcend family ties by making of a more diverse company "mother, father, brother and sister," keeping the interpersonal and the domestic in their style of living and caring. A first step in good liturgy is the ritualization of core activities and things of community life and community care. The sacrament is not actually the common table itself, or the nursing given to the sick, or the domestic and agrarian uses of water, but it is the ritualization of these acts, the expression of their meaning in some simple but aesthetic form, such as the breaking of a loaf of bread, the pouring of water, the sharing of a common cup, the laying on of hands. Such ritualized forms must allow participants both to see their lives and fundamental acts of shared care and identity reflected in them, and at the same time to stand back from life and its activities in order to perceive their meaning and the larger perspective of mystery within which they belong. Discussions about the correct bread recipe, or about what oil to use, or about who may lay hands on whom, are at bottom perverse, since they fail to understand that the intent of basic ritual instruments and gestures is to let the things of life stand forth, in beauty and in mystery. Hence the value of a simple place, of a table, of bread and wine, of oil and water, of lights and shades of darkness, of care-full touch, of the awe apparent in a kiss of peace. In effect, for Christian liturgy this does mean a return to the most primitive and most simple symbols, even though the bread recipes are different from the one used in the upper room.

Such basic symbols and rituals, however, have to be paired with the challenge to barriers and divisions enunciated in the story and remembrance of Jesus Christ. The natural ritual tendency may be to sacramentalize one's own family or kin, one's own ethnic group, one's own social class where one feels at home, one's peers in age and profession, since such are the groups in which one is most secure, and indeed instinctively most aware of the sacred powers that govern life, and most protected against the chaos that could intrude. The challenge of Christian remembrance is to perform the same gestures of sharing and intimacy, to respect and reverence the things of common life, to stand in awe before the sacred and in trust against evil, in settings and groups where divisions and discriminations have no entry. Perhaps this might be stated by saying that Christian worship has to express in ritual, and at the same time parabolic form, an ethic of compassion, where it is the vulnerability of life, the suffering of the other person, the being denied respect and reverence and even name, that calls forth the common bond of faith in God's promise. Each one enters into Christian worship conscious of personal vulnerability, naked before Christ and naked with Christ, and alert to this reality in those with whom the gathering is formed, and open to whomsoever approaches, seeking compassion and blessedness. This is why though the ritual act as such is distinct from the meal, it remains bound up with a meal, why "the sharing of food and drink with each other, the celebration of a meal especially among those who are well-to-do and those who have nothing, is essential to the celebration of the Christian eucharistic meal."[19] The beatitudes of the poor and the meek are the qualities of heart that Christians bring to the ritual of the shared table, and to the rituals which invite or restore to that table, or relate mortality and sexuality and power in the community to that table.

Sacred power, sacred place, sacred time, all undergo a transmutation in Christian worship which is a subversion of the carefully established ways in which religious organizations order them, possibly aware of a deep conscious instinct for security in face of the enigmas of power, place, and time. Evangelical place and time are qualitative, not quantitative, and hope is accordingly eschatological, not apocalytic. "Constantly," writes Simon de Vries, "the human mind strives to offset the dread of confronting something entirely unique by reducing it to categories of intellectual understanding, either by way of measurement or by way of comparison. Quantifying measurement enters into use as an abstractive process by which one "time" is correlated with others purely on the basis of the passage of moving objects (the sun, moon, stars, timepieces, and the like) within a regular orbit or recurring routine. So also the qualifying approach that reduces temporal experience to analogies. Identifying a particular day for its special characteristics, the analytical mind makes intellectual and then linguistic comparisons with other days perceived to be somehow like it. Ultimately, all of life and history may be regularized and brought under control of man."[20]

In contrast with this, de Vries notes: "The essence of the qualitative non-objectifying, apprehension of time is an awareness that God *has* done something 'from the beginning to the end.' One day is not simply related, numerically or categorically, to another day. Rather, each day is seen as transcendentally significant in itself; i.e., each is seen as at least potentially revelatory of God's purpose. A day may be different from all other days, not only because it may be the occasion of a decisive event in the history of men and nations, but because it may be the opportunity for a crucial confrontation between God and man."[21]

In ritual, one can find holy days marked off and described as "time out of time," because they are days that provide a sacred pattern for all time, and allow people to reduce their sense of living in time to a reproduction "on other days" of what is represented on the holy day. On the other hand, however, holy days may be seen as significant of the openness of any day to God's promises and decisive action. In practice, though some days are set aside for celebration, any day is open to being a holy day, sanctified not on a calendar but by the gathering of the believing community to remember, make intercession, rejoice, and look forward in hope. Early Christians had to look for a space of time on the first day of the week to come together to hear the word and break the bread, and to see to one another's needs. Today, for most people the time is set apart for leisure and it is not work which interferes with gatherings. It may be just as important for households of faith to make space on other days—or indeed to make space on Sunday—to entertain in their midst those who do not enjoy leisure. It is the Lord's Supper which sanctifies the day, not the day which sanctifies the Lord's Supper.

One could make similar remarks about sacred place and the places where Christians gather. If the place is given some quality of its own, independent of the community, or if it is recognized as the place of a carefully circumscribed divine presence, one can say that the community has missed the point of God's presence in the community itself, in the word spoken, and in the table shared. As any time is qualitatively open to a divine event or inbreaking, so also is any place, and the gathering of believers in a place is for them indicative of this openness. The return to a more domestic setting, the celebration of eucharists in homes, the construction of very simple buildings for communities in the shadow of larger basilicas, is simply a quest on the part of evangelical Christians to discover a true sense of place, where worship is given in spirit and in truth.

The locus of God's power is the community itself, for the reality of power is the Spirit of Christ poured forth into our hearts. The symbols of the presence of the Spirit are those which signify interaction between the members in mutual charity and service. Without in the least questioning the place of the sacrament of order in the church, it is necessary to recall that the liturgy is the gathering and action of the baptized, and that it is enlivened by the many services of the Spirit, so that the reality of the apostolic and evangelical community may be shaped. The statement that the one who presides is as the one who serves, is not merely rhetoric or an exhortation to leaders to be humble. It is rather the significant declaration that Jesus is present to his community in both actions, or in any action of the word, prayer and mutual charity, and in any exercise of the gifts of the Spirit. Indeed, the ultimate reality before which all else fades into the background is the reality of the body of the Lord, and the ultimate ground of the Lord's presence is the community of faith, not any particular gift or ministry. Evangelical communities are conscious of the gifts of the Spirit in their own midst, and trusting of the Lord that they will be provided with the ministries which they need. They are therefore free of stereotypes and ready to discern the gifts of word, of service, of prayer, of presidency, that are most suited to their prophetic and evangelical presence in society.[22]

Because of their historical and eschatological openness, and because they recall the Lord's passion as the act of God's solidarity with the poor and suffering, evangelical communities give significant proportions to the function of narrative in liturgy, whether as a distinct act or as part of the prayer of blessing. From relatively early patristic times, the representation of Christ's mysteries in sacrament and liturgy has often been sought in signs and actions, or in some declaratory words. It is, however, much more in keeping with the Jewish roots of Christian liturgy to recognize the importance of *haggadah*.

The mimesis of the Lord's death and resurrection is not captured in signs or actions figuratively representative of his cruel death, of his descent into Hades, or of his rising. It is found in a story which redescribes the events in such a way that they present a ground for hope, and something to imitate in the freedom of new invention and and in freedom in front of all human power structures and expectations. This introduces a creativity into the telling of the story, as well as an actuality, something unfortunately largely lost in liturgy for some centuries. That the narrative of the passion and resurrection may be told in different ways, for different communities, we already know from the Gospels. These of course remain the unique canonical source, but they can be returned to for fresh inspiration in narrative construction, rather than simply repeated.

There is a particuarly important Christological insight in today's believing communities, which is a new ground for more narrative creativity in liturgy.[23] This is the emancipatory nature of the Christ story, and the solidarity of that story with

the story of the world's forgotten and unnamed. Jesus is remembered as the one into whose suffering all suffering is tak-
en, as the one in whose name all those left without a name are
named, as the one in whose remembrance the forgotten of the
world are remembered.

Chaos, senselessness, and meaninglessness are part and par-
cel of actual human experience, but they can be so massive, so
terrifying, that whole societies are built on the capacity to forget. It has been remarked often enough of our own age that
senseless death is so daily, that it is so massive, so global, so
imminent to each of us, so prone to reduce thousands to a
kind of nonliving or daily death, that peoples ignore it, suppress it in what they choose to remember. The memory of Jesus in worship can be such as to make room for the expressions of fears, of terror, of emptiness, of blindness, of the
offense and the cruelty, present not only in his death and history, but in all history and in present society, to wit of all that
tends to be suppressed because apparently uncontrollable, or
at least dismantling of our favorite ways of being. It is possible
to express all this, because in the pasch there is a vital hope, a
hope that is hope only because it takes all this into account. It
is a hope which alerts the community to the recalling of all
those who in suffering, and in opposition to society's collective forgetting, show faith and courage and trust and a belief
in life.

In remembering Jesus, therefore, we are allowed to remember "that all human enactments require criticism, revision, and
reenactment—and that this process is within God."[24] The
hopes that this memory evokes are not dull hopes that see
people as "better off" in heaven, but hopes that a fuller life is
possible, that the past whatever it has been may yet be redeemed, that reconciliation may be effected, that minds and
hearts may be opened to compassion, that the material world
may be part of God's history, not something to be left behind,
and that the poor and the desolate and all who live a shadowy
existence will be vindicated.

Such remembrance gives rise to two types of song, namely,
to lamentation and to doxology.[25] Communities have to be allowed to grieve, to express their fears and terrors, to lament
over the denial of life that is found in alienation, over the refu-

sal of death, over exercises of power that lead to despair. Lamentation is in fact the basis to Christian doxology, because doxology engages us in the promise of newness that comes with the Spirit, who heals, unites, and empowers. That which is remembered in grief is redeemed, made whole, renewed. In doxology, in the hope of a new Jerusalem among us, lament turns into rejoicing.

CONCLUSION

Evangelical communities come to this kind of remembering, grieving, and praising out of their own concrete quest for ways of living that are an alternative to the quest for power and happiness that crushes all before it. In living as it does, in remembering Jesus, Christ and Spirit-giver, and asserting its oneness with society rather than accepting to be made marginal to it, a community of faith expresses the reality of God's power active in a concrete historical time and place. The community gathered around such a memory is by its very being and gathering critical of all that is hopeless and alienating in religious and civil society and organization. Because of its belief in God's freedom, it is at the disposal of a God who is not co-opted by human power structures, and so it is free to continue to practice the evangelical way of life, and to speak prophetically to the renewal of society.

An evangelical way of life, a compassion with the poor, a resistance to the institutional and noninstitutional violence of the times, a common life enriched by many ministries, awe towards the sacramentality of life and of matter, a remembering of Jesus Christ which is also a remembering of all the forgotten, of things suppressed, of hopes dismissed, a lamenting before God's face, and praise and thanksgiving for the hopeful newness of the Spirit's creation, these appear to be marks of the households of faith in the coming church.

Notes

1. Franz-Xaver Kaufmann, "The Church as a Religious Organization," *Concilium* 91 (1974) 77.

2. Niklas Luhmann, "Institutionalized Religion in the Perspective of Functional Sociology," *Concilium* 91 (1974) 54.

3. Quoted by Nazareno Fabbretti, "Francis, Evangelism and Popular Communities," *Concilium* 149 (1981) 34.

4. Michel Mollat, "The Poverty of Francis: A Christian Social Option," *Concilium* 149 (1981) 27.

5. Lester K. Little, *Religious Poverty and the Profit Economy in Medieval Europe* (Ithica, NY: Cornell, 1978) 114.

6. Ibid. 116.

7. Ibid. 113.

8. Ibid. 116-117.

9. Marie-Dominique Chenu, "Fraternitas, évangile et condition socio-culturelle," *Revue de l'histoire de la spiritualité* 49 (1973) 385-400; Little, *Religious Poverty* 171-217.

10. Lester Little remarks: "The matter of who held power, of who was making the basic decisions for the community or who had the right to define the community, was critical in determining whether initiatives in the direction of change were looked upon as authentic and thus to be accepted or as alien and thus to be rejected. When those in power were not receptive to innovation, the cost of advocating innovation ran perilously high." In "Evangelical Poverty, the New Money Economy and Violence," in *Poverty in the Middle Ages*, ed. David Flood (Werl/Westf.: Dietrich-Coelde, 1975) 26.

11. One thinks especially of the christologies of Edward Schillebeeckx and Johannes B. Metz.

12. Edward Schillebeeckx, *Ministry: Leadership in the Community of Jesus Christ* (New York: Crossroad, 1981) 79, 136-137.

13. Richard K. Fenn, "Recent Studies of Church Decline: The Eclipse of Ritual," *Religious Studies Review* 8 (1982) 128.

14. Ibid. 126.

15. Fenn, *Religious Poverty* 16.

16. See *Vaudois Languedociens et pauvres catholiques*, Cahiers de Fanjeaux 2 (Paris: Edouard Privat, 1967) and Little, *Religious Poverty* 134-145, on the Cathars.

17. Little, *Religious Poverty* 142. For details of the ritual, see *Rituel Cathare*, introduction, texte critique, traduction et notes par Christine Thouzellier, Sources chrétiennes 236 (Paris: Cerf, 1977) 87-136, 222-224.

18. Kurt-Victor Selge, "Caracteristiques du premier mouvement Vaudois et crises au cours de son expansion," in *Vaudois Languedociens* 131-132.

19. Elisabeth Schüssler Fiorenza, "Tablesharing and the Celebration of the Eucharist," *Concilium* 152 (1982) 10.

20. Simon de Vries, "Time in the Bible," *Concilium* 142 (1981) 4-5.

21. Ibid. 8.

22. See Peter Eicher, "The Age of Freedom: A Christian Community for Leisure and the World of Work," *Concilium* 142 (1981) 50.

23. Schillebeeckx concludes his volume *Christ: The Experience of Jesus as Lord* (New York: Crossroad, 1980) with a homily and a eucharistic prayer.

24. Stephen Happel, "The Structure of Our Utopian Mitsein (Life-together)," *Concilium* 123 (1979) 101.

25. See Walter Brueggemann, *The Prophetic Imagination* (Philadelphia: Fortress, 1980), *passim*.

8

Liturgical Praxis:
A New Consciousness
at the Eye of Worship

THESE DAYS, IT MAY WELL BE WITH SOME FEAR AND TREMBLING THAT we gather for worship in Christian churches. It is not with the wonted tremble with which people enter the presence of the awesome, the numinous, the almighty, but rather with a trembling that comes from the fear that our liturgical traditions may have displaced the gods with idols of human making. We may tremble because of the ideologies that surround and encumber the naming of God and the remembering of Jesus Christ. We may tremble because when we hearken to the word, God's sole claim to holiness breaks through, and God's naming of the holy challenges the sacralization of objects, roles, and rituals that is so integral to liturgical practice. We may well tremble as our memories of Jesus Christ are compelled to embrace the memories of the victims of sacralization and of the religious legitimation of powers, both civil and religious. Tremble we must, as we discover that the powers of the weak reveal more to us of God's holiness than do the powers of the consecrated, whether priest or king.

As a new consciousness of the human and of the cosmic emerges within our culture, we are engaged in some kind of night battle with liturgical traditions, some struggle with the gods that emerge from dark realms within our minds and claim our fidelity. It is the engagement with life that we need to bring to worship, the readiness to be challenged to self-understanding by an affirmation of the holy that gives perspective to the appropriation of new social and inner experience. There is an extraordinary power of revelation latent in the rituals and the symbols and the poetry of liturgical traditions, for those who would do battle with them, wrestling with God as Jacob wrestled, so that only those who are wounded can give testimony to the existence of angels. Too hieratic a consciousness can still the voice of angels, prevent the engagement with life from being brought to the breaking of the bread, and deny the knowledge bred in the marrow bone.

As we finger a way through the Gospel art of the peasants of Solentiname,[1] or browse through the pages of Rosemary Ruether's *Womanguides*,[2] we can see that there is a new consciousness taking shape through the engagement with life, and finding its way into the gatherings where two or three come together, seeking to name the Christ in whom redemption comes. Struggling with biblical and liturgical traditions, and reviving suppressed and forgotten streams, they listen and speak and celebrate, out of their own experience of being victims, out of submerged and now revived memories, and out of the hope born from the discovery of gifts of the Spirit, long neglected and now burgeoning. It is upon that consciousness that I want to reflect as the "eye" of worship, the still center at the heart of the storm that beats against liturgical houses built on sand, the centering point for remembrance and lamentation and thanksgiving, and for building hopes more durable on the recollection of things past.

> O where does the dancer dance —
> the invisible centre spin —
> whose bright periphery holds
> the world we wander in?
> For it is he we seek —
> the source and death of desire;
> we blind as blundering moths
> around that core of fire.
> Caught between birth and death

we stand alone in the dark,
to watch the blazing wheel
on which the earth is spark,
crying, Where does the dancer dance —
the terrible centre spin,
whose flower will open at last
to let the wanderer in?[3]

There are clearly then new experiences of self, and of earth, and of struggle, new engagements with fuller life, that cry out for the completeness of worship, but that are often given but a small place in it. How much church leaders can deny the place of the weak in the community of faith as they forge ideologies of the sacred could be researched at length, but there is one blatant piece of evidence of recent origin that is worth quoting. It is the letter of the Congregation for the Doctrine of the Faith on the minister of the eucharist of August 1983. Finding in the discussion of the right to the eucharist of newly emerging or long forgotten, laity-based communities of faith, only a claim to lay presidency instead of the larger issue of ordination practices, the Congregation, with what reads as cynicism, chose to remind all that where there is a *votum sacramenti*, or desire for the sacrament, there is no need for the sacrament itself, since God accords all necessary graces to those who have this sincere desire. With an axiom taken out of context, the Congregation thus blithely disposes of God's dispensation to be among us in the earthly realities of tangible signs and symbols, replacing God's desire to be among us in fleshly forms with a desire for the pseudosacral of the clerical order.[4]

Such an apparent subterfuge, willful or otherwise, gives an edge to the sense of the holy that has been made known to us in Jesus Christ. As Mary Collins commented some years ago, "only when the church is diaphanous is it sacred. By contrast, all theocratic claims of church authorities to possess the authority of God and to act in God's place, as vicar, as representative, *in persona Christi*, negate the difference between the holiness of God and the divinely willed profanity of every created thing [including the church]. The result is pseudosacralization."[5] Behind the making of such images of the holy, there seems to lie a fear of what Christ makes known as the truly holy, namely, the capacity for self-gift that does not stop short at losing one's life—or at least one's vantage point in the order of things. To those accustomed to the argument for God's existence from the perceived order of the universe, it is discomfitting to perceive the revelation of God's holiness in Jesus' self-gift, in contradiction of the forces of order, and it is disquieting to have to live from this point as the center for the conduct of human affairs and of the church. The location of God outside the appointed order seems menacing and chaotic. God must be joking, so we quickly baptize the self-gift of Jesus with sacral names like sacrifice and priesthood and incorporate its ritual enactment into an ordered hierarchy, ignoring the fact that the original predication of those names in Christian tradition was indeed a divine comedy. As Collins names them, the "self-protective schemes evident in human religiosity"[6] have a tendency to take over. When they do, they obscure the revelation and presence of God in the memorial of Jesus and his discipleship, with its unexpected disclosures, and in the believing community's capactiy for self-gift and for identification with the world's victims. The need to confront temple and sabbath ideologies is as great today as it was in the time of Jesus, if in remembering him we are to discover the remembrance of the covenant built on the twin commandments of the love of God and neighbor, inherited from a nomadic people to whom idols were forbidden. The new consciousness of committed groups makes this confrontation possible, as it also has the centering force to renew eschatologically oriented memories.

THE NEW CONSCIOUSNESS

I live my life in the growing orbits
which move out over the things of the world.
Perhaps I can never achieve the last,
but that will be my attempt.
I am circling around God, around the ancient tower,
and I have been circling for a thousand years,
and I still don't know if I am a falcon, or a storm,
or a great song.[7]

It is within a consciousness freed of the pseudosacral that

authentic remembering can take shape. What emerges in this freedom is a fresh perception of the human and a fresh perception of humanity's oneness with earth and cosmos. This is a renewed centering point for gathering in the memories and hopes of the Judeo-Christian tradition and for bringing them to song. To come to an understanding of this free consciousness and its potentiality, I would like to look at some of the critiques addressed to hieratic consciousness.

Feminist writings point to the human enslavement that follows from the habit—and from its philosophical and theological justification—of seeing all reality as hierarchically ordered, the lesser governed by the greater, each species having its due place in the ordered universe. Transferred to church order, this perception upholds a graded clergy, the distinction between clergy and laity, and of course allots womankind its appropriate place. Such allotments and distinctions are sanctified by the adopted model of liturgical ordering, which remains discriminatory as long as it is mandatory, despite protests to the contrary which affirm the church's belief in the fundamental equality in baptismal dignity and its nondiscriminatory attitude toward women.

An alternative vision of the church is well expressed in these words of Elisabeth Schüssler Fiorenza: "The gospel . . . is the communal proclamation of the life-giving power of the Spirit-Sophia and of God's vision of an alternative community and world. The experience of the Spirit's creative power releases us from the life-destroying powers of sin and sets us free to choose an alternative life for ourselves and for each other . . . The Gospel calls into being the church as the discipleship of equals that is continually recreated in the power of the Spirit. Jesus' ministry, his healings and exorcisms, his promise to the poor and challenge to the rich, his breaking of religious law, and his table community with outcasts and sinners made experientially available God's new world . . ."[8] Later on in the text she notes: "As long as women Christians are excluded from breaking the bread and deciding their own spiritual welfare and commitment, *ekklesia* as the discipleship of equals is not realized and the power of the gospel is greatly diminished."[9]

Besides this critique of the hierarchical perception of church and human society, there is another critique of the established consciousness that feminists share with all who wish to be united with the earth and cosmos in a companionship for the future, and to forestall a destruction which threatens us because of earth's misuse. This critique looks at the dualism that affects the ordering of life in the western world, and so much of the action that has resulted from technological progress.[10] It is a dualism which unfortunately was fostered by elements in the Christian tradition that opposed the works of the flesh to the works of the spirit, and looked for the domination of spirit over matter.

So deep-rooted was this dualism in the western soul that even when Christian faith was shed by the enlightened, the dualism was passed on as part of the cultural heritage and has grossly affected technological advancement. While the good of creation was handed over to technology in an effort to free it from hierarchical control and from the constraints of a hierarchically conceived universe, the cultural ideal of human domination and a mechanistic perception of nature prevailed. Nature has been made to serve what is conceived as the good of human beings; it is emptied of its own holiness, and humans think themselves competent to probe and master the secrets of the universe. Now the scientists are counting the cost in terms of the destruction of earth and of the threat to living species, including the human. Even the secular prophets are calling for a revival of the religious sense. However, it is not to Christian religion that they look but to more ancient and cosmically sensitive forms that revere the holy in the cosmos. One writer, for example, states: "While improvements in the technologies that are used to support human life and affluence can help to ameliorate the extinction crisis [the writer is refering to the extinction of living species], and to a limited extent technologies can substitute for lost ecosystem services, it would be a lethal mistake to look to technology for 'the answer.' In my opinion, only an intensive effort to make those improvements and substitutions *combined* with a revolution in attitudes toward other people, human numbers, what life is for, and the intrinsic values of organic diversity, is likely to prevent the worst catastrophe ever to befall the human lineage. Scientific analysis points, curiously, toward the need for a quasi-religious transformation of contemporary cultures. Whether such transformation can be achieved in time is, to say the least, problematic."[11]

Social critics, such as Jurgen Habermas, are now asking whether in the interests of the future of society and of the cosmos, it is possible to retrieve the contribution of religious attitudes, without having to subscribe to the established religions.[12] We may thus well ask whether Christians have in their heritage, when it is freed from its grosser ideologies, the power to proclaim a changed attitude to nature, to bring to human consciousness the sense of how much human fate is one with the fate of the cosmos, of how much companionship with the vital energies of the universe, rather than a subjection of them, is inbuilt into eschatological hope.

> Strength plays such a marvellous game —
> it moves through the things of the world like a servant,
> groping out in roots, tapering in trunks,
> and in the treetops like a rising from the dead.[13]

Thus the poet Rilke. What of the roots of Judeo-Christian worship in traditions that enhance bodiliness, that show awe for the mysteries of earth and cosmos, that wed humanity with God through earthly and cosmic symbolisms? Somewhere along the way, Christian tradition appears to have lost touch with these roots, so that now, instead of finding in Christian liturgy a bastion against the inroads of dualism on culture, and a power to transform attitudes to nature, we have to bring *to it* a new ecological consciousness and commitment, one that can gather back in the bodily, the earthly, the cosmic eschatologies of the tradition.

Neophytes that do not know the cleansing and life-giving power of fresh running water, oil that does not flow with fragrance, wine that is imported in a bottle and bought at inflationary prices, bread that is nonnutritional and not produced by human hands, communities that do not gather around a table, and still less around a sick bed or an open grave, vigils that are held before sunset, are all signs of our alienation from the cosmic order. Despite the elemental nature of its core symbols of water, grain, seed, vine, olive, light and darkness, and seasonal change, liturgy is often nothing more than the precise enactment of causal functionalism. We may justly rebel against the idea that our lives are ruled by the stars and planets, knowing them to be open to the gratuity of grace, but in the process have we lost sight of the destiny that links our faith with theirs?

To this state of things we can bring a newly developing consciousness of cosmic oneness, appropriating it in remembrance as we appropriate the vision of grace that speaks within the poetry and even the conflicts of the Christian heritage. This is a consciousness of humanity's participation in, rather than domination over, cosmic history, and a consciousness that humanity's own history will be determined by the capacity to live in harmony with the vital energies that pervade all things, great and small. The development of individual consciousness in its more differentiated states is in effect the development of a consciousness of participation and interpenetration, beyond the stages of naiveté, but yet fraught with awe and wonder, and above all humility. It is possible for humanity's relations with the cosmos to lie latent and unexplored in consciousness. We are nonetheless preconditioned by such participation, and risk being destructive if we remain unreflective.

REPRESENTATION

I have tried to describe a new consciousness that is taking shape within our culture, and that is apparent in Christian groups and gatherings that share a larger cultural struggle for freedom and hope. I have asked what this means for worship when a new sense of human and baptismal equality develops in a world and in a church still ordered largely by patriarchy, or what it means when an awareness of oneness of being with cosmic forces emerges in a world threatened by the powers of hubris, and in a church befuddled by a limited vision of natural law.

It is often a misconception of what representation means that prevents sensitivity to baptismal equality, as it prevents sensitivity to earthly and cosmic symbolism. In other words, certain approaches to the representative actually impede the new feminist and ecological consciousness from having a part in the shaping of forms of worship. If representation is confused with imitation or the work of the reproductive imagination, then the possibilities of representing Christ's presence in community, word, and sacrament are severely limited. Classicist theories of representation would have us see the represented made visible in the sign or symbol, whereas authentic representation is rooted in the affect and the psyché, and engages memories that allow for the elusive quality of that to which symbol or sacrament refers. Such representation is a search for meaning and looks for a way of uniting with what is represented, rather than pretending to an imitation of something or some person clearly known.

There is a painting by Caravaggio in London, entitled "Supper at Emmaus," wherein Christ is blessing the bread in front of two startled disciples. The power of the painting relies on the fact that Jesus is unrecognizable. Caravaggio was careful not to use any of the usual images of Christ known at his time. It is only in the blessing of the bread that Christ is recognized. As far as his own bodily appearance is concerned, he remains *in alia effigie*, in another form, an alien likeness. Among his followers, the risen Christ is to be known in symbolic action and agapic practice, not in human forms and representations.[14]

Authentic and disclosive representation cannot be understood as the attachment of a name to a reproductive image. It is a transfer of names or, more properly, a naming process. Well it is that the bishop may be called the figure of the Father or the icon of Jesus Christ, but the deacon too represents Jesus Christ and the deaconess the Spirit, and to each other Christians are all fathers and mothers, sisters and brothers in Christ and in the Holy Spirit. The naming is a searching, a predicating within a larger context, and ought not to serve as a fixing of images and names that stills the poetic sense, or as the canonization of hierarchical order. Ossification of images is what causes damage and prevents reflection upon the workings of human subjectivity that lead to representation.

If representation is merely the work of the reproductive imagination, it is misleading. The image may be allowed to occupy the place of the reality imaged, rather than inviting to thought about it and about our relation to it. When some person or thing is genuinely represented, then the absence of the represented is taken into account. It is present in a way which means that it cannot be seen or touched. It is known at the stage of removal proper to symbolism. Representative images are the casting of our desires as they seek reality and truth, and they need to be traced back to their psychic origin and to the memories from which they spring. They have to be taken as the expression of the affective in order to be given their true cognitive force. Representing is a predication, a seeing as, an expression of relations between the one who represents and what is represented, the draw of the reality that eludes us upon our quest for meaning.

Every image or name has to be caught in the middle of the sentence where it occurs. Whatever is visual in the imaging has first to be negated, in order to be retrieved, within the boundaries of language. The visual is then valid in a way that does not allow it to stand as reproductive image. Let me speak to one of the most important examples of representation, one that is also party to divisions among Christians. If a bishop or presbyter is called the representative of Jesus Christ, or is said to act in the person of Christ, to catch the proper meaning of this statement it has to be seen in its originating context. In other words, we have to go back to some statement such as the following: in liturgical action, within the assembled congregation of faith, the one presiding acts or speaks in the person of Christ. Only when it is appreciated that he is not in his own person and figure an image of Christ does the meaning of the predication become clear. Then attention is drawn to the action, the prayer, the blessing, the ritual, and we see this *as if* it were Christ who prayed, blessed, or baptized, seeking in that way to capture the power of the word or the action to disclose a godly presence and grace, or a communion of the divine and the human. The bishop is like the Christ in Caravaggio's Supper at Emmaus: not recognizable as Christ except in the action of blessing and breaking bread with the community of faith.

Jesus Christ defies figurative representation, and can now be represented among us only in forms that steer away from reproductive imagery. The child in the manger defies pictorial representation, for it is always in memory the contradictory sign of human weakness and covenant fidelity given by God to the human race that would prefer to find the godly in the royal or priestly figure. The crucified Christ defies reproductive representation, for who can ever enter hell "lost in plungings of wilder depths," to step forth again, "possessor of pain," "on the tall tower of his endurance"?[15] The crucified and tortured Christ is known in the pain and in the onslaught of death, and what imagery could reproduce such truth? The risen Christ defies human representation, and is among us *in alia effigie*, for in the one transformed in the Spirit there is too full a merging of earthly and cosmic, of male and female, of Jew and Greek, of matter and spirit, to be presented in forms other than those eschatological which point to the community to be built among people and between humanity and cosmos, or the transformation of all being that is to come about in the coming of the Human One. The Christ bequeathing us his memory and abiding presence at the Supper equally defies imaging, choosing to transfer all force and power and grace to the bread and cup, blessed, broken, poured out, and shared among a people engaged in this action as the high point of their life engagement in discipleship.

Authentic representation, being the free play of the imagination, moving in keeping with fundamental desire and in response to the revelatory word, is at the service of exploring the traces of God in history. These traces are in conflict with the tendencies of the reproductive imagination, which belongs in the order of the pseudosacral among the self-protective "schemes of human religiosity." The traces of God are found in what challenges and disrupts order as humankind creates it. The language of God's presence and action is the language of metaphor, the nonrepresentational imagery that belies figurative reproduction. It is free linking and visually dissonant, and finds its place with story, not at the center of history as we write it, but at the edges. The imagination of faith seeks to name God between the cracks.

THE RETRIEVAL OF WISDOM

Let me recapitulate before proceeding a step further. Believing the consciousness brought to the renewal of the liturgical

books, and to the functioning of liturgy, to be still largely hierarchical and dualist, I have spoken of a new consciousness of
human and baptismal equality, and of a consciousness of the
unity in destiny of humanity and cosmos, and of the energy
that permeates the universe. In connection with this, I have
addressed the type of representation that blocks this consciousness. It is this new consciousness, which leads people to
specific types of engagement in life and action, that can center
worship and enable the church to retrieve the tradition's powers of transformation.

To do this, it has to take shape in story, ritual and blessing,
in a new, if ancient, naming of earth, of victims, of Christ, and
of God (yes, all in one breath, one *pneuma*). This means retriev-
ing what has been suppressed in human and religious experience. In this venture we do not have an ordered system whereby to replace another ordered system, but are involved in
explorations and creativity. By experience we learn from experience. In such a situation, I suggest that the recovery of the
name of *Sophia* or Wisdom, for God, for Jesus, for the discipleship of Jesus, will play a prominent part. This is precisely because of its practical focus.

Wisdom is acquired experientially, by living by an open
and playful imagination. It is the gift given to those who cope,
in trust, with reality, taking it as it comes in all its apparent
ambiguity. This does not mean that we can look to a body of
experiential knowledge to be mastered in life situations. Wisdom is a discipline of mind and spirit. It is the flexibility of
heart that assists one in discerning the right time and the fitting place for the appropriate behavior.

Human wisdom is an attitude of trust, which believes in a
divine wisdom that wills the wholeness and humanity of ever-
yone, and that binds together *ethos* and *cosmos*, the sphere of
the world and the sphere of human action. The divine gift of
wisdom gives rise to the *pathos* of actively assumed suffering,
the suffering of those who refuse the easy answers of order
and retributive justice, and of a theodicy of reason, and brings
compassion to those whom the world would condemn or exclude, knowing that it is these very ones whom divine compassion embraces.

Sophia is the name that we can give to the God of Jesus, and

Sophia's messenger, the name which we can give to Jesus himself. As Elisabeth Schüssler Fiorenza writes, out of a woman's memory: "The earliest Palestinian theological remembrances and interpretations of Jesus' life and death understand him as Sophia's messenger and later as Sophia herself . . . It was possible to understand Jesus' ministry and death in terms of God-Sophia, because Jesus probably understood himself as the prophet and child of Sophia. As Sophia's messenger he calls 'all who labor hard and are heavy laden' and promises them rest and *shalom*."[16]

This reality of God-Sophia is spelled out in the preaching, healing, exorcising, and table community of Jesus and his disciples. The discipleship itself is a wisdom community, which gathers in the suffering and outcast, and anyone else who can believe in God, in spite of death and in confidence in the superabundance of God's motherly embrace. Remembrance of the God whom Jesus preached, of the divine action in which he engaged, of the godly presence that others discerned in his ministry and death, can be forged, in this age of doubt and new consciousness, through the images of Sophia.

At the same time, this naming (which is not the work of the reproductive imagination) can become the focus for the consciousness of human and baptismal wholeness, and of the relation between *ethos* and *cosmos*, that I have suggested need to be woven into liturgy. This is not without precedent. The wisdom literature of the Jewish tradition is highly cosmic. Paul, in his letter to the Corinthians, discerned the revelation of wisdom in the cross of Christ, and the original proclamation of the resurrection was the fruit of the visionary-ecstatic experience of the women who, even in his death, recognized in Jesus the faithful messenger of divine wisdom. For the resurrection community of discipleship, the raising up of Christ and his transformation in the Spirit are testimony to that wisdom whereby the God who dwells in the cosmos, dwells in a people who through the *pathos* of suffering and compassion become a community in which there is neither Jew nor Greek, neither slave nor free, no male and female. This persuasion shapes the world in which, in the name of Christ, Christians are invited to live, and to which they can, in the same name, invite all humanity to enter.

LITURGICAL PRAXIS

Within our liturgical practice, the symbols, memories, and rituals of this wisdom are there to be retrieved, but they are often to be found between the cracks. The principal points that I have sought to make in this chapter can be set out now under the explicit heading of *liturgical praxis*. By praxis, I understand a conscious doing of whatever we are doing, a doing that is open to reflective critique. A liturgical praxis that would retrieve the traces of wisdom can only be buit upon an ethical and agapic praxis, as well as on a noetic praxis pertinent to the whole of human existence. It has to integrate these, as well as its own specific attention to the uses of language and symbol.

First of all, Christian communities acknowledge the glory of God in an authentic social, agapic action, that in the name of divine wisdom transforms ecclesial, cultural, and social horizons and values. Such is the engagement that in practical action touches the victims of history and human technology and embraces them in compassion and hope. These victims find a ready place at the heart of liturgical remembrance that is rooted in community reality.

Second, to avoid the pitfalls of deceptive representation, communities have to be invited to that noetic praxis which offers a differentiated understanding of the human subject. Liturgy has to integrate a fuller consciousness of cognitive and affective desires and expectations, as well as that sense of energy which calls for an interpenetration and conscious fusion of humanity and cosmos.

Third, it behooves us to be open to a poetic praxis attentive to the fullness of language. We need an eye for metaphor and an ear for the dissonance which dissolves the domineering tendencies of man over man, of man over woman, of humanity over cosmos, and allows us to hear the voice of God between the cracks. There is a wager in this use of language, which is the wager of hope in the service of freedom and the fullness of being for all. The task is to grasp the symbols of the sacred, rooted in the oneiric and the cosmic, in the psyché and bios, and catch them at the point at which they enter, and are transformed by, the history of a people's search to be free, in the gratuitous gift of the God who makes self known in the ordinary and the painful. The water is the water of agapic praxis. The power of the holy is relocated, companionship is found with the awesome. Hope and the holy are found at the heart of anguish, when this is the pathos of an active suffering, of suffering assumed in hope for, and with, whosoever and whatsoever, is diminished by the claims of others or of the processes of socialization and culture. Such is a poetics that spills over into the service of a more human community, and of the transformation of the world in the glory of the crucified Christ. Language that engages authentic desire needs to be twin to the action that is commitment to a hopeful, social, cultural, and cosmic transformation.

Words have their power, when they yield it, humbly, to that of which they speak. As the poet, Judith Wright, sings to the flower:

> Now I come to lock you here in a white song.
> Word and word are chosen and met.
> Flower, come in.
> But before the trap is set,
> the prey is gone.
> The words are white as a stone is white
> carved for a grave;
> but the flower blooms in immortal light,
> being now; being love.[17]

Notes

1. Philip and Sally Scharper, eds., *The Gospel in Art by the Peasants of Solentiname* (New York: Orbis Books, 1984).

2. Rosemary Radford Ruether, *Womanguides: Readings Toward a Feminist Theology* (Boston: Beacon Press, 1985).

3. Judith Wright, "Song," in *Selected Poems: Five Senses* (Sydney: Angus & Robertson, 1978) 121.

4. Letter of the Congregation for the Doctrine of the Faith. "Individual faithful or communities who because of persecution or lack of priests are deprived of the holy eucharist for either a short or longer period of time, do not thereby lack the grace of the Redeemer. If they are intimately animated by a desire for the sacrament and united in prayer with the whole church, and call upon the Lord and raise their heart to him, by virtue of the Holy Spirit they live in communion with the whole church, the living body of Christ, and with the Lord

himself. Through their desire for the sacrament in union with the church, no matter how distant they may be physically, they are intimately and really united to her and therefore receive the fruit of the sacrament." *Origins* 13 (1983) 232.

5. Mary Collins, "The Public Language of Ministry," *The Jurist* 41 (1981) 219.

6. Ibid. 292.

7. Rainer Maria Rilke, *Selected Poems*, a translation from the German with commentary by Robert Bly (New York: Harper & Row, 1981) 13.

8. Elisabeth Schüssler Fiorenza, *In Memory of Her: A Feminist Theological Reconstruction of Christian Origins* (New York: Crossroad, 1984) 344ff.

9. Ibid., 346f.

10. Cf. Gibson Winter, *Liberating Creation: Foundations of Religious Social Ethics* (New York: Crossroad, 1981).

11. Paul R. Ehrlich, "Mankind and Extinction. The Loss of Diversity: Causes and Consequences," *The Washington Book Review* 1 (1986) 5.

12. Jürgen Habermas, *Autonomy and Solidarity: Interviews*, edited and introduced by Peter Dews (London: Verso, 1986) 53f.

13. Ibid., 33.

14. Cf. Charles Scribner III, "In Alia Effigie: Caravaggio's *Supper at Emmaus*," in *Art, Creativity and the Sacred*, ed. Diane Apostolos-Cappadona (New York: Crossroad, 1984) 64-79.

15. "Christ's Journey to Hell," in *Rilke Between Roots*. Selected Poems rendered from the German by Rika Lesser (Princeton, NJ: Princeton University Press, 1986) 14f.

16. Fiorenza, *In Memory of Her* 134.

17. "Nameless Flower," in Wright, *Selected Poems* 98.

9

The Church's Calendar:
Are the Saints Neglected
or Misrepresented?

IN THE CATHOLIC CHURCH AT PRESENT, DEVOTION TO THE SAINTS seems to be at a point where people are asking what it is all about. It would be wrong to conclude that such devotion is on the point of disappearing, since some popular devotions, universal or regional, are still strong. On the other hand, there seems to be considerable uncertainty about the meaning of devotion to the saints and about the place which their commemoration ought to have on the liturgical calendar.

One of the principles enunciated at the Second Vatican Council for the reform of the liturgical calendar asked for the priority of the celebration of the mysteries of Christ over the commemoration of the saints.[1] In effect, the feasts of saints were so numerous that even in times like Lent and Advent the liturgy of the season was often overshadowed by the feasts of the saints. The reading of their lives or legends risked taking up more time and imagination than the reading of the Gospels. Moreover, reverence for the divinity of Christ and the adoration of Christ in the blessed sacrament did not allow for a just appreciation of his priestly intercession, and in times of need, both spiritual and temporal, it was in the intercession of Mary and the saints that people had confidence rather than in the priestly prayer of Christ to the Father. Attention to the seasons of Lent, Easter, Advent, and Christmas, as well as to the Sundays throughout the year, was designed to restore a better sense of the mystery of Christ. Its purpose was to replace the practical priority given to the saints with communion with Christ in his mystery, through the reading of the Scriptures, the prayers of the season, and participation in his priestly worship.

In ordering the commemoration of the saints in the liturgy, concern was shown for greater historical accuracy in structuring the calendar and in composing texts for the feasts.[2] Eliminated were purely mythical figures as well as the apocryphal elements from the legends of the saints. This concern with the historical had in fact already emerged in hagiography. From the early part of the century, in connection with general advances in historical studies, writers sought greater accuracy and documentation in putting together the lives of such persons as Vincent de Paul, the Curé of Ars, Thérèse of Lisieux, Ignatius of Loyola, Bernadette Soubirous, or Francis Xavier. The day of the Golden Legend was already on the wane before the Second Vatican Council and its reforms.

Implementing these principles sometimes went counter to people's devotion. The story of Saint Philomena was dismissed as the result of a misreading of a Greek tomb inscription, so that her feast was abolished. Some popular (though not liturgical) novenas, such as that to Saint Jude, were suppressed in parishes and sanctuaries. There was also a rather wholesale removal of the statues of the saints from churches, especially from the sanctuary space, as church buildings were remodeled to allow for liturgical changes. Consequently, people were denied ready contact with saints, which contact they sought through images and relics.

As far as the actual devotion to the saints is concerned, attitudes among the faithful seem to be at odds with each other in the wake of these liturgical reforms. One reaction is to ask for some restoration of the saints to their place in the church's prayer, and indeed of their statues to church buildings. Sometimes this springs from people's attachment to devotions, such as those to Saint Anthony of Padua, Saint Jude, or Saint Rose of Cascia; sometimes from a more sophisticated avowal that veneration of the saints is an intimate part of Catholic belief about grace and the afterlife. Even in admitting a previous imbalance between the commemoration of the mysteries of Christ and devotion to the saints, some argue that the commemoration of the saints is more substantive to Catholic tradition than liturgical reformers have allowed. All in all, despite efforts at reform, it must probably be admitted that the liturgy has not completely worked out consistent forms for the commemoration of the saints, and seems not to have been thoroughly in touch with the roots of the practice in early tradition.

The generic preface for the commemoration of holy men and women in the new Roman Missal praises God for giving us their example, their friendship, and the power of their intercession.[3] As these three modes of relation to the saints are worked out in the liturgy or in other practices, they appear to be allied with a cosmology of the afterlife with which a contemporary perspective is not at ease. The cosmology, brilliantly celebrated by Dante in the *Divinia Commedia*, is that of heaven, hell, and purgatory, and is accompanied by a sense of time sequence which allows for the particular judgment, for time in purgatory after death, and for the fulfillment of blessedness in heaven directly after death or after purgatory.[4] It also allows for modes of contact between heaven and earth which make it possible for the dead in general, or the saints in particular, to be in touch with the living and to take their needs to heart, and even to play a direct part in their lives. This defies the more literal imagination of our day and presumes a certainty about the other world that leaves even many believers uncomfortable. There is also discomfort with taking some of the saints as exemplars, since their lives and erstwhile earthly concerns seem very remote from ours. The mind more readily turns to the peace-makers such as Martin Luther King, Thomas Merton, Oscar Romero, and Mahatma Gandhi, or to such as Anna Frank and Edith Stein who in hope survived the demolition of all hope. The revivial of devotion to past figures such as Hildegard of Bingen, Meister Eckhart, Teresa of Avila, or Ignatius of Loyola comes from the perception that their way of bringing faith to bear on the human dilemma can be retrieved in a way that is pertinent to contemporary issues and struggles.

LIGHT FROM TRADITION

As is well known, the cult of the saints has its historical origins in the cult of the martyrs. It may not be as broadly recognized that the cult of the martyrs has its roots in the more general practice of the commemoration of the dead.[5] This was based on the sense of an abiding communion between the living and the dead who had died in the hope of Christ and of the resurrection from the dead. It may be difficult for us to appreciate the power of the belief in the resurrection of the dead as it is expressed in the New Testament and in early Christian piety. This was not reducible to the belief that each individual person would rise again from the grave at the end of time. It was a belief that had a more corporate quality, being linked with the sense of the church as the holy people or the elect. In the resurrection of Christ it saw the promise not only of future life for the dead but of the destruction of death itself. Not merely would the dead continue to live and be raised up in their bodies, but death as the enemy of humankind and of the earth was to be destroyed. Christians who died continued to be partners in this hope, and this was the basis for their commemoration in the gatherings of the church at liturgy or in visits to their places of burial. The celebration of the *refrigerium*, or festal meal, and later of the eucharist, at the site of burial on appropriate days, especially the anniversary of death, were apt symbols for the expression of this common hope, shared by the living and the dead.[6]

Two other factors, however, affected this remembrance and communion. One was the conviction that the hope had to be realized for all simultaneously and at the resurrection of the body. The dead therefore had to endure a period of waiting before enjoying the full fruit of Christ's sacrifice and rising in the common resurrection. The piety of the living was expressed in the prayer that this waiting would be spent in a place of refreshment, light, and peace. The other factor influencing communion with the dead had to do with a gradual differentiation between the common dead and the martyrs. In dying in the very profession of their faith in Christ, these latter had reached the point of total configuration to his death. Therefore it was to be expected that they would be given total configuration to his resurrection and already enjoy the final overcoming of death. The geography of this resurrection was no more clearly worked out than was the geography of Christ's own resurrection or the geography of the resting place of those awaiting final resurrection. It was remembrance that affected the nature of communion. Remembrance of Christ's *martyrion* determined the faith and hope that came from his mysteries. Similarly, remembrance of the *martyrion* of those who died in the profession of their faith gave rise to a sense of a different sort of communion with these privileged dead.

Keeping this communion was marked by two devotional activities. The fundamental one was that of remembering the martyrs by reading the acts of their martyrdom in church assemblies.[7] Through such reading, they could be said to have served as examples and as reminders of the power of Christ's death and resurrection working in the lives of the faithful. The second form of devotion was the appeal to their intercession, which at first was closely allied with appeal to Christ's own intercession. In the sermons for the anniversary of his own ordination, a homilist as relatively late as Leo the Great ascribes the power of the apostles to the testimony of the martyrdom with which they sealed their preaching of the Gospel of Christ, and to the way in which Christ had chosen to associate their heavenly prayer with his own priestly intercession.[8] For Leo, this was but the culmination of the choice of Christians as a priestly and prophetic people, in whom the power of Christ's sacrifice continued to live and through whom its testimony was noised abroad.

In short, devotion to the dead in this early period of church history is an expression of the abiding communion in a common hope that transcends the boundaries of death and that is rooted in the remembrance of the paschal mystery. This hope is expressed in such images as priestly people, parousia, final judgment, resurrection from the dead, the new heaven and the new earth, and the defeat of the ultimate enemy which is death itself.[9] This last is the most powerful and important of all.

Many things assisted the transformation of this cult into one that changed the figure of the holy person and the perception of saintly intercession.[10] One of these was certainly the displacement of the hope of the parousia or final end, which seemed less immediate than in early Christian days. Another was the sense that the power of Christ was as much at work in resistance to the allurements of the world as in the death of the martyrs, who in any case became in large part figures of the past rather than persons of living memory. The power of an Anthony was something to be reckoned with, and who could deny his full participation in the life of Christ after death? Stress on the awesomeness of the divine majesty and on the divine nature of the Word made flesh also called for advocates who were more suppliants before God's throne than coheirs allied with Christ's own intercession. Unfortunately, hagiographical details and the later official procedures of canonization contributed to the evisceration of the saints so that they appeared to have little to do with human life on earth.[11] The less they appeared to have been concerned with things of earth, the more the deceased seemed to become candidates for sanctity. To favor this notion of sanctity, at times the real concerns which preoccupied them during life were obliterated from the official record. When, for example, Saint Charles Borromeo was canonized, the official bull recognized his devout practice of prayer and of the virtues of humility, patience, and pastoral zeal, but omitted all mention of his valiant and sometimes controversial efforts to implement in the church of Milan the reforms decreed by the Council of Trent. The defoliation of the figures of Bernadette Soubirous and Thérèse Martin in the name of holiness hardly needs to be recalled, but it is central to the rather problematic aura surrounding the commemoration of the saints.

RETRIEVING THE TRADITION

In finding the place for the commemoration of the saints on today's calendar, lessons might be learned from the early tradition which could be allied with the contemporary forms of hope that are nourished by the dangerous memory of Christ's death and resurrection.

First, there is the question of the most apt way to express Christian hope. If early Christians hoped for the defeat of death in the resurrection from the dead, and if medieval Christians hoped for quick access to heaven after death, how would contemporary believers express their hope?[12] This question is asked in the persuasion that shared hope is the foundation for communion between the living and the dead, and so for the commemoration of the dead. Today again disciples of Jesus Christ look to his memory for the hope of the defeat of death in all its destructive power. This death, however, is not seen simply as the physical ending of the life span but as a destructive force that can make life a kind of living death, reducing it to mere survival, in pain and in despair. The thirst for peace and justice and for an earth on which life can be lived in dignity is a vital feature of hope today, as is the sense that the dead continue to share this hope with us.

To foster such hope, there are two kinds of dead that may be most readily remembered. The first are those who in life were powerless and without voice, who did not enjoy the possibility of living life to the full and who were deprived of the power to leave a mark behind them. The sense is growing that such persons continue to live in hope for themselves as well as for all the oppressed, and that the living have a duty in piety to bring their lives to memory and to make them a part of the living history of humankind. On the other hand, there are the dead whose stories inspire us, who have faced the enigmas of life or grappled with suffering and oppression and thus become integral to our living history, either as a challenge to take action against evil or as an assurance that God does not abandon the weak and powerless.

The vital foundation for such commemoration is found in remembering the story of the dead and in seeing it in relation to the story of Christ, as well as in relation to the building up of a present hope. The way in which communion between the living and the dead is expressed depends on how the story of the dead is remembered and how it expresses a hope in Christ for humanity or for a particular people. The sense of future which is integral to this storytelling and communion certainly cannot be identified with the early Christian expectation of the parousia. Neither is it in harmony with the medieval cosmology of heaven and earth, and its sense of time consumed in eternity through attainment on death of the beatific vision.

The imagery of the overcoming of death may be more oppor-
tune, when death is portrayed as, paradoxically, a vital energy
that destroys life in many ways, that already lays waste upon
earth and reduces many a human existence to something powerless and oppressive. This vision of death is already present
in the connection made in Saint Paul's letters to the Romans
and to the Corinthians between sin and death, the great enemies of God and of the human race. For him, neither reality is
reducible to a particular act or to a particular moment. They
are all pervasive forces and are destructive of the very possibilities of life. Death does not simply end life. When it con-
quers, it is a power that makes nothing out of life, or makes
life nothing. Today people more readily believe that hope for
the overpowering of this destructive force on earth is closely
allied with eschatological hope, in whatever this promises by
way of divine finality. Consequently, they look to stories of
those who have persevered in this hope, in word and action,
until the end of their own lives on earth, and it is this perse-
verance which is taken as the guarantee of their continuing
life, whatever form this takes.

THE CANON OF THE LIVING DEAD

A church constitutes its canon of Scriptures as the originating expression of its faith, and it constitutes its liturgical canon
as the traditional norm of its worship. In a comparable way, it
constitutes its canon of the living dead as the group of those
whose lives it believes were exemplary of the following of
Christ and of participation in his mystery, so that their deaths
warrant their continued share in the blessings of the paschal
mystery. As there is something analogously normative about
the scriptural canon and about the liturgical canon, so there is
something normative about the canon of the dead. However,
just as the scriptural canon was in a sense betrayed as a living
memory, to be continuously interpreted in relation to life, by
being envisaged as a deposit of truths, so the canon of the
saints can be betrayed by taking the process of canonization as
an authentication of virtues practiced, without adequate reference to living memory. If there is lack of interest in some of

the canonized saints today, or if there is some indifference to the process of having persons canonized, it is because the relation of this process to living memory and living hope is not well focused or respected.

The early process of canonization, before Rome took a more authoritative role in it, had its roots in the remembrance and piety of the people. It then culminated in the official admission of the name into the church's liturgy by episcopal leadership. It was indeed this naming in the church's worship that constituted, and still officially constitutes, the naming of a saint rather than any formal decree about the heroicity of virtues. Unfortunately today, though the act of canonization is a liturgical act, the official decree seems to take pride of place. A deep-rooted remembrance in the liturgy is not in fact assured because there is no rooting in communal remembrance and devotion.

In actual fact, the earlier process of canonization is in some respects being recovered. It is without the use of the title of saint, and often without any kind of formal ecclesiastical approval, because its inclusion is not allowed for in the fourth canon, which is the canon of law. However, people in their faith are calling up the memory of those who exemplify hope for them and are often in act including their naming in public acts of worship. This is in essence the process of putting persons on the calendar, but it still lacks the formalities which would allow for some new kind of official approval. Among Catholics there is hesitation to include the recent dead in litanies or to read from their lives in liturgical assemblies. The reason is a feeling that such action requires official approval. Yet it is in this very naming and acclaiming that the devotion to the living dead begins. Perhaps it is not without aberration, but it does offer the beginnings of a revival of the cult of the saints in new form. For those who believe that communion between the living and the dead in a common hope is a substantive part of the Catholic tradition, such new beginnings are more welcomed than feared. Since they are integral to the renewal of the dangerous memory of Jesus Christ, it need not be feared that they will take away from the truth and vigor of his memory and living presence in the midst of the church.

Notes

1. Constitution on the Sacred Liturgy no. 108.

2. On the revision of the calendar, see Sacra Congregatio de Cultu Divino, "De Calendariis Particularibus atque Officiorum et Missarum Propriis Recognoscendis" 18, 19 (AAS 62, 1970, 658). English translation, "Instruction on Particular Calendars and on the Selection of Mass and Office Propers" (Washington, D.C.: USCC, 1970).

3. Roman Missal, Preface 69, "Preface for Holy Men and Women II."

4. On the development of the religious and social imagery of purgatory, culminating in the poetry of Dante, see Jacques Le Goff, *The Birth of Purgatory* (Chicago: University of Chicago Press, 1981) 289-355.

5. For references on the cult of the martyrs see Herman Wegman, *Christian Worship in East and West. A Study Guide to Liturgical History* (New York: Pueblo Publishing Co., 1985) 105-107. The classical work is H. Delehaye, *Les Origines du culte des martyrs* (Brussels: Société des Bollandistes, 2d edition, 1933).

6. See Cyrille Vogel, "The Cultic Environment of the Deceased in the Early Christian Period" in AA.VV., *Temple of the Holy Spirit* (New York: Pueblo Publishing Co., 1983) 259-276.

7. On the reading of the Acts of the Martyrs in the liturgy see B. De Gaiffer, "La Lecture des Actes des Martyrs dans la prière liturgique en occident," *Analecta Bollandiana* 72 (1954) 134-166.

8. Leo the Great, Sermons on the Anniversary of His Ordination. Critical edition in *Sources chrétiennes* 200 (Paris: Editions du Cerf, 1973); partial English translation in NPNF 12, 2, 115-118.

9. See, for example, the anonymous Paschal Homilies in PG 59:723-732,735-746. English translation in Adalbert Hamman and Thomas Halton, *The Paschal Mystery* (New York: Alba House, 1972) 50-74.

10. See Peter Brown, "The Rise and Function of the Holy Man in Late Antiquity," in *Society and the Holy in Late Antiquity* (Berkeley: University of California Press, 1982) 103-152.

11. See Pierre Delooz, "The Social Function of the Canonisation of Saints," *Concilium* 129 (1979) 14-24.

12. See Christian Duquoc, "Heaven on Earth," *Concilium* 123 (1979) 82-91; Stephen Happel, "The Structure of Our Utopian Mitsein (Life-Together)," ibid. 92-102.

FORMS OF WORSHIP

10

When to Worship
Is to Lament

You are my life,
God, over and over my life,
Will you hear me
say it, will you understand it,
a living death
is all I lead, body and soul.
People treat me already as the ghost I am.
I sprawl like a
battlefield corpse in a fresh grave,
You forget where
You buried it, You feel nothing.
You threw me here,
no light, no limit to this place,
but I feel You
raging at me, the weight of You
splitting me off
from friends; they think I am hateful;.
You lock me in.
I lose sight of You in this hole.[1]

This is a terrible psalm, desolate and awful, its only saving grace being that it is still addressed to God and not to the person's own soul. Its furor is even more terrible than the anger of Psalm 137 with its dreadful cursing of the enemy. One can understand somehow the yearning for vindication, even grasp the kind of faith in God that leads to it. But the desolation of Psalm 88 is overpowering. Still, though it is the lament of an individual, it may not be without resonance as paradigm for the collective lament of this failing century.

A child is terrified by a tornado, and in the dark cellar where it is hiding with its parents from the storm it is mindful of the lesson of creation. Being told in answer to query that God created tornadoes along with all else, it ventures the opinion: "Maybe God made a mistake." Might this not well be the believer's response to many of the day's calamities, whether of violence, or racial hatred, of hunger, or of earth's waste? If there is such dread and such unbelief in the midst of faith, how can we worship?

There is a story in Elie Wiesel's book *One Generation After* that strikes a responsive chord in anyone beset by evil. After the six-day war the Talmudic scholar asks the survivor of the concentration camp, who had not up to that point returned to synagogue worship: "From now on will you believe in miracles?" The narrator goes on:

> "Yes,"I answered.
> "And you'll no longer deny God's blessings?"
> "No."
> "Well then, young man, it takes very little to please you."
> "The rebirth of a sovereign nation extinct for twenty centuries, you consider that little?"
> I had never seen him so angry with me. "You don't understand," he said, enunciating each word carefully. "There is Israel and there is your reaction to Israel. I am thankful to Israel, but you disappoint me. The present and the future make you forget the past. You forgive too quickly."[2]

In reading the closing line of the story, we ask: forgive whom? As Christians, it seems to be too much to ask to admit that in face of some realities God's fidelity may be called into question. Religious people, and Christians in particular, want to reconcile their belief in God with the horrors and the evil that they experience or see about them. Natural evil is squared off with notions of providence, and calamities in human life are squared off with predications of sin. If lament is allowed in any measure, it is in the form of confession of sin or of lament over the sins of others. It is hard to find a place in public prayer for the complaint against God by those who find no reason for the things that have occurred.

At the close of his book *Praise and Lament in the Psalms* Claus Westermann's verdict was: "Something must be amiss if praise of God has a place in Christian worship but lamentation does not. Praise can retain its authenticity and naturalness only in polarity with lamentation."[3] Elsewhere in the same book he remarks of this omission:

> Jesus Christ's work of salvation has to do with the forgiveness of sins and eternal life; it does not deal, however, with ending human suffering. Here we see the real reason why the lament has been dropped from Christian prayer . . . The impression [thus] given is that although Jesus of Nazareth actively cared for those who suffered and took pity on those who mourned, the crucified and resurrected Lord in contrast was concerned with sin and not at all with suffering.[4]

If there is no place in worship for lament, there is no way in which churches can wrestle with God over human suffering, and hence no accepted reaction to suffering other than to endure it with resignation. On the other hand, the promise of liberation cannot be anesthetized as though it meant waiting for God's good time. There needs to be a stronger cry against suffering if the promise of liberation is to have substance.

WHAT IS LAMENT?

To find the place which lament may have in Christian worship, and to understand its nature, we may begin by turning to the laments in the Book of Psalms. Westerman lists the components of psalms of lament, found in variable measure according to historical circumstances and the perils faced, as follows:

1. an accusation or complaint against God, deriving from a situation that seems incompatible with the promises of the Covenant;

2. a contrast with God's past actions in favor of the people;

3. complaint against the enemies of the people;

4. a sense of solidarity which makes the people see themselves threatened precisely as a people, and not just as individuals;

5. a vow of praise that reaches into the past, whereby the people do not belie God's past favors but continue to praise these, while looking to them as a basis for the hope of God's action in the present;

6. sometimes, a confession of sin or fault, committed either by this present generation or by their forebears.[5]

While the confession of sin occurs in some songs of lament, it is not a necessary part of this kind of psalm. Where it does occur, it is not necessarily recalled as the reason for present calamity. Indeed, the people's sin can hardly be the reason for present distress, since the very recall of God's mercy and Covenant is a remembrance of divine forgiveness. In the long run, the threat to the people's existence can only be seen as a contrast with God's past generosity and mercy, whatever their past or present sins. It is impossible not to see it as a threat to the very idea of Covenant with God and as a question put to Godself, uttered with all the force of complaint.

Westerman also distinguishes various stages in the development of the form of lament in the course of Israel's history. This development reflects the history itself and the efforts of the people to cope with calamity in the face of God.

In the early days of the nation, there is the lament of those oppressed by enemies of superior strength, such as, Psalms 74 and 79. At a later stage there is a distinction between lament in the face of natural catastrophe, for example, Psalm 83, and lament in time of conflict with enemies, such as, Psalm 137 and Jeremiah 14. There is, however, always some hope in these laments, a basic confidence that the Covenant, the worship of Yahweh, and the prosperity of Israel will be restored as, for example, in Chapter 9 of the Book of Nehemiah, a remarkable example of how in lament and in God's praise the story of the Covenant is reconstructed to account for evil. Indeed, in Nehemiah and in Ezrah 9 there is a marked tendency to get over what appears as God's faithlessness by the prominence given to the confession of sin and the recall of the sins of the forebears. The complaint against God is quite direct, but it is balanced with the confession of sin.

Lament became really critical in 527 B.C.E. when there was no longer any temple in which to worship. Since the worship of Yahweh was essential to the recall of divine beneficence and thus essential to the very nature of the Israelite people, this was an almost insuperable calamity. Westermann remarks: "the national lament took on special meaning, for after the destruction of the temple in Jerusalem lamentation became the only possible way left for worshiping god."[6] In intertestamental times, as reflected in the pseudepigrapha, the complaint against God returns in radical and bitter fashion. Here it is even kept out of official worship, as though introducing it into worship would risk suppressing it in favor of the praise of the Covenant.

Westermann points to 4 Ezdra 3:20-36 as an example of this bitter complaint. It is a lament in face of the incomprehensible fact of the destruction of Jerusalem. Ezdra turns over in his mind the events of world history, beginning with creation. Other peoples that sinned have been left to prosper, and only Israel, supposedly God's chosen one, is subjected to such destruction. The song concludes with this bitter complaint over the doom of the city:

> Then I said in my heart. Are the deeds of those who inhabit Babylon any better? Is that why she has gained dominion over Zion? For when I came here I saw ungodly deeds without number, and my soul has seen many sinners during these thirty years. And my heart failed me, for I have seen how you endure those who sin, and have spared those who act wickedly, and have destroyed your people, and have preserved your enemies, and have not shown to anyone how your way may be comprehended. Are the deeds of Babylon better than those of Zion?[7]

This lament rejects the explanation that the people's sin, their transgression of the Covenant, is the reason for their downfall and destruction. Over against the sins of the nations and their prosperity, such an explanation cannot hold. Hence the songster begins to doubt God and the Covenant. What Westermann points out is that this complaint is Ezdra's own and is not given voice within the assembly. Consequently there is no association with thankful remembrance, but only the brutal contrast between past and present, without apparent hope for the future.

There is a dilemma here which not even the psalms of Israel fully resolved, namely, the maintenance of a hope even in the worst of calamities and without benefit of an appeal to the people's sin by way of explanation. Is there room in public worship for the contrast between God's past deeds and promises on the one hand, and the apparent dereliction of the people without reason on the other? Is it possible to maintain the vow of praise and the praiseful remembrance, when God appears in all logic to have been unfaithful? In other words, how can the people take God to task and still render thanksgiving and express praise? More graphically, could Ezdra's complaint be uttered in the common prayer of the people before God and then, in faith rather than in doubt, terminate in a prayer of thanksgiving?

This is the dilemma with which the Jewish people have labored down through their checkered history and their manifold calamities. It is one with which they have been faced in this century in a way that they have never before experienced with such force. The Holocaust put the whole reality of the Covenant into question. If the Covenant were to be kept as the foundation of the people's existence and identity, they felt the need to be able to recall it in a way commensurate with their awful sense of abandonment. How would it be possible to celebrate Passover service as long as it were not possible to find a way of containing the horrors of the Nazi hatred and violence within the remembrance of the Pasch.[8] This was not a simple thing to do, for it was not possible to return to the kind of confidence in God that could be expressed before the Holocaust. Here was an event which had to either obliterate remembrance or be recalled within some hitherto unperceived sense of the Covenant and the Pasch. Does a people silence this remembrance in order to continue to worship, or can it take issue with God over a brutality to which there is no divine response as far as any meaning is concerned and yet render praise in hope?

Clearly such a dilemma is not resolved simply by writing a text. It is dealt with in the heart, the individual heart and the corporate heart. So many times in the course of their history, in the aftermath of pogrom, the Jewish people have faced this anguish. They have always had to redefine themselves through fresh ways of recalling Covenant and story in order to keep up their worship, their solidarity as a people, and their hope. Yet there has been no time comparable to the horror of the concentration camps and the trampling underfoot of both people and culture by the Nazi regime. It is not a memory that allows of easy return to synagogue or Pasch, nor is it a memory which in the name of humanity can be allowed to disappear from human record. As we know, some of the people sustained identity and hope by a silencing and even a relinquishing of Yahweh's name, resorting to a sense of historical and cultural solidarity as a people in place of an avowed faith in the Covenant as divine intervention. This ought not to be put down too quickly as unbelief or abandonment of faith. It is an effort to retrieve from their own history what the accomplishment and vigor of this people have been, so that in such memory they can retain their sense of identity and build a future. When Yahweh's promises are in doubt, there is strength in such human faith.[9]

Oddly, it is this human faith which may lead back to an avowal of Yahweh as the people's savior, and not only theirs but the world's. This may be expressed relatively simply, by saying that if the strength of the people survived even such oppression, then it must be by God's gift, and it is in this that God has kept the Covenant. I have a suspicion however that such explanation smacks overmuch of Western Christianity and of a certain rationalism, and is not really true to Israel's spirit. The return to praise seems to be regained by them rather by a rather unique way of considering the Covenant. This is to view it as a partnership, where not only are the people dependent on God but God on the people. The Nazi onslaught does not need in any way to be seen as God's doing, nor does it have to be reconciled with notions of providence. It is, in effect, God's failure. God now needs the Jewish people if the Covenant is to be kept and if any further such inhumanity of peoples to each other is to be kept from ever again recurring on the face of the earth. Believing Jews find their origins and their identity in God's saving action and Covenant, and their hopes for the future have to do wholly with Yahweh. But there is now a moment in human history which requires a remembrance of Holocaust, a testimony and an action on the people's part, if this awful moment of human history is to be gone beyond and if humanity is to be saved from such unnameable and inexplicable evil. This is the route by which the complaint against God and the chiding of God is reunited with Covenant and thankful praise.

Christian Churches on the whole were wanting in their response to the Holocaust and the plight of the Jewish people. It seems to have taken some decades before Christian people began to realize that the Nazi persecution of the Jews called their own faith into question. They still do not know quite how to express this. One way of putting it is to say simply: "The Holocaust forces us to think . . ."[10] There is a beginning in that. Some thoughts have turned in the direction of the Holocaust as a sign of humanity's failure, most particularly the humanity of the more developed world, with its enlightenment confidence. Others have looked to it as a way of making us mindful of all genocidal tendencies and dangers, dark warnings as it were of the beast in the human heart and dire reminder of the inclination to compromise, even among the best. Some find the churches called upon to make confession and to lament their collective failure. Finally, there are some who recognize that it is a question to our faith in Jesus Christ, an event that has to be incorporated into that faith.[11] For these last, on the one hand it makes Christians ask what place God intends for the people of Israel in the repetition and fulfillment of eschatological promise. On the other, it requires that in both theology and worship faith in Jesus Christ finds an expression which heeds the sign of contradiction given in the Holocaust.

DISORIENTATION AND REORIENTATION

Quite clearly the victory of evil, or of the evil one, over the believer is a violent disorientation of beliefs, practices, and prayers which cuts to the very identity of a people in God. Christians need to face up to such disorientation and find a way of remembering God's apparent failure without loss of hope in the resurrection. The alternative is to think simply that the resurrection can be expected only as a reward for present suffering, so that there is no evil in this world great enough that cannot be harmonized with the promises of redemption in Christ.

It seems to me that for faith's own sake it is time to admit some disorientation into the harmony of the Christian world and world view. For this reason I would like at this juncture to consider some ideas of Walter Brueggemann on the psalms, as found in *The Message of the Psalms*.[12] Brueggemann divides the psalms of Israel into three categories: psalms of orientation, psalms of disorientation, and psalms of reorientation. Psalms of orientation express a vision of the world and of history in which God's power, election, and mercy hold sway, so that even the factor of petition in them expresses deep confidence. Allowing lament to interrupt praise and thanksgiving is to allow disorientation, for it disrupts this ordered world. As complaint against God, lament arises from a perception that God has not been predictable, that divine fidelity is unreliable. The disorientation is all the more acute when it seems that the divine presence is not after all identifiable with what were thought to be the guarantees of Covenant and of divine action. What can the people do or say when the temple, the priesthood, the king, and the nation are either not guaranteed or are allied with the forces of evil, or when even the prophets make oracles in Yahweh's name that cannot be trusted?

To continue in the address to God, remembrance has to confront the contrast between the past activity of God and the present apparent inactivity, with its corrosion of certainty. This brings about a sense of crisis, religious, social, and historical. It is historical because it brings the historical identity and future of the people into doubt. It is social because it has to do with the doubt about the regime and the world view which were thought to be guaranteed by divine fidelity and in turn its guarantor. The nature of God's relation with the people is in question, and the divine presence has to be relocated. In another of his books, *David's Truth*, Brueggemann shows how differently David is remembered in different traditions.[13] In the one case, he is the hero, the very anointed of God, the representation of Yahweh to the people. In another, he is shifty and untrustworthy, more interested in his own personal and familial ambition than in the good of the people. In a third, he is a frail and beaten character, overcome by his enemies, the beginning in person of the story of Israel's miseries. The three versions of the Davidic tradition reflect in fact Israel's way of dealing with the social reality of king and kingdom, in remembrance of God and in face of its own historical vicissitudes. For some, the recall of the great David as heroic figure is a prop to hope in times of doubt. For others, the recall of his moral ineptitude is a reminder of the religious and social dubiousness of the kingship and a caution against placing trust in it. For still others, to note the downfall of one who had been so mighty and so divinely favored is a necessary if disturbing question about the very nature of the promises of the Covenant. It is like asking the question "Where, then, is Yahweh?" In these last two instances, the lament is not merely a matter of crying out: "How long, O Lord, how long?" But even more deeply it is the cry: "What were and are you doing, Yahweh?" What is a social crisis affecting an understanding of history and institutions and so expectations about the future, is also a religious crisis because it touches the very image of God and the people's expectations of God's promises.

It may be easier to tone down the sounds of lament, or to evade it all together, rather than to admit its disorienting influence into prayer. It can be evaded through resignation in face of calamity, as though this came from God. It can be toned down if without remainder it is identified with the confession of sins, so that catastrophe finds its explanation in human sin and is not allowed to raise issues about divine fidelity. Neither way faces the crucial questions about Godself and about God's presence, because they are both based on the hope of a return to a glorious past or of vindication and reward. They do not allow what true lament has to do, that is, within the very act of remembering confront doubt and reshape the memory and the hope, this being a task taken on by psalms of reorientation. Faith is not simply restored; it is renewed by wrestling with the images of God and with the effort to relocate divine presence. One way in which this hope was renewed in the tradition of Israel was through the growing confidence in the presence of God in people's fellowship rather than in temple or kingly institutions. Another way was by finding the hero in the *anawim* or the poor of Yahweh rather than in historic leaders like Solomon and David.

CHRISTIAN DISORIENTATION

Here we have seen the depths of Israelite lament when it is voiced as complaint against God and when it affects the levitical, davidic, and even prophetic institutions which are so closely allied with the notions of Covenant. Even further, especially when we come closer to our own age, we see how this complaint touches on the very identity of the people as people and on their historic future. If lament is made, it is because there is cause for lament, and its place in the shaping of tradition and hope is to face the doubt and not allow a sense of security, however justified by doctrine, to undermine faith and fidelity. Can Christians allow the place of such lament in their traditions? Or must they need do so to be found faithful to the name of Jesus Christ?

The official books of Christian worship are primarily of an orienting sort, if we are to adopt Brueggemann's categories. They have a creedal foundation and express clear beliefs about God and secure expectations about the future, most often having to do with life after death rather than with life on earth. Whatever passing lament is allowed in Christian worship does not carry the full blow of corporate lament. The individual may be permitted to sorrow, or even a whole body of people to mourn, but it is always gone beyond in the confidence of the fidelity of God's benevolence and promise. Much of the time this is quite adequate and is one with a cultural appropriation of faith that is clearly oriented through belief and moral commitment.

In the present time of cultural disorientation and reorienting, there seems to be place for a fuller use of lament in Christian assemblies, but this requires the courage to let beliefs about God and about providence be questioned. We may indeed grieve over suffering and oppression, bewail the calamities of the Jewish people, weep over the raped earth, look with sorrow on the church's treatment of women, but do we ever allow this to be a complaint against God? In the address to God, do we ever allow the questions that a postcritical age puts to the inmost nature of God and of God's relation to the world enter into remembrance and prayer? Confronted by issues of biblical tradition, church teaching and structures, or by doubts about the church's stands in the past on vital issues, may we not complain that God stands aloof from so many things that have been presented as securities of divine word and guidance? Does not the very sacramental tradition in which we say Christ and the paschal mystery are represented seem at times to have been less than adequate? What has God got to say to that? Where is God, if not there? And if there, why in so clumsy a way?

FOUR CAUSES OF LAMENT

There are four realities of contemporary existence and of Christianity's part in it which call for lamentation at the very heart of worship. If lamentation is not allowed to enter there, the disorientation of belief and life which is necessary to an appropriation of faith adequate to experience will not take place. In brief these four realities are: the fate of the Jewish people in our time; the suffering of humanity and of earth which defies acceptance; the dualism of the church's own traditions; and the patriarchy which pervades the Judeo-Christian tradition and which has such an enormous effect on human and religious life.

In worship Christians remember the story of God in Jesus Christ. Doing this, they draw on biblical, cultural, historical, and archetypal images. They profess that the story of God and the story of the world converge. Every human story has to be remembered and retold for what it tells of the godly power manifested in divine grace and for what it challenges in our ways of affirming faith and of remembering God.

The Jewish people tell and collect their tales of extermination attempted by the pogroms and concentration camps.[14] If these events are forgotten, God can no longer be questioned; but if this happens, the recall of the Covenant has to change. Sometimes God is put on trial and, when judged guilty, worshiped. Sometimes the story is told *as if* there were no God, as if God were totally absent, or totally negligent, or totally uncomprehending, because faith in the God of Abraham and of Moses demands that this *as if* be wrestled with. Sometimes the question is asked whether Godself hangs upon the gallows, or enters the gas chamber, or fights with fellow prisoners over a crust of bread, and—if this is so—what is to be made of the Covenant?

These stories are as much for Christians as they are for Jews. This is not only because such atrocities as those committed by the Nazis would question belief in God were they committed, as in part they have been, by any race against another. Not only is it so because what we call the Holocaust stands as a modern expression of the myth of *homo homini lupus* and a reminder of all attempts at genocide. Not only is it so because Christians cannot dare to forget their corporate complicity, however blatant or ignorant or unknowing, in this racial hatred. Indeed, all these things are reason enough not to forget the Shoah and to tell the stories over and over again even as we speak to God, but they do not constitute the most important reason for remembrance, the reason that needs no other reason. The fact is that this is the suffering of the *Jewish* people, the people of Yahweh's Covenant and promise. They are a people who held to the realization of prophetic promises within history, to their realization in this world, even when Christians tended to defer them till heaven or eternity. If God so suffered this people to suffer, what is to be made of God's Covenant with the world and with human history? What do Christians deny in their own tradition, so rooted in the history of the Israelite people, if they choose to forget the people's suffering and with it their hope beyond hope?

There certainly has to be a large moment of repentance in Christian worship in face of these stories. Pope John XXIII stopped a Good Friday service in mid-course in order to remove the charge of perfidy against the Jewish people. This was only to touch one symptom of a deeper ill. Even from the time the Gospels were written, Christian expression has been accomplice in, and even cause of, antisemitism. The memory of Jesus Christ has been tarnished by it. Hence what is called for is a corporate response, an acknowledgment of solidarity. Christians, however, cannot stop at repentance. They need to admit the question to faith into their ways of remembering, thanking, and interceding.

There is a sense in which we are introduced to a remembrance of the larger suffering of humanity through recollection of the suffering of the Jews in face of and despite God's Covenant. What Christians profess about the reign of God in Jesus Christ, about the victory of the resurrection over death, about the hope of the resurrection of the body, about the promises made to those who believe, have to be reconstrued in face of satanic victories in a world whose creator we proclaim as good. So powerfully do they suggest a divine absence that they have to be told over and over again in ways that are not so much an affirmation of a divine presence as a search for it.

It is all too simple to say that Christ has put away sin and death by his sacrifice, or that Old Testament history is a reminder of how human beings put divisions between themselves and God by sin. Can we tell and celebrate the story of Jesus Christ convincingly on the fiftieth anniversary of the outbreak of a World War which terminated in the discovering of the extermination camps? What has Christ to say to massive famines that could be averted by human endeavor but which in fact are worsened by racial and ethnic controversy? What metaphors and symbols and plot introduce the remembrance of Jesus Christ into such calamity, where he will not be remembered if he is not remembered in the midst of violent death? What are we to say of the cosmic Christ and of the God of all creation in a world which may in time not be fit for human habitation because human greed has so exploited it? How powerless can the God of Might become? Are only promises to be held out, promises which have to do with the afterlife or a new creation beyond time and history?

As we confront such issues in the effort of faith, is it the descent of Jesus into Sheol that makes sense of creed? Is it his hanging between two thieves? Is it the comfort to endure, and in enduring to testify, that he gives to Thecla or Perpetua or Lawrence? Is it the judgment pronounced in the passion narrative against the judges? Is it the fortifying presence among the oppressed of Martin Luther King or Oscar Romero, which says that even in their impotency the promises must rage against this world's evil and distress?

Out of the chaos of the world around us, a third cause for lament looms up. This is Christianity's past and even present tendency to harbor dualistic attitudes and to countenance the slight of human development and of care for the earth. It is at times as if the only eschatological hope offered to humanity and to earth has to do with what happens beyond time, and that all present spirituality is grounded in a yearning to be done with the attractions of life here and now. Surely we have to lament the God who asks this of us. Christians have contributed by apparent contempt to the rape of the earth in many ways in the manner in which they express the promises of the divine kingdom and the hope of a blessed paradise. They have contributed more actively and forcefully by actions justified in the name of the stewardship or lordship of creation given to human beings by God. All too often such stewardship has put the things of earth totally to the service of human progress, as though the earth and atmosphere did not have claims of their own, by virtue of their own nature and finality.

The rising of women's consciousness has played a role in the Jewish remembrance of the Holocaust.[15] Not only do the tales of suffering, heroism, and faith include those of women and children. Women's voices have pointed to factors in the Judeo-Christian tradition, factors dating back to the common canonical Scriptures, that are not unassociated with the history of western culture which found its most brutal expression in the Holocaust. Christian history has incorporated these faults, already present in Judaism, to an even greater degree and allowed them larger place in the tragic outcome of an enlightened and rationalistic and technological western civilization.

This gives rise to the fourth and cruelest cause for lament, that aroused by an overidentification of God, of Christ, or of the Spirit, with specific modes of canonical communication. Is there not an element of divine deceit in what the churches have made of the Scriptures, of sacrament, of priesthood, and of church authority? It may be next to impossible to rediscover the ways in which these represent the presence of the triune God in our midst, if we do not, not only in theoretical works but in prayer itself, learn to weep over the ties that have bound God to particular ways of viewing these canonical and ecclesial realities. The complaint against the patriarchy of Scripture and church seems to come to the heart of this dilemma and to bring us to the point where faith is either at its weakest or its strongest. Does the androcentric language of the

Scriptures not defy the recurring proclamation: This is the Word of God? Does the barring of women from ministry not question the confidence of the proclamation: The mystery of faith? The fact of the matter is that the dubious identification of God with text, representation, and structure occurs at the very heart of Christian worship, even in the celebration of the Lord's Supper. How then can remembrance of Jesus Christ as savior and redeemer be retrieved from suspicion and reoriented, if we do not complain and lament this divine fallacy? It is not possible to locate the memory of Christ and the presence of the Spirit in the struggle and hope for liberation if this kind of overidentification continues. The dangerous memory of Jesus Christ can be effectively regained only through the power of a lamentation that enables Christian people to acknowledge the fallacies of belief and that frees them from false securities that blind to reality.

FORMS OF LAMENT

Much that has to do with these four causes for Christian lamentation is already active in the Christian conscience and imagination, but it is much more on the fringe than at the heart of Christian worship. They need to be invited into the assembly. There is too much that is de-energizing in the ways that calamity is covered over, for us to be able to dispense with the release and the energy that come from lamentation.

One forceful way of allowing lament to be heard in worship is to give heed to the voices of victims. This has been the way of remembrance for the Jewish people on Yom Ha-Shoah, with the telling of stories and the plaintive liturgy of the extermination camps, inserted into the Kaddish for the dead.[16] John Paul II on his visit to Mauthausen gave an example of the kind of plea that could well be given a place in Christian liturgy, when he called on the dead of this and other extermination camps to speak to this age.[17] Jesus' own lament can be heard in such a context, his lament in solidarity with all the suffering of the world, for—as Westermann points out in his work—the lament of the mediator belongs among the prayers of lament and is found in the mouth of Jesus.[18]

There is clearly a need in Christian prayer for that part of lament which is repentance. At the beginning of the Sunday liturgy, instead of the rather bland petitions for forgiveness, there is room for litanies that allow victims to speak and prompt the church to a corporate penance and metanoia.

Beyond repentance, or as a necessary sequel to it, there are recollections that disorient our remembrance of God's promises, and ask for a thanksgiving that is heedful of them and ready to recognize the presence of God in the midst of suffering, and indeed even in the suffering itself. Here too the Jewish people teach Christians some of the forms of praise to which one may return from the disorientation of lament. As one listens to the stories of the Holocaust, one hears the presence of faith in the midst of absurdity and death; there is also the example of how this remembrance and this kind of praise now form part of Jewish corporate worship.[19] We also need to gather in the faith-filled story of women down through the ages and heed how they have found and praised God in the midst of life and of death.

So important is the reorientation of Christian prayer, that it has to occur at the very heart of worship. When faith's vision is disoriented, the vow of praise holds firm but is, for a while, inarticulate. Taking new memories and perceptions into the thanksgiving act of worship does not come easily, but it is the challenge of the time.

It is not enough to couple lament with memorial thanksgiving and supplication, to pass tranquilly on, catharsis completed, to the customary praise. Lament does not have to do with threats to faith to be rid of in order to be able to praise as is the wont, but with questions to faith that have to be admitted in order to change the manner of praise. It is of the very substance of memory, not only its antecedent. In other words, catharsis has to be not only of mind and heart but of the memorial thanksgiving and ritual affirmation themselves.

Troublesome questions have to be admitted into the act of remembering that the churches put at the center of their worship. Where is God in the Covenant when the Jewish people have been so allowed to suffer as to be subject to the threat of extinction? Where is God in creation when the earth is raped? Where is the savior of the poor when the poor die by millions on our television screens or in the backyards of drug dealers, where death itself is acted out as comedy? Where is the Christ in whom there is neither Jew nor Gentile, slave nor free, male nor female, when these distinctions work themselves into the very fabric of our celebration and into the language of proclamation? If our memories have led us to deceptive assurances, how can they be redeemed except where they have been wont to occur? Only if we cry out to the God who has led us to this impasse, to the now almost nameless God, will we be able to come to a renaming of the holy in which human hope does not perish but is born anew.

Notes

1. Translation of Psalm 88, in Francis P. Sullivan, *Lyric Psalms: Half a Psalter* (Washington, D.C.: The Pastoral Press, 1983) 77f.

2. Elie Wiesel, *One Generation After* (New York: Pocket Books, 1978) 165.

3. Claus Westermann, *Praise and Lament in the Psalms* (Atlanta: John Knox Press, 1981) 267.

4. Ibid. 275.

5. Ibid. 162-213.

6. Ibid. 270.

7. 4 Ezdra 3:28-31 (RSV)

8. On this, see Lawrence A. Hoffman, *Beyond the Text: A Holistic Approach to Liturgy* (Bloomington: Indiana University Press, 1987) 139-143.

9. It is only in this light that one can understand the reestablishment of the State of Israel.

10. Thus the title of the essay, Emilio Baccarini, "The Holocaust Forces Us to Think . . ." SIDIC 24 (1989/3) 20-24.

11. See, for example, the contributions of Christian writers to the symposium *Jews and Christians after the Holocaust*, ed. Abraham J. Peck (Philadelphia: Fortress Press, 1982).

12. Walter Brueggemann, *The Message of the Psalms* (Minneapolis: Augsburg Publishing House, 1984).

13. Walter Brueggemann, *David's Truth in Israel's Imagination and Memory* (Philadelphia: Fortress Press, 1985).

14. Among others, see the collection of stories and prayers for Yom Ha-Shoah in *Siddur Sim Shalom. A Prayerbook for Shabbat, Festivals and Weekdays*, edited, with translations, by Rabbi Jules Harlow (New York: The Rabbinical Assembly. 1985) 828-843; Elie Wiesel and

Albert H. Friedlander, *The Six Days of Destruction. Meditations towards Hope* (New York: Paulist Press, 1988).

15. See A. Roy Eckardt, *Jews and Christians. The Contemporary Meeting* (Bloomington: Indiana University Press, 1986) 116-131.

16. *Siddur Sim Shalom* 840-843.

17. John Paul II, Address at Mauthausen, June 24, 1988 *Origins* 18 (1988) 124.

18. Westermann, *Praise and Lament* 275-279.

19. Hoffman, *Beyond the Text* 139-143.

11

Hope Is the Joy of Saying Yes

IT HAS BEEN QUESTIONED MORE THAN ONCE WHETHER CHRISTIANS bring much joy to their lives and to the celebration of redemption, or whether the state of singing in churches is not a sign of radical disengagement from the Christian story. In many a parish church or other place of assembly, one can note the stillness, the complacency of ritual, the illusions of sacred quiet, and the bored and apathetic assistance of those who go to church because they must. Such are a people in exile. Yet there are places where songs are raised up, and though the exile may not be ended, there are Christians alive who can sing of themselves:

> When the Lord restored the fortunes of Zion,
>   we were like those who dream.
> Then our mouth was filled with laughter,
>   and our tongue with shouts of joy;
> Those who go forth weeping, bearing seeds for the sowing,
>   shall come home with shouts of joy,
>   bringing their sheaves with them. (Psalm 126)

The 1986 regional NPM Convention in New Orleans took as its theme "the heart of ministry." Story, song, and people were respectively referred to by this title. Putting the three together, however, we can say that the heart of ministry is a people who come together in mutual service, sharing each other's stories and above all the story of Jesus Christ, to sing and to celebrate.

175

One the one hand, we cannot do without a song that is rich in memory, at times heavy with the tragedies that afflict the universe, but nonetheless vibrant with hope and exultant with the God-given capacity to say "yes" to past, present, and future, despite, or even because of, the ability to penetrate the reality of finitude and suffering. On the other hand, the capacity to tell and hear the story is vital to Christian existence and to Christian ministry. To serve is to bring the story of Jesus Christ to life in the midst of a people, so that their perception of their own lives, of humanity, and of the world is renewed, and they are enriched with the capacity to say "yes" to the mystery that is at the heart of the universe.

The power of the Christ story truly comes to life when people can interweave it with their own stories. It then comes to life in song and celebration, for there is no denying that the energy of God appears to come to the fullness of life in song. There are few passages of the Old Testament that have the vibrancy of the dying song of Israel's great leader and prophet, Moses (Dt 32). It is a doxology in which God's freedom comes to voice in the freedom of this man condemned not to see the promises fulfilled but still transformed by hope, and in the freedom of the people who have learned to sustain this hope, even as they see themselves deprived of Moses' leadership. There are, likewise, few passages in the New Testament that have the vision and power that is to be found in the song of Mary, the daughter of Zion (Lk 1:46-53), whose "yes" to the incarnation is the "yes" of all the poor in the world who even in their poverty marvel at God's reversal of humanity's vainglory.

CHANGING PERCEPTIONS

While narration is the fundamental mode of storytelling, the recall of story is not reducible to this. It cannot make its point without the witness of the storyteller (the parabler become parable), and the arts are needed for its meaningful transmission. Certainly, no story is complete until it is given voice in song, whether by way of ballad, or by way of exultation that flows from the energy it contains, or by way of lament over the tragedy that it unfolds, or by way of a contemplation that introduces into the heart of the tale. Other arts, too, must share in the task and are vital to remembering and transforming lives in virtue of what is remembered.

> The man bent over his guitar,
> A shearsman of sorts. The day was green.
>
> They said, "You have a blue guitar,
> You do not play things as they are.
>
> The man replied, "Things as they are
> Are changed upon the blue guitar."
>
> And they said then, "But play, you must,
> A tune beyond us, yet ourselves,
>
> A tune upon the blue guitar
> Of things exactly as they are."[1]

In this small section of Wallace Stevens' poem, "The Man with the Blue Guitar," we catch some sense of what story does, and of how music enhances its power. It has the capacity to change the perception of reality, and yet leave the reality empirically recognizable. The words of the poem, "things as they are," with the adverb "exactly" interjected the second time around, bespeak the transformation. The people ask for a tune beyond themselves, yet themselves. The musician is expected to tell of life as it is recognizable in the daily grind or the daily achievement, the daily joy or the daily sorrow, yet also to give an insight into its reality, a way of looking at it that makes it different. Story and music and art reveal some truth as we pass from moment to moment, from day to day, from year to year. They are vital to a ministry that enables people to come to grips, as fully as possible, with the realities of life, political, economic, and social life, giving a vision of the world in all its complexity as the work of a divinely creative love.

Some specific examples can serve to show how art changes perceptions and may thus be suggestive for ministry. In the Museum of Modern Art in New York, there is a painting by Picasso, entitled "Girl before a Mirror."[2] In the painting there are two larger than life female figures, one apparently imaging the other, reflecting it in a mirror, yet one with it in its reality.

The reflected image is more sensuous and voluptuous than the original, the breasts and thighs are brought out more prominently and artfully, earning for the painting the acclaim of being a celebration of sensuality. What Picasso does in this painting is to make a trivial every-day concern of young girls a matter of great moment and at the same time to reverse a traditional theme of Vanity in painting, wherein the reflected image is that of a death's head. The obvious censure of any young girl absorbed enough in her own developing femininity to spend time inspecting herself before a mirror is turned by Picasso into a celebration. He makes fun of the traditional moral admonitions about vanity, and allows his model to take delight in her sensuality. This is indeed a tune beyond herself, beyond the awkwardness of developing sensuality and beyond the censoriousness of social inhibition.

A second example is taken from a musical composer better known for "Cats" than for his Requiem. In this latter composition, Andrew Lloyd Webber contrasts the world of the child and the world of the adult as they are both brought face to face with death. As the music and chant develop, the tendency of the adult singers is to come to terms with death, to leave the sorrow behind in favor of paschal joy, even, indeed, in the *Sanctus*, giving themselves over to a sort of skittish exuberance. Death and bereavement have to be put in their place, for life continues.

The children's plaintive tone, however, serves as an undercurrent to the entire piece, and it is the boy soprano's sweet toned *perpetua* that closes out the Mass. There is an irony at work in this, for though in the written text of the liturgy the word *perpetua* clearly qualifies the *lux* or light that God bestows upon the deceased, in the sung melody it may well qualify the enduring quality of the child's sorrow. Though adults will pass over their sorrow and grief with whatever consolation comes their way, even risking to forget or put out of mind both death and the dead one, the child does not forget and is not so easily consoled. Peace and hope may indeed be offered to us in Christian faith, but not at the expense of forgetting, or in avoidance of the tenacity of sorrow. The adult may be safe, but the child is wise and sings of things as they are, exactly as they are.

Passing to a third, more directly pertinent example, consider how the Byzantine liturgy, in its watch at the tomb on Good Friday, celebrates the dead Christ. Among the many dirges of the burial, we find the following:

> The centurion cried out: O Christ,
>   even dead I know you are God.
> Joseph and Nicodemus trembled and said:
>   O God, how could we touch you with mortal hands?

And in another part the chant takes Mary's voice:

> When our most pure Lady
> beheld you laid out, O Word of God,
> she shed tears of agony.
> O my precious Son, my God,
> you crushed death by your death
> through the might of your godhead.
> O my son, I praise you
> for your great compassion
> which moved you to suffer this death.[3]

This is a striking liturgical example of life celebrated in agony over death, but this kind of piety is not confined to the East. What the oriental liturgy does with its watch at the tomb of Jesus Christ, the popular piety of Latin countries and peoples does with the procession of the dead Christ, which makes up an important part of the people's annual commemoration of the mysteries of our salvation.

The magnitude of Jesus' pain is immense, the sorrow of his death overwhelming, the grief of the mother overpowering, the wretchedness of his friends who bury him insurpassable. There is no escaping the pain, for the pain is both brute reality and revelation. Death's hold over Jesus is that beyond which we cannot believe. But for both Byzantine liturgy and Latin piety, in the intensity of the grief there abides the belief in the godhead, in the amazement at the death there is the depth of hope in the power of the dead one. Joseph's fingers tremble as he takes down the body of the dead Christ whom he in this very service acknowledges as God; Mary's tears of agony become the song of praise in which at the death, as at the conception, she sings the song of God's liberation, of death itself overpowered by death.

These three—Picasso's girl before a mirror, Lloyd Webber's Requiem, and the Byzantine vigil at Christ's tomb—are examples of how through art form something paltry (an adolescent girl worried about her breasts) sorrowful (a child bereaved), or tragic (the magnitude of Jesus' pain and death) becomes revelation, participation in the mystery of love and life. Irony is integral to the art, for it reverses wonted perceptions, according to which the girl is vain, adults deal better than children with death, the death of Jesus is a paschal mystery and part of the divine plan. Art replaces this commonplace with a fresh vision and fresh power: the girl is made for love, the child teaches the adult not to forget, the ones who weep most over the death of Jesus are the ones who speak most powerfully of his godhead.

STORY TOLD AND RE-TOLD

One of the marvelous things about storytelling is that the story is seldom told the same way twice. We have different ways of getting into the story, according to where the teller or the listener stands. As stories take their place in a tradition, the people of the tradition never stand on the same ground twice. Social sands are always shifting. The realities to be faced change color. The better a story, the more able it is to give a way of seeing life and its mysteries to generations that live differently and face different issues. But to achieve this end it does require the conspiracy of the artists and storytellers who pass it on, not only with some kind of critically constituted accuracy (as with exegesis) but with power.

Consider the many ways in which the story of Abraham and Isaac has been narrated and artfully embellished. We are most familiar with the account given in Genesis 22, and with the celebration of that story as the story of Abraham's faith, as we find it in Paul's letters. But behind the biblical story there is another story of the end of human sacrifice among semitic peoples—not all, but among those who make covenant with Yahweh. The biblical narrative has already been able to put aside that aspect of the tale, for the issue of human sacrifice is no longer an issue of any consequence for it. Instead, it uses the tale to extoll the faith of Abraham in the promises of the bewildering, contradictory God who has led him from his own land.

Among the Jewish people the story has a rich literature handed on outside the biblical canon under the title of the *Akedah*, or binding of Isaac.[4] This is a story more about Isaac than about Abraham. Isaac is portrayed as a young man—in some versions he is thirty-seven years of age—perfectly aware of all that is going on. He is the willing, if innocent, victim of an inevitable and even cruel death that mocks not only Abraham's but the whole people's hope in the future. There is no apparent cause for the death, no good reason why it has to take place. But take place it must and Isaac is willing and still trusting. The *Akedah*, as it passes on from generation to generation, often has Isaac actually killed (for to a people who know cruel death, what use is a tale in which death's power is held back from slaying its victims?). Sometimes it has him raised up again, but the main point of the story is that the hope of the future for the people lies in the one who is the innocent but believing victim of senseless death. Even God seems to have no say in this, for Yahweh is depicted as apologizing to Abraham and Sarah and Isaac for what cannot be otherwise if the people's hope is to be guaranteed.

The story defies reduction to an intelligible plan, to one in which good reasons can be given for Isaac's binding. Its strategy is to make the hearers see that the future is given for all through the one who says "yes" both to death and to God, to God in death, who gives testimony of trust in the Covenant of God with the people, even when there are no reasons for what happens, and the testimony itself must be the reason. No hearer can say "yes" to the "yes" of Isaac without weeping. And God can only apologize.

While this story was taken up by Paul as a celebration of faith into the Christian tradition, and while in later generations Isaac became the figure of Jesus Christ, it is a story that continues to ravage the Christian memory and to be probed in different ways for its meaning for humanity.[5] In the sixth century Ravenna mosaics, the story is given a tranquility and order that it does not possess even in the Genesis account. It is an epiphany of the priesthood of Christ and of the priesthood of the church, a divinely intended type of Jesus Christ as priest and victim. To less serene minds and for more troubled ages, neither the pain of Abraham nor the pain of Isaac could be so readily reduced to ordered intelligibility. In the paintings of Caravaggio and of Rembrandt it is the pain of the father who must sacrifice his son that rivets the attention. In the face and flesh of Caravaggio's Abraham there is anger and rebellion even as the deed is done. In the face of Rembrandt's Abraham there is a sorrow and a puzzlement, which, as one critic puts it, one feels must have remained with him all his life, even though the child is reprieved by God's command. One could not expect this man to see the end of the story as a happy one, for it will never be clear to him why he should have been pushed to such an extremity. I doubt that Rembrandt's Abraham ever heard God apologize.

The story of Abraham and Isaac has been taken up again in our own country and in our own time, in the sculpture made by George Segal to commemorate the students killed at Kent State University in 1970 in a confrontation with the National Guard. In this depicting, Abraham and Isaac are protagonists in a tragedy of misunderstanding, where two generations, both moved by good will, fail to understand one another and are brought inevitably by misunderstanding to violent confrontation. Though the new generation, the one that has not found its place in the established order of things, appears to be the one that is overcome or defeated in this confrontation, the sculpture's hope is embodied in the resolute and pleading face of the kneeling Isaac. It is inevitable that he will be struck down by the brutality of the "good man," Abraham, who must save order at any cost, but one knows that the passionate desire of the younger man will not pass away with death.

One is drawn quite readily from this sculpture, kept not at Kent State but at Princeton, to the figure of the crucified woman exhibited in the church of Saint John the Divine in New York.[6] Everything, even the scandalized uproar surrounding its exhibition, says that such yearnings as here depicted must be suppressed, suppressed even in the name of the good God. It is only the passion, the witness given in the passion, that says they will live. In this case, as in that of Isaac, the passion of the one who is passioned is the hope. Only that. Even that. Indeed, that.

Segal's Isaac and Almuth Lutkenhaus' Crucified Woman are recollections from Jewish and Christian tradition that in so tragically bespeaking our age—through a new telling of the traditions—challenge and unsettle our remembrance of the Jewish heritage and of Jesus Christ. This, of course, is what they are deliberately doing: out of the very unsettling of our settled way of being and conceiving and doing, they are raising up new hope. It is impossible to gaze upon Segal's figures and ever again read Genesis 22 with an easy act of faith. One cannot look upon Lutkenhaus' crucified woman and ever again think of Christ in the same way.

THE MEMORY OF CHRIST

The Christian people's memory of Christ has to immerse itself in the tragedy of the age, lest both church and world be left without priest or prophet or artist or songster, but it has to do so at the cost of relinquishing blithe answers to faith's questions. God is in the conflict now almost without a name, and one cannot say "yes" to God, or to what Christ now becomes through the passion of this world, without saying "yes" to the conflict and the passion. Rather than escape, faith is the door of entry into the conflict and the passion. Joy is for those who are not afraid. It was never promised to those who try to avoid tragedy.

We are so accustomed to hearing the Gospel narratives about the ministry, death, and resurrection of Jesus Christ that we fail to realize how unsettling they were from the beginning. We are also so accustomed to imposing doctrinal interpretations upon them that we fail to realize how deeply they continue to question so many of our assumptions about God and about godly order in the world. I would like to take only two factors in the Gospel story to show how it disoriented, in order to re-orient, remarking only in passing that many readers may be familiar with current studies on the parables which pinpoint in them just this capacity to unsettle assumptions about God and about the good, in order to introduce new perspectives.

The first thing to which I would like to point in the Gospel story about Jesus Christ is that it portrays Jesus as in conflict with the good. That is to say, many of his enemies were those who would have been looked upon as "good people," trying to serve the best interests of society and of the Israelite people, or indeed of world order. Or they were what we would call the forces of order, the establishment that tried to serve the economic, political, and religious interests of the people. One of the ways in which the passion narrative shows how Jesus and his Gospel reverse social and religious values and perceptions is its use of the metaphor of judgment. On the one hand, Jesus is judged by those who represent order and established interests: the high priests and sanhedrin, representing religious traditions and interests; Herod, representing the local political interests of one sector of the population; and Pilate, representing the power that by incorporating Palestine, along with other nations, had brought order and tranquility to the Mediterranean basin and beyond. On the other hand, however, as far as the Gospel narrators are concerned, this judgment becomes a judgment on the judges: God's judgment is not that which is spoken by the representatives of order, but resides rather in the victim who is judged. God pronounces in favor of the very things of which Jesus is accused, and the manner in which divine judgment is given is not through a ruling but through the testimony and witness of the one who is done to death.

Such a manner of recounting the story can lead us today to incorporate all of Christian and indeed human history into the remembrance of Jesus Christ under the heading of "the memory of victims." To the history that is often officially or most popularly proclaimed, there is an alternative history, and it is that of the underside of human events, of those whose place in human affairs is more easily consigned to oblivion. For an Irish people, for example, it is the story of the people who perished or took exile in the years of famine, remembered according to popular tradition until 1966 in the *De Profundis* said at the end of every Mass. For the American people today, must it not be the story of the slaves who did not come to the country through Ellis Island, or of the refugees who are refused entry because they too readily fit the description on the base of the statue? And for the church, must it not be the readiness to see Christ represented in its own history, not simply in the priesthood or magisterium, but in the women so consistently denied power or voice, but who have their own story of fidelity, their own life in the Spirit, their own ways of testifying to God's liberating grace?

But most fundamental of all to the Gospel story is the way in which the witness of Christ's death is central to the story and to its meaning. That a person be raised from the dead is not in itself all that amazing: Jesus is recounted to have raised people from the dead on a few occasions. What is amazing is that his own resurrection derives its meaning from the fact that it is evidence of the meaning of death, testimony to the reversal of death's power by a death. In his dying Jesus himself is transformed, and in him the whole cosmos. His death is like the grain of wheat falling into the earth, and in dying becoming something totally different, a new form of life, one with the very earth into which it falls. Jesus descended into the bowels of the earth, into the very abode of death; he was placed in the rock. Not only did he become one with dying humanity, but he was absorbed into the earth, becoming one with the cosmic energies represented in the parable of the grain of wheat. Death is reversed, not simply by the promise of a return to life, but by becoming itself a becoming, a transformation into new forms of life. The darkness of Jesus' death is that it gives the lie to known forms of life: its light is that it witnesses to a new kind of life, which eye has not seen nor ear heard. Henceforth, Christian believers find life in death, not merely a promise of life after death.

In picking out these two aspects of the Gospel story, namely, judgment reversed and death reversed, I have taken the elements that I believe need to be woven into today's ways of retelling the story or the singing of the story, if it is to be a "yes" to the life which we are called upon to live and a testimony of hope for a tragic world.

There are a number of things in our world today that simply do not make sense. They can be factually traced in their origins, but they can be given no meaning, either human or divine. Can we give witness to life in the name of Christ by saying "yes" to being part of this situation, by doing no more than expressing solidarity with a victimized people and a victimized earth, without trying to impose godly reasons on all that has and is taking place? Is our faith in God's power, our hope of life, great enough to be able to affirm them, without having to understand and explain what is beyond explanation and understanding?

In referring to the world's tragedy, I have three things in particular in mind: (1) the extent of world poverty and the abominable difference between rich nations and poor peoples; (2) the structures of domination that determine the political, the economic, and the ecclesiastical order and which are most tellingly represented in the position of woman in society and church; (3) the destruction of the earth and the cosmos, which results from the failure to perceive ourselves as an element in a cosmic order and not the lords of it. Can we, in the memory of Jesus Christ, find the energy whereby to give witness to God's love for the poor, to the power of the weak, and to the claims that earth and cosmos have upon humanity? I do believe that by retelling the story of Jesus Christ by focusing upon the renewal of human judgments and established orders, and by finding God's witness and new life in the death of entering into tragedy, we will be led to a discovery of that energy. But it is a rather hearty reversal of many established human, political, economic, and religious perceptions. We have to look for mentors in such artists as Picasso and Segal and Lutkenhaus. Is any of our church music as affirmative of the energy and vitality to be found in the despised or the victimized? Or as ready to recognize who these victims are?

What, for instance, are the songs of creation? The psalms have long served us as paradigm, or even provide us with the very words we use. Study of the psalms has shown how they themselves are a reversal of some pre-Israelite or early Israelite songs. The risk of finding godly manifestation in the wonders of earth, sea, and sky was that human beings were made subject to the inevitable forces of creation, and had to placate the divine by satisfying the gluttony of nature. So Israel sings of God's entry into human history, and of the service that creation itself, as in the waters of the flood or of the Red Sea, was made to render to the chosen people. This introduced something of a balance into the relation to the earth, for God's magnificence could still be glorified in the splendors of the cosmos, while, however, the mountains skipped with glee over the fortunes of the people and the command to dominate the earth could stand ground for the introduction of new economic policies. It is the command to dominate that has worked its way into western humanity's ethos and, as a result, Christianity has made a large contribution to the vicious exploitation of the earth that we now know. How do you sing of God's manifestation in sky and water when you know they have become our victims, by being made, bit by bit, our providers instead of the great and wondrous reality of which humanity is only a small, if intimately joined, part? Can we find our way first to saying "yes" to being part of this tragedy in order to then discover how to say "yes" to a new mode of being part of the earth—in the name of Christ, Word Incarnate, Creator who must redeem creation from our very hands?

EUCHARISTIC PARADIGM

We can find ways of assenting to being part of the world's tragedy by the ways in which we celebrate Christ's supper. And by being led thereby to this assent, we will find new energy and hope. In the dangerous memory of Jesus Christ we can include the memory of other victims. Instead of giving priority to the structures of domination, we can come to expressions of mutuality in a sharing of gifts and a sharing of a common table, where the structures of domination are negated. In the reverence we express for bread and wine, we find a new harmony with creation, where the bread and wine are not camouflaged as sacred things but wept with for their adulteration.

At Christ's table, art and priestly ministry converge around the bread and wine. Their nature is to be revealed in action, word, and song. We need to be brought face to face with the truth that true bread and wine are revealed in their inmost being as Christ's body and blood. We have to rediscover the scandal of the wine that is sometimes spilled and of the bread that crumbles, in order to discover the truth of Christ's presence in our midst. The very depths of the being of Jesus as the Christ of God are rooted in the realities of bread and wine, provided by the bounteous earth, kneaded and pressed by human hands and feet, and shared at a table which is common before it becomes the common table of the Lord's Supper. The ultimate truth of the Incarnation is that God's love takes being in the world in bread and wine, shared at a common table, where they are treated with reverence because they are the earth's fruits, without which reverence cannot truthfully be revered as Christ's body and blood. The creative word of transformation is the creative word of revelation, the word that lets being stand forth. This is so little recognized that we may well ask how we can sing the song of the Lord in an alien land. In the eucharist, however, where there is a people united in the memory of victims, in oneness with the earth, in the hope of all humanity, and renewed in the power of the Spirit of Christ, there is indeed the power of the new creation. There is the Christ, in whom there is neither Jew nor Gentile, slave nor free, male nor female, earth nor humanity. There is the new people, the new heavens and the new earth, the new creation in the Spirit of God.

CONCLUSION

In this essay I treated first the ways in which story and insight into story of artistic forms change our perceptions, of how, like the man with the blue guitar, they change reality for us. Then I treated of how the same story, taking the example of the binding of Isaac, can be told in many different ways, and of how the power of a story, such as that of the dangerous memory of Christ's Passover, lies in its capacity to become the heart of a multiplicity of situations. Third, in the energy that comes from the story told and celebrated I placed the source of the power to say "yes" in hope, to finitude, even to tragedy, in the trust that in the passion is the victory. Fourth, I treated briefly of today's tragic situation and how remembrance of Christ allows us to enter into it in witness of God's solidarity with the poor, the dominated, and with the earth itself, and therefore in the joy of hope. Fifth, I pointed to the eucharist as the celebration of the new creation by the community of those who place their faith and hope in the memory of Christ and in the power of the Spirit that transforms.

In conclusion, let us return to the girl before the mirror, as to a parable. What does she see, this young girl? She sees her unformed figure. But what does she see, this anxious girl? She sees, as human wisdom tells her, a vain young person, foolish in her vanity, a very death's head. Yet, what does she see, this happy young girl? She sees, in deeper wisdom, a creature lovely and beloved, the desire of infinite love. There is ecstasy in her gaze, and her song is this:

> Wisdom, the fashioner of all things,
>   taught me
> For in her there is a spirit that is
>   intelligent, holy,
> unique, manifold, subtle,
> mobile, clear, unpolluted . . .
> steadfast, sure, free from anxiety,
> and penetrating through all spirits,
> that are intelligent and pure and most subtle.
> Wisdom is the breath of the power of God,
> and a pure emanation of the glory of
>   the Almighty;
> therefore nothing defiled gains entrance
>   into her.
> . . . against wisdom evil does not prevail.
> (Wis 7:22-30)

Enriched with wisdom, which is the wisdom of Isaac passionate and pleading, of the crucified woman, of the wine poured out and the bread broken, of the Christ who is one in eucharist with broken humanity and disemboweled earth, the energy of a new and transformed life, may our mouths be filled with laughter and our tongues with shouts of joy.

Notes

1. Wallace Stevens, "The Man with the Blue Guitar," in Wallace Stevens, *Collected Poems* (New York: Knopf, 1954) 165.

2. See Melinda Wortz, "Theological Reflections on an Image of Woman: Picasso's Girl before a Mirror," in *Art, Creativity, and the Sacred*, ed., Diane Apostolos-Cappadona (New York: Crossroad, 1984) 297-303.

3. Joseph Raya and Baron José De Vinck, eds., *Byzantine Daily Worship* (Allendale, NJ: Alleluia Press, 1969) 829, 830.

4. For a summary, see G. Vermes, "Redemption and Genesis

XXII," in *Scripture and Tradition in Judaism*, Studia Post-Biblica 4 (Leiden: Brill, 1961) 193-227.

5. See Jane Dillenberger, "George Segal's Abraham and Isaac: Some Iconographic Reflections," in *Art, Creativity, and the Sacred* 105-124.

6. See Rosemary Radford Ruether, *Readings toward a Feminist Theology* (Boston: Beacon, 1985) 105-133, with reproduction of the image on p. 104.

12

On Blessing Things

BY GIVING ATTENTION TO THE BLESSING OF THINGS, IT IS HOPED THAT
in this way the meaning and intent of blessings will be illustrated and insight given into the uses of power. Here we will
consider those blessings that are given outside a distinctly liturgical context, for example, at a meal, or to the blessing of
objects intended for use in daily life, such as oil, water, fruits,
scapulars.

Studies on the eucharist in recent decades have drawn attention to the Jewish *berakah* or blessing prayer. As a result,
there is a tendency to model all Christian blessings on it and
to emphasize the note of thanksgiving or praise addressed to
God in blessings. On the other hand, there is a persistent demand on the part of the faithful to have things blessed in order to plead divine protection. This can even lead to a tension
between an official mentality and a popular mentality on
blessings. When the Paschal Vigil was restored in the fifties,
the blessing of homes and food-stuffs that used to take place
in some countries on Holy Saturday was put off until some
day in the paschal season. Priests doing their rounds after
Easter found that the people's disappointment over the failure
to have their Easter table blessed greatly tempered the welcome given to them. One could multiply examples of this sort
to show how in blessings people find a source of divine pow-

191

er, a mediation of good health, peace, favor, and safeguard against evil, which is more readily captured in an invocation of God's name over an object, or in a gesture such as the sign of the cross, than in an act of thanksgiving or of praise. Does this necessarily denote superstition? Is the emphasis on praise and thanksgiving imposed by ecclesiastical tradition? What is to be said from tradition about connections between human energy, demonic energy, and divine energy, to which blessings are addressed?

HISTORICAL SURVEY: EARLY CENTURIES

The precise relation of Christian blessings to Jewish blessings is unclear, partly because of uncertainties in our knowledge of the Jewish tradition, partly because of obscurities in the Christian. Discussion over the berakah[1] are too many to rehearse here. Suffice to recall that Joseph Heinemann, who notes the dominance of the motif of praise in Jewish blessings, also notes the recurrence of the invocation of divine power. Thus of the daily Tefillah or eighteen blessings he writes:

> The principal content and purpose of these blessings is to give praise and thanks to God for the abundant goodness which he has bestowed upon his creatures and, at the same time, to obtain permission from him to enjoy the fruits of this world, for "the earth is the Lord's, and the fulness thereof". On the other hand, most of the eighteen benedictions . . . are petitionary in content. To be sure, each of these petitionary prayers concludes with a eulogy formula, and is thereby infused with elements of thanksgiving and praise to him who satisfies the needs of all his creatures . . . Nonetheless, the primary purpose of the weekday Tefillah is unquestionably to petition for Israel's necessities out of the firm conviction that the Lord will hear these supplications and respond favourably to them.[2]

While this is said of blessings for the people, it denotes the general sense of all blessings in Israel at the time of Christ and of the early Christian Church. The interweaving of praise, thanksgiving, and petition carries over into the Christian tradition.

Eucharist, Eulogy

When turning to blessings over things as practiced in the early church, attention is first given to two blessings pronounced in the course of a meal, whose sacramental meaning is often discussed. These are the prayers over the bread and the prayer over the cup found in the ninth chapter of the *Didache*.[3] Leaving aside the issue of their relation to the celebration of the Lord's Supper, these prayers can certainly be taken as paradigmatic of the blessing of things in an early Christian tradition, still much under the influence of Judaism. The blessing over the bread reads:

> We thank you, Father, for the life and knowledge which you have revealed to us through Jesus Christ your child. Glory to you through all ages.

In this Christian form of blessing it is the thanksgiving motif rather than that of praise which is chosen, though the eulogy or praise at the end is typically Jewish. The object of the blessing is the life and knowledge given in Jesus Christ, rather than the divine providence evidenced in the produce of the bread from the fields, as accented in Jewish table-blessings. In the blessing of the cup at the end of the meal, one notes the invocation of the name of Jesus Christ. This is the Christian turn given to the invocation of the divine name found in Jewish traditions, an invocation which expresses both awe of the divine mystery and expectation of divine care.

In the two blessings from the *Didache*, while they are pronounced over bread and wine to be shared in the fellowship, little is said of the significance of bread and wine in themselves, since all attention is given to the share in the blessings of Christ which the table mediates. This should not lead us to think that early Christians had no mind for the provident attention given to the production of earthly fruits. A good example of this is found in the blessing of first-fruits found in the *Apostolic Tradition*. Though the prayer begins with a formula "We thank you, God," the body of the prayer is a eulogy or praise for God's action in creation and providence.

> Through your word you have made them grow; you have commanded the earth to bear all its fruits for the joy and nourish-

ment of humanity and all the animals. For all this we praise you, O God, and for all the blessings you give us when you adorn the whole creation with all kinds of fruits, through your child, Jesus Christ, our Lord.[4]

In the lucernary or blessing of light at the beginning of the evening meal, it is the motif of thanksgiving for the benefits of redemption which is developed. Picking up on the natural symbolism of light, the prayer then celebrates the gifts of redemption through an extension of this symbolism, referring it to Jesus Christ.[5]

If only the form of blessing is taken into account, one could say that in these two texts we have an example of a difference between a eucharist or thanksgiving, and a eulogy or praise. However, when the compiler of the *Apostolic Tradition* makes a distinction between a *eucharistia* and a *eulogia*, he does not seem to have this in mind.[6] He uses the former term to signify either the prayer said at the celebration of the Lord's Supper, or the bread and wine which, being blessed, become the body and blood of Christ. *Eulogia* is then used to designate the prayer said by the bishop over the bread blessed at the beginning of a common meal or over the first-fruits and flowers which the people offer, or the bread and fruits which when blessed are shared.[7]

According to this distinction, where the intention is to distinguish all else from the sacrament of the eucharist, the thanksgiving for the evening light would be classed as a eulogy, despite the etymological sense of praise attached to this word. This would lead to the conclusion that prayers of blessing over objects developed either in the form of thanksgiving or in the form of praise. From the two examples given from the *Apostolic Tradition*, one gets the impression that sentiments of praise dominated when thought was given to the works of creation, whereas thanksgiving prevailed in considering the work of redemption, though this is not to be taken as a hard and fast distinction.[8]

Eulogy, Exorcism

It would also seem that in some cases eulogy had associations with the invocation of the divine name over objects, an invocation which amounted to a petition for the mediation of divine blessings or divine protection to those using the objects. This sense of blessing is found particularly in the East Syriac tradition, and a good example is to be had in the *Acts of Thomas.*[9] It is disputed whether this blessing of bread is a eucharist in the Lord's body. Whatever about this discussion, the prayer has its origins in the Jewish blessing of bread at the beginning of a meal and seems to give evidence of the Syrian Christian tendency to convert this blessing into an invocation of the divine name. The text is here quoted from an early Greek translation, rather than from the extant Syriac, since the latter seems to have been corrupted by later "orthodox" interferences with the textual tradition.

> Bread of life, those who eat of which remain incorruptible: bread which fills hungry souls with its blessing—thou art the one to receive a gift, that thou mayest become for us forgiveness of sins, and they who eat thee become immortal. We name over thee the name of the mother of the ineffable mystery of the hidden powers and dominions, we name over thee ineffable mystery of the hidden powers and dominions, we name over thee the name of Jesus. May the power of this blessing (*eulogia*) come and remain in this bread so that souls who receive it may be washed of their faults.[10]

In this text it is clear that the bread blessed is intended to mediate divine blessings upon those who eat it, particularly the forgiveness of sins and immortality. While this, of course, takes on particular significance if what is intended is the sacrament of the eucharist, in a more general sense it reflects the power of *exorcism*, that is to say, the protection against the ills of body and spirit which is mediated through a share in blessed things. It is also to be noted that the core of the prayer is an invocation of the name. This invocation would seem to mix the name of the Spirit (the mother of the ineffable mystery) with the name of Jesus, reflecting an early East Syriac inclination to blur the distinction between Christ and the Holy Spirit. In any case, it has been suggested that the root of this blessing is the invocation of the divine name in Jewish prayers of which the most important is that said over Jerusalem in the daily synagogue prayer or *Tefillah*.

Some items about blessings in the *Apostolic Tradition* bear comparison with this exorcism or invocation of the divine name for care and protection against evil. For example, while the blessed bread given to the baptized at the end of a *synaxis* is called a eulogy, the bread given to the catechumens is called an exorcised bread.[11] As the name given to the bread for the baptized derives from the type of prayer said over it, so the bread given to the catechumens is probably derived from the type of prayer pronounced over it. The bread thus blessed was intended to mediate to the catechumens the divine power which they needed in their combats against Satan.

Though the word *exorcism* does not recur, the sense that things can mediate protection against ills of mind and body does crop up in the blessing of oil, cheese, olives, and water. While the rubric or directive for the blessing of oil, cheese, and olives says that the bishop is to give thanks over them in a prayer similar to the eucharistic *anaphora*, the compiler actually furnishes a text which constitutes a request for the solace and health of those who use the objects. The prayer develops a redemptive symbolism from the natural symbolism of the things themselves.

> O God, in making this oil holy thou givest holiness to those who use it and who receive it. Through it thou didst confer anointing on kings, priests and prophets. Let it procure likewise consolation for those who taste it and health for those who make use of it.[12]

> Make this curdled milk holy by uniting us to thy charity. Let this fruit of the olive never lose its sweetness. It is the symbol of the abundance which thou hast made to flow from the tree (of the Cross) for all those who hope in thee.[13]

The note of exorcism, with more attention than in the *Apostolic Tradition* or the *Acts of Thomas* to demonic powers, is highly developed in the blessings of oil and water at the end of the Sunday synaxis in the *Euchology of Serapion of Thmuis*.[14]

> In the name of your only-begotten Son, Jesus Christ, we bless these creatures. We invoke the name of him who suffered, who was crucified, who rose from the dead and sits at the right hand of the Eternal, on this water and oil. Give these creatures the power to heal, let them drive out every fever, every demon and every sickness. Let them become for those who use them a healing and reviving remedy, in the name of your only-

begotten Son, Jesus Christ. Through him, glory to you and power, in the Holy Spirit, now and for ever and ever. Amen.

Of this prayer, several things may be noted. First of all, it is a blessing in the form of an invocation of the divine name, revealed to us anew in Jesus Christ. Second, it is a petition for divine power, a power that is invoked indeed over material things, but that is mediated through them to human beings. Third, it expresses the feeling that all of human life is affected by the redemption, so that people may pray for health of body as readily as they may ask for forgiveness of sins and grace. Fourth, the prayer closes with the doxology customary to other forms of blessing. Fifth, and perhaps most significantly, in developing the imagery of the demonic the text conjures a sense that all creation is caught in a struggle between demonic powers and the divine power that saves and redeems.

Peter Brown sees this sort of consciousness of the demonic as something which came to the fore in the third century, rather than as something to be found in earliest times. He writes:

> Men who had discovered some inner perfection in themselves, who felt capable of intimate contact with the One God, found the problem of evil to be more intimate, more drastic. To "look at the sum total of things," to treat human miseries with detachment—as so many regrettable traffic-accidents on the well-regulated system of the universe—was plainly insufficient. It made no sense of the vigour of conflicting emotions within oneself. Hence the most crucial development of these centuries: the definitive splitting off of the "demons" as active forces of evil, against whom men had to pit themselves . . .[15]

At the same time, the author notes, these demonic powers, all-embracing agents of evil in the affairs of the human race, were held in check by the divine power mediated through the community, especially through the agency of holy persons.[16] The exorcism pronounced over objects to be used by the faithful seems to have been part of this check, assurance of a divine protection and deliverance. The exorcism of early prayers, it will be noted, is not intended to free things themselves from demonic control, but to free humans who use them in their daily life as a kind of sacramental mediation.

Offering

A survey of early Christian blessings would be incomplete if note were not taken of the fact that offering is at times associated with them. In the *Apostolic Tradition* the oil, olives, cheese, flowers, and fruit blessed by the bishop are offered by the faithful.[17] It is also said that when the bishop says the eulogy over things, he offers them,[18] while on the other hand the thanksgiving over the light is apparently not understood to constitute an offering.[19]

The language of offering in the early church was polyvalent, and is therefore at times obscure to contemporary readers. It was a matter of assuming the language of offering and sacrifice into a way of life and of worship wherein the accent was on growth in the Spirit and upon the gifts that God gives. To call the bishop's blessing an offering is in line with the notion that Christian prayer, especially that of praise and thanksgiving, is a new form of cult, constituting in itself a spiritual offering. For the people to offer things of the earth (which were then going to be used by them at home or shared in community) was to adopt an old covenant perception of first-fruits as offerings to be made to God within a Christian context. This offering symbolized acknowledgment that all good things come from God, as well as the hope that God through provident care would attend to the health of mind and body of those who believe in Jesus Christ as redeemer, the one in whom the world of creation is recapitulated, to use the imagery of Irenaeus.

Conclusions

This fairly summary sketch of blessings in early Christian centuries allows us to draw some conclusions. First of all, we find that three forms of prayer were in vogue, namely, acts of *thanksgiving* over the goods of creation which focused on their redemptive symbolism, acts of *praise* which expressed wonder at the providence of God manifested in the fruits of the earth as well as a sense of reverence in their use, and acts of *petition*, invoking the divine name or divine power on things, so that they might serve to mediate divine care and divine protection to those who used them. This distinction is based on the historical evidence, but is not to be taken too rigorously, since any prayer could include all three forms or any one or two of them.

Second, we can note how the earth and its fruits were increasingly looked upon in redemptive perspective. While one might be inclined to say that they represented God's creative power, Christians saw the whole world and humanity's relation to it within the horizon of Christ's redemption, or recapitulation.

In the third place, invocation of divine power over things for the sake of those who use them was as much a part of an early blessing tradition as was thanksgiving. This did not reflect a separation of the sacred from the profane, nor the idea that things blessed were sacralized. Rather it reflected an understanding of sacramental power, that is, the sense that redemption included all creation and that through the things of daily life God mediates protection and love.

In the fourth place, it seems that the request for divine mediation was gradually developed in terms of the need for protection against demonic powers. The idea was not that Satan had power over the things of the earth, but that the human persons who made use of them could be subject to Satan. Apparently it was felt that God was so close to creatures in the good things of the earth, so provident of them, that protection against Satan might well be mediated through this agency.

Fifth, all blessings from this age have fundamentally that significance which is rooted in the eucharistic blessing, namely, that all things are redeemed in Christ and that in all the uses of the things of this earth believers share in the grace and goodness of the redemption.[20]

Finally, account has to be taken of the action of holy persons or charismatics in giving blessings. The texts that we have are largely in canonical collections and so reflect what was done in assemblies, the prayer given by the bishop. However, this should not cloud the fact that divine power was thought to be mediated through persons rather than through formulas, however well constructed. One would have to pursue the investigation further to show that the role of charismatics in blessings and healings, the recourse to hermits against the powers of devils, are an integral part of the history of blessings in the early Christian centuries. In any case, we have to remember that in the ordination tradition of the time it was a holy person who was sought out for the office of bishop, so that there was no danger of isolating his role in the community from the power of his prayer before God or from his power as a person to mediate divine blessings. Activity in prayer was grounded in a sense of the Christian person as mediator of God's blessings, and only secondarily in the mediation of office as such.

THE MEDIEVAL WORLD

The Multiplication of Blessings

Peter Brown in his work on late antiquity notes that between the sixth and ninth centuries less attention was given to the blessings mediated by holy persons and more to the holy things themselves as agents of protection, or images of divine presence. The holy things made God visible or tangible and conveyed the patronage of the saints to whom they were dedicated.[21] Along with this went an increasing accent on exorcism, not now simply in the sense that through blessed objects God would give love and care to their users, but more and more in the sense that things themselves had to be rescued from Satan's power.

In his work on blessing A. Franz has given many examples of the blessings of things in the Middle Ages.[22] Rituals and pontificals reflect a growing concern with the subjection of the world to the demonic. The increasing number of exorcisms in the form of exsufflation of devils shows more interest in the safeguard from evil than in the sharing between Christians of divine graces. The tendency is then to attach a blessing, completed often by an exorcism, to everything. The *benedictio ad omnia* is typical of the Middle Ages. Though rituals supply innumerable blessings for things in the home and things in the fields or other places of work, this blessing provides for the unforeseen occasion, when a specific blessing is wanting.

As a principle of interpretation, one should note that the meaning of blessings cannot be derived from the texts alone. One has to imagine the world which is reflected in such an abundant collection of exorcisms and blessings. For example, the text of the *benedictio ad omnia*, preserved from medieval texts in the 1614 Roman Ritual, is very close in terms to early church blessings. Through an invocation of the divine name, the prayer asks for the health of mind and body of those who will use the blessed object. However, the very existence of such a blessing, alongside many specific blessings for such things as cornfields, granaries, kitchens, pots and pans, as well as the increasing need for exorcism and protection against the devil, suggests the transactions (spiritual and no doubt monetary) that went on between people and priests. The people seem to have prevailed upon priests to invoke God's name frequently over domestic and utility objects, as well as over objects of devotion that would serve as guarantees of divine surveillance or heavenly patronage. The actual words of blessing may often have mattered little, more merit being attached to physical acts, such as the sign of the cross or an oral exsufflation of the devil.

The Blessing of Water

The blessing of water obtained increasing importance in the medieval world. Like the *benedictio ad omnia* it was something that provided for all necessities. With blessed water on hand, people had an ever-ready protection against sickness and other kinds of evil, and a constant agent of God's care to be sprinkled on whoever or whatever stood in need.

The text of the blessing of water, destined for sprinkling in the home, that is found in the Gelasian Sacramentary, gives a good example of how the symbolism of water was developed. The idea behind the blessing is that the water may be used to protect homes against Satan. Old Testament episodes are evoked to convey this meaning. On the one hand, the water is likened to the blood of the paschal lamb sprinkled on the doorposts of the Israelites prior to the exodus to protect them from the hand of the avenging angel. On the other hand, the water was apparently felt to have an ambiguous relation to God, since it had to be sweetened (by the infusion of salt), as Elijah sweetened the bitter waters with his axe-head.[23]

Blessings and Saints

The importance of blessings given by holy persons in early Christian centuries has already been noted. However, as early as Paulinus of Nola, Franz has indicated the connection made between blessed objects and saints.[24] Among other gifts sent to his friends either with or for a blessing, Paulinus seems to have sent the relics of martyrs or other holy persons, with the intention of sharing together in the divine blessings evidenced in the life of the venerable deceased. Other examples are also given by Franz: the *Vita Severini* calls a relic *sancti Johannis Baptistae benedictio*, and Gregory the Great speaks of the relics of Mark, Peter, and Paul as *benedictiones*. Such usage probably derives from the practice of blessing these objects with a prayer that invoked the name of the saint. What we have in these examples is the fusion of devotion to martyrs or other holy deceased with the practice of sharing communion in an exchange of blessings, as well as with the practice of mediating divine power through whatever is blessed.

Through the Middle Ages the cult of the saints intruded more and more on blessings. The martyr or saint took on the role of patron, that is, one who had the ear of God and could therefore exercise power and influence on behalf of devotees. Not only were relics blessed, but their use in blessings to touch people was a tangible guarantee of patronage and protection. It is not surprising that the Blessed Mary's patronage is often invoked in blessings and that special blessings were attached to a number of her feasts.

Different Worlds?

One cannot look for an even and uniform development of blessings in the Middle Ages, for this would be to assume a logical, coherent, and universally similar spirituality. Besides the blessings that emphasized the need for the protection of God's power against demonic power, there were already those that accentuated the distinction between the profane and the holy. Already in the Gelasian Sacramentary, one finds that everything connected with public worship had to be blessed or consecrated.[25] Churches, altars, vestments, and vessels for worship are all provided with blessings. The texts themselves are quite appealing, since they do not attach any specific power or holiness to the objects themselves but are concerned with priestly service in spirit and in truth. However, the withdrawal of things from profane usage, the Old Testament imagery of priestly cult, and the setting-off of the ecclesiastical world from the popular are significant factors in these blessings. Contemporary with the emergence of these specific blessings is the fact that all blessings seem to have become the preserve of priests, so that the power of the priest as such even intruded into the world of popular blessings. There were apparently two kinds of power recognized by the people, both of which they accommodated to their needs: the power of the holy person, now identified with the saints in heaven, and the power of priestly office. They had to be brought into league with one another, for the protection of the people in a world of woe and dangers.

Another kind of world is reflected in other blessings, of which a good example is the blessing of a knight's sword at his investiture, such as is found in the tenth century Romano-Germanic Pontifical.[26] This quite beautiful text belongs to that quest for lay spirituality which would allow lay persons their part in the conquest of the world for God in what had become a clerically and monastically dominated society.[27] The knightly or crusader spirituality was not the only one whereby people in those centuries sought their place in the kingdom of God, but it was one that allowed a lay person to claim a role as one who defends the kingdom against its enemies, tributary to other dominions, and as one who protects its most vulnerable members, the widow and the orphan. The blessing reads:

> Hear, Lord, our prayers, and with the power of your right hand bless this sword with which your servant wishes to gird himself. May he use it for the defense and protection of churches, of widows and orphans, and of all those who serve God, against the savagery of pagans. May it strike all those who attack your church with fear and trembling.

The blessing ceremony included the singing of Psalm 45, with a special accent on verse 3: "Strap your sword upon your thigh, O mighty warrior."

From one point of view, this text might seem to reflect the subjection of the temporal to the spiritual order and the tendency of the church to sanctify war when it seems to suit its own ambitions to power. From another point of view, however, it has to be seen in its own time as an attempt on the part of the laity to find their own due place in God's kingdom. The blessing was probably composed more as an accomodation of the clergy to the spiritual aspirations of the knightly class than as an attempt of clerics to arraign this class to their service. In a comparable category of blessings one would place that of the rough robes of the mendicants, for this would represent a kind of accomodation between clerical and monastic holiness, on the one hand, and that of the new order of those who sought holiness by an evangelical poverty in the world of the poor, on the other.

Careful attention, then, to the blessings of things that developed during the Middle Ages over a period of centuries reveals the, at times uncomfortable, accommodation of different worlds to one another. In the first place, there was the ecclesiastical world in which the sacred was separated from the profane and cult imposed a special status on its practitioners. All the laity suited themselves to this world by accepting that blessings had to be mediated through the agency of the clergy, even when some challenged the power of the clergy by demanding that the sanction of a holy life was required for the exercise of office. In the second place, there was the world of the more socially and politically powerful laity, who wanted to find their own place in God's reign and saw themselves particularly as its defenders against the onslaughts of the evil one. In the third place, there was the world of the common people, subject to dire necessity and to poverty, people often without protection or patronage against the uncertainties of nature or the exigencies of the powerful, a world wherein recourse to heavenly patronage and divine protection seemed the only viable safeguard. These three worlds interlocked and interplayed, but the people in them mapped their course by different charts.

THE POST-TRIDENTINE WORLD

In ecclesiastically approved rituals during the centuries that followed on the Council of Trent, it is the distinction between the sacred and the profane that seems to dominate the blessing of things. Whatever was to serve in the sacred order had to be withdrawn from the profane. Exorcisms are linked with blessings because things have to be wrested from the sway of the devil.[28]

At the same time one has to note all during this period the devotion represented by the blessings and wearing of scapulars in honor of Mary and the saints, as well as other particular blessings such as that of the cords of Saint Philomena. Blessings of such objects as bread, wine, or water in honor of a particular saint also continued, and the blessing of fields or fishing fleet could be done with great festivity.

Vestiges of this proliferation of blessings and blessed objects remained in the appendix of the 1614 Roman Ritual even after its revision in 1925 to meet the requirements of the 1917 code of canon law. The euchology of these blessings retains the ancient demand for *sanitas mentis et corporis*, but it accentuates the hope of heaven. To introduce the hope of heaven was the ecclesiastic's way of orienting the need for help in the world of the common people. The people might have recourse to blessings and blessed objects in a world of powerlessness, in the hope of a supernatural prevention of illness or of protection against impending calamities, or in the trust that God could dominate nature in such a way as to give them abundance of sea and harvest. The priests, however, possibly dreading the superstitious or ineffectual inclinations of such hopes, or fearing that dissatisfaction could lead to something more crass, directed the people's thoughts to heaven. The world could then be lived in, in the hope that God and heavenly patrons would assuage the necessities of this life, and in the knowledge that suffering endured would be merit for the joys of the after-life.

REFLECTIONS

This short and necessarily partial survey of the history of the blessing of things gives rise to some reflections, pertinent to their form and usage today.

Forms

In the canon of church tradition there is no stereotyped

form of blessing, but from earliest times, as noted above, one finds a mixture of forms, inclusive of praise, thanksgiving, invocation of the divine name, exorcism, and even offering. In the early tradition the underlying faith to which expression is given is that the whole world is suffused with divine power, and all things and their usage are affected by God's creative and redemptive love. Later traditions, wherein protection against demonic power is the prevalent sentiment, or the patronage of saints is invoked against calamities, or the holy is separated from the profane, are departures from this early conviction.

Eschatology

The tone and purpose of blessings necessarily change as a people's or an age's eschatological perspective changes. Early blessings belonged to the *eschaton* of the covenant community, which believed in the advent of God's reign, and sharing in natural things shared thereby in the divine blessings of creation and redemption. A later age was tributary to a world wherein all things were seen to be caught up in the combat between God and Satan, between the powers of the two kingdoms. There were different perspectives on this combat, the one seeing all things as corrupt and the other seeing them corrupted by human misuse. A vision of the universe that separates the sacred and the profane is still another perception of God's presence and power in the world, and many blessings belong within an eschatological view that life in this world is a time of suffering, preparatory to the hope of heaven.

Interpretation

As already observed, blessings have to be interpreted not only according to the text but within the world to which those who transact them belong. It is quite possible for different persons to share the same ceremony with divergent meanings. Blessing is a transaction between persons and one has to ask what benefits the different parties deem themselves to derive, and what power they exercise over one another and over the things of God and the things of the earth. While in the medieval and modern worlds the clergy have been acknowledged as the ones who mediate divine power, and the doctors and scribes who composed the texts appear to have had adequate knowledge of early traditions and euchology, one always has to ask how much it was the people who determined the field wherein these divine blessings were invoked. How much reflects the accommodation of ecclesiastical authority, with ambiguous intent, to people's demands upon them? How much reflects the compromise whereby priestly and ecclesiastical power could be held secure, even while allowing the people and their needs to set the agenda for devotion and blessing?

Powerlessness

The relation of blessing to powerlessness and to the powerless seems to be one of the major factors to be taken into account in a proper understanding of the blessing of things. The fundamental meaning of blessing, whatever form it takes, is that God's power redeems the powerless. Earliest Christian communities, sects to the prevalent religious and temporal cultures of their time and place, could see themselves made powerful in Christ. They found their way of dwelling on earth and using among themselves the things of earth by reason of their strength in Christ. This depended on the strength of being a community in him. The community's protection of the widow and the orphan, that is, of its own powerless, is a necessary underpinning to the praise of God and the invocation of the divine name over the things of the earth, which all shared in common.

Without the privilege and support of a close community, flung upon a world where they could have no earthly protection, the poor of later times had typical resort to heavenly patronage and to the hope of divine intervention. Even the more wealthy among Christians could lack the power that goes with status and dignity, so that they too had recourse to patronage and blessing. *Dignitas*, we know, was an important theme in early medieval Christianity, and its influence on the fascination for the blessings given in honor of saints, looked upon as patrons, is not to be discounted.

It is, however, those who have little or no source of worldly power, whether of wealth or of dignity or of influence, who appear to have the most frequent recourse to blessings. Prelates and the new *kleros* of the educated often regard this interest in blessings as a superstition, or at least as prone to superstition, and there is no doubt that it has in places survived with little else left of Christian faith or practice.[29] This fear of superstition seems to be one of the reasons for the current trend to let the form of thanksgiving have pride of place in blessings, over petition or the invocation of God's name. However, one does not meet the reality simply by laying traps for superstition. Future development in the pratice of blessings depends on how the church sees the power of God to be given to the powerless of the earth. What kind of liberation does the Spirit of Christ bring to the helpless? What personal sense of power does the Gospel give them? The underpinning of community, with its corporate strength, will be necessary to such development. The language of their demands defines the world in which the poor live, bereft of power but possessing their own independence and dignity. This self-definition is to be respected, not tampered with.[30] Only if this language is comprehended, only if it can be expressed how God's power comes to people in a world defined by that language, will it emerge what it can mean to bless God in such a world, and what it means to invoke God's blessing.

Notes

1. See Jean-Marie Tillard, "Blessing, Sacramentality and Epiclesis," *Concilium* 178 (1985) 108.

2. Joseph Heinemann, *Prayer in the Talmud: Forms and Patterns* (Berlin and New York: De Gruyter, 1977) 18.

3. W. Rordorf, ed., *La Doctrine des douze apôtres*, Sources chrétiennes 248 (Paris: Cerf, 1978). The translation given here is taken from Lucien Deiss, *Springtime of the Liturgy* (Collegeville: The Liturgical Press, 1979) 74.

4. B. Botte, ed., *La Tradition apostolique* (Münster: Aschendorff, 1963) no. 31. The English translation is taken from Deiss, *Springtime* 148f.

5. Ibid. no. 25.

6. Ibid. no. 26.

7. For a similar use of *eulogia* in a Latin text, see the journal of Aetheria: *Ethérie: journal de voyage*, H. Petre, ed., Sources chrétiennes 21 (Paris: Cerf, 1957) 106/7, note 1.

8. According to Hippolytus, first-fruits and flowers were to be offered and blessed, but not vegetables. See no. 31.

9. On these blessings, see G. Rouwhorst, "Bénédiction, action de grâces, supplication: les oraisons de la table dans le Judaïsme et les célébrations eucharistiques des chrétiens syriaques," *Questions liturgiques* 61 (1980) 211-240.

10. E. Hennecke and W. Schneemelcher, *New Testament Apocrypha II*, trans., R. McWilson (London, 1973) 427.

11. *Apostolic Tradition* no. 26.

12. Ibid. no. 5f.

13. Ibid.

14. F.X. Funk, *Didascalia et constitutiones apostolorum II* (Paderborn, 1905) 158-194. The English text given here is taken from Deiss, *Springtime* 198f.

15. Peter Brown, *The World of Late Antiquity* (Singapore: Harcourt, Brace, Jovanovich, 1971) 53.

16. Ibid. 101.

17. *Apostolic Tradition* no. 5f.

18. Ibid. no. 28.

19. Ibid. no. 27. "He does not say: 'Let us lift up our hearts' because that is said at the moment of the offering." Above all, the author does not want anything else to be confused with the sacrament of the Lord's body and blood.

20. Tillard develops this thought in "Blessing, Sacramentality and Epiclesis."

21. Brown, *The World of Late Antiquity* 182-187.

22. A. Franz, *Die kirchlichen Benediktionen im Mittelalter*, 2 vols. (Freiburg-im-Breisgau: Herder, 1909). This remains the authoritative work on blessings.

23. L. Mohlberg, ed. *Liber sacramentorum romanae aeclesiae ordinis anni circuli (Sacramentarium Gelasianum)* (Rome: Herder, 1960) nos. 1556-1557.

24. Franz, *Die kirchlichen Benediktionen*, vol. 1, 239-246.

25. *Sacramentarium Gelasianum* 689-702.

26. C. Vogel and R. Elze, eds. *Pontificale Romano-Germanicum*, vol. 2 (Città del Vaticano: Biblioteca Vaticana, 1968) CCXLIV, p. 379.

27. See A. Vauchez, *La spiritualité du moyen-âge occidental: VIIIe-XIIe siècles* (Paris: Cerf, 1975) 65-74.

28. See A. Gignac, "Les Bénédictions: sous le signe de la création et de l'éspèrance évangelique" in J. Gelineau, *Dans vos assemblées*, vol. 2 (Paris: Desclee, 1971) 579-593.

29. For an interesting perspective on this, see Roger Bastide, *The African Religions of Brazil: Toward a Sociology of the Interpretation of*

Civilizations (Baltimore and London: Johns Hopkins University Press, 1978) 349-352.

30. Compare André Aubry, "The Feast of Peoples and the Explosion of Society—Popular Practice and Liturgical Practice," *Concilium* 142 (1981) 35. At the time of writing this essay, an analysis of the new *Book of Blessings* for the Roman Rite was not possible. This would now need to be done to complete this overview.

SIN, SICKNESS, DEATH

13

The Sacramentalization
of Penance

AT THE END OF THE 1983 SYNOD ON PENANCE AND RECONCILIATION
some had the impression that the bishops had not adequately
addressed the issues involved in the renewal of the sacrament
of reconciliation and the church's penitential discipline. From
one point of view, the synodal documents concentrated too
much on one element of the process of forgiveness and reconciliation, namely, the confession of sins to an ordained minister. From another point of view, it did not show much insight
into the nature of the confession of sins as such and its overall
place in the Christian life. To address the present situation, it
will be helpful to consider the tradition of penance, to look at
the three forms given in the new order, and to address the language of confession of sin.

CONFESSION

The confession of sins as an act of the Christian person is
clouded by current sacramental structures, its nature obscured
by canonical obligations and by an excessive preoccupation
with what has come to be known as the integrity of confession
necessary to the reception of sacramental absolution. That it is
more than a listing of sins and their submission, with a con-

trite heart, to judgment is made clear by some words of Pope Paul VI that have been integrated into the 1972 Order of Penance. Paul VI describes *metanoia* or conversion as a *profound change of the whole person* whereby one begins to consider, judge, and arrange one's life according to the holiness and love of God.[1] This perception of one's life is mediated by an act of confession, made with a contrite heart and leading to acts of penance that serve to change the habits and outlook of one's life.

For Christians of the western tradition, the model for confession is always in some sense the *Confessions* of Saint Augustine. In this work one finds a profound attempt by the author to see his life as a whole, both backwards and forwards, to find in it the signs of sinfulness and aberration along with their causes, but more profoundly to unfold the continuing traces of God's grace and mercy. Acts are examined not simply in themselves, but in their motivations and in their relation to what Augustine became in performing them. They are placed in the setting of the person's ineradicable desire for the good, which is at root the thirst for God, however much this may be obscured in the course of life. Life is re-ordered by this confession, with its narrative form and its attention to desires and motivations and to the wholeness of a person's existence from start to eternity. Because it is addressed to God and invokes the grace of Christ, it cannot be a confession of sin without at the same time being a confession of faith and a confession of praise.

This attention to the roots of sin, to the tension between sin and grace, and to the re-ordering of life by attention to deep motivations, is a constant and integral part of tradition, though often expressed in different ways. The narrative form, however much to be recommended, is not always kept, for practical interest can choose other modalities of scrutiny, such as the listing of capital sins.[2] The capital sins did not serve quite the same function as a later listing of the ten commandments in models for the examination of conscience, since the capital sins were not viewed as deeds to be acknowledged but as tendencies of the heart found behind many actions. These were to be brought to consciousness and confessed before God if deeds themselves were to be changed and the cancer of sin removed. This effort to get at the roots of conduct appears to be much more important in the early penitential tradition than a precise enumeration of misdeeds, though it exists in tension with that kind of attention to precise acts of which some persons are only capable.

For great spiritual writers, and here one might think not only of Augustine but of such persons as John Cassian and Isidore of Seville, confession of sins is ultimately a matter between God and the sinner. It is a constant need of daily Christian living and serves to forge and deepen a relationship with God. None of the prescriptions about canonical penance or of the admonitions to monks to confess to spiritual guides can obscure this fact. There was indeed the role that the confessor or spiritual guide could play in helping the person examine heart and conduct and in choosing appropriate penances, and thus in mediating sound confession, but this mediation was not exactly the same in canonical penance and in personal guidance. In the former it had to lead to some appropriate public acknowledgment of being a sinner and to public reconciliation with the church.

When the boundaries between canonical penance and other forms of confession and penance dissolved, the confession of sin related to the sacrament in new ways, and was more constantly, and for all, related to sacramental practice, even though the possibility of confession to laypersons remained for a long time. This confession to priests served in the first place as an intensification of the Christian life and as a means of receiving guidance from priests. It could and did also serve as a control on beliefs, made concrete in the law of confession to one's own pastor, as well as a control on ethical behavior and universal norms of conduct in society. The more precision was asked in confession, the more these purposes were served, but the precision could also adversely affect the quality of the act of confession itself. One way of getting around this problem was to separate the act of contrition from the act of confession, but this disjunction does not really serve very well. There is a wonderful model for the celebration of penance between confessor and penitent in the work of Lanfranc of Canterbury, where he presents them as co-penitents looking to the mercy of God and united together in confession and penance in a way that reflects the unity of Jesus Christ with the Father.[3] This model acts as a counterbalance to the juridical model, but unfortunately it can all too readily be displaced by it.

In the light of this historical development of the uses of confession, it is important to note that it is the failure of the role of integral confession in mediating commonly accepted ethical standards that has served most sharply to alert us today to the deficiencies and inadequacies of the sacramental practice. In other words, today's penitential practice as prescribed by the church canons and ritual does not adequately serve the naming of sin. Quite interestingly, this failure is illustrated by an increasing appeal for collective absolution (repeated by a number of bishops at the synod) and by its relative success. The quest for this form of forgiveness and reconciliation appears to be rooted in the difficulties experienced in confessing personally. These do not spring simply from an unwillingness to recognize oneself a sinner or to deal with sin in one's life. It has more to do with an uncertainty over what constitutes sin and consequently with how to name it. Collective absolution provides a port of re-entry to a shared religious identity and a shared acknowledgment of sinfulness for many who cannot take the route of individual confession in a sacramental forum. In effect, it provides a communal sign of a social nature which actually allows for a divergence of opinions on categories of sins, thus defusing the threat of a broken communal ethic. People can have resort to personal guidance and even personal confession outside the sacramental forum, while still finding a common ritual that expresses the desire for community, forgiveness, and reconciliation.

Even while seeing the benefits of a less inflated use of individual sacramental confession, and the desirability of communal rituals of reconciliation, one has to recognize the problematic affecting not only the sacrament but confession in its larger form. The diverse ministries that serve the building up of the church in its witness in society have to be addressed more specifically to the question of how to discern and name sin, and to allow people this possibility in their individual and collective lives.

How many priests hearing a series of confessions today

would feel that they meet the admonition of Halitgar of Cambrai (d.830) to pray, weep, and do penance with the sinner? How uncomfortable would they be with the reasoning that it is impossible to take away one's burden, unless it is carried with the penitent?

> As often as Christians come to penance, we assign fasts; and we ourselves ought to join with them in fasting for one or two weeks, or as long as we are able, lest that be said of us which the scriptures say of the Jewish priests: Woe to you, men of the Law, for you load men with burdens hard to bear, and you yourselves do not touch the burdens of one with your fingers (Lk 11:46). Nobody can help the man who has fallen beneath a burden, unless bowing down he gives him a hand: no doctor can heal wounds, if he is afraid of infection. Likewise, no priest or bishop can heal the wounds from which a sinner suffers, or take away the sin, if he does not suffer and pray and weep with him.[4]

The text quoted above belongs to the early centuries of private or auricular confession. It shows, as do some of the rituals of the same period,[5] that the role of the confessor went beyond the hearing of sins, the imposition of penance, and the giving of absolution. He was personally involved in the conversion of the sinner and in the conferring of mercy. Since that time, greater emphasis has been given to the ritual efficacy of the sacrament and to the judiciary aspect of the priestly action. To renew penitential procedures in the church today, we have to take into account the limits of the legal analogy, and to be aware of the many ways in which the reality of Christian penance takes place.

PRINCIPLES OF INTERPRETATION

The term "sacramentalization" in the title of this article indicates the basic principle which is employed. The sacraments of the church are understood to be symbols and rituals which affirm and bring to being the Christological and ecclesial reality of human life. As such, they permit us to interiorize this reality.

An increasingly common way of explaining the sacraments

relates them to the symbolic structures of human existence.[6] The human elements are integrated into sacramental structures, not merely juxtaposed to them. The *verbum fidei* transforms the human in its totality. This is applied to the major events of human life, such as birth, marriage, and death, as well as to certain basic and common actions, such as washing, eating and drinking, anointing, touching. Thus a broader symbolism, and human events themselves, are taken into the order of grace and sacramental meaning. The personal intentionality and desire experienced and stressed on these occasions is related to Christ through the liturgy.

This kind of explanation can also be used to foster understanding of the sacrament of penance. It is possible to examine the human structures used in this sacrament, and the intentionality inherent in attitudes to sin and reconciliation. This is a basis for a discovery of the symbols inherent to the Christian tradition of penance and forgiveness.

To talk of sacramentalization in this way shows why the history of the sacrament has known such growth and change. This causes no problem when the church herself is taken to be the primordial sacrament of Christ. Ritual forms develop as expressions of her life and witness. There is no need for a *historicizing* interpretation of the origins of the sacraments, which attempts to trace any particular form back to Christ or to the apostolic church, or forbids further development on the basis of such explanation.

> Without prejudicing or challenging an immediate historical association of certain sacraments with Jesus in his pre-Easter ministry and teaching, we can state simply that the sacraments in general have been instituted by Christ because and to the extent that, the Church originates with him. The precise meaning of the expression *institution by Jesus Christ* is to this day a controverted question in theology . . . A historicizing exposition is not required, since both the Council of Trent and medieval theology as the authoritative witness refer this expression not to history but to the efficacy of the sacraments.[7]

The sacrament of penance must equally be related to the eucharist, and this can be done in keeping with the above understanding of sacramentalization process. Recently, some writers have spoken of the eucharist as the principal sacrament of reconciliation in the church, since liberation from the slavery of sin and communion in Christ are central to its meaning.[8] Penance is a sacrament of reconciliation and forgiveness only in as much as it is related to the eucharist. Insight from anthropological and religious studies may serve to shed light on how this is so.

Much is now said in these studies about rites of passage or transition, whereby the individual is related to the social group and its value systems. These rites, usually associated with adolescence, marriage, and change of role-status, enable the person to find a new place in the group, and the group to change its attitude toward the person. The time spent in such passage is a "liminal" period, during which the person or group of persons lives, as it were, on the threshold of the community and society, part of it, yet segregated from it. It is a period of purification, discovery, and change, one in which stress is on human lowliness and on the vital forces which serve to create interpersonal communion. Status and structure, even though recognized as necessary to the community, are given little importance in rites and periods of passage. The community ideal, meaning, and myth, have to be personally discovered and appropriated. For this to happen, a person has to realize both one's own lowliness and personal worth, and to find the true force of communion in shared meaning and value, rather than in social structure.[9]

This model of passage can be applied, with changing nuance, to the forms which penance takes in the church. If a person's deviation from the eucharistic ideal is serious and manifest, segregation may be imposed and purification exacted before re-entry to full community sharing. In case of lesser sins or "daily faults" the individual submits to a ritual of self-examination, purification, and confession, whose aim is personal conversion, to a life more in keeping with the eucharistic symbols. This is in part a fuller discovery of the meaning of these symbols, an appropriation of them which affects moral choice and its motivations. Finally, an entire community may choose to live periods of penance as periods of passage or "exile," of communal poverty and humility, learning thereby to live more fully the reality of reconciliation in Jesus Christ as an ongoing process.

THE HISTORY OF PENANCE: SOME OBSERVATIONS

For the history of penance one can draw on such authoritative sources as Vorgrimler or Vogel.[10] I do not want to add to that history, but only to make some observations about the meaning which it conveys, or the factors which need further understanding.

The relation of penitential procedures to the eucharist is very evident in early church practices. Certain sins excluded a person totally from the eucharistic community. Yet this did not necessarily mean that God's forgiveness was withheld. What it did mean was that as far as the church was concerned, one had not kept that holiness of life which sharing in the eucharist requires. When reconciliation was allowed (and the fluctuations of that history are well known), public penance and public rites of reintegration were required. The hardness of the discipline even gave rise to the curious situation wherein the sinner, having repented of sin, was allowed the eucharist, without having been fully reconciled with the church because the exacted penance had not been performed.[11] This reconciliation could well be given in danger of approaching death, because then there was no further risk of the anomalous situation of a person living full church membership without having done public, or at least necessary, penance. The meaning of this needs to be further probed, as do the exact implications of the penances prescribed by the *Libri Penitentiales*, which maintain something of the offical and social character of penance beyond the age of canonical penance. In other words, what is to be asked is the meaning of acts of penance and purification, when these do not simply envisage the conversion of the individual, but have a bearing on membership of the church community.

Besides canonical penance and its medieval offshoots, the early church had other forms of sacramentalizing penance and conversion, which were applicable to all the members of the community. These were fasts, vigils of prayer, almsgiving, and pilgrimage. Origen's list is typical: besides baptism and martyrdom, which he lists in first and second place, and canonical penance, which he lists in seventh, he mentions four other ways whereby sins are remitted according to the Gospel: "The third is almsgiving, the fourth is fraternal forgiveness, the fifth is fraternal correction, and sixth is charity, which covers a multitude of sins."[12]

The explication of the quality of the church's life in such "sacraments" (as an older terminology would have called them) serves to affirm that the church is a body always on the way of conversion. On such occasions and in such acts, the whole church places itself in a liminal situation, as the community of the redeemed which lives out its life and witness in the expectation of the *eschaton*.

We are accustomed to the idea that auricular confession came into vogue as the normal form of penance in the Middle Ages. This should not allow us to forget the pressure in earlier centuries of the one-to-one personal relationship between spiritual father and penitent. Origen, for example, spoke of the sinner's need to have a counsellor and guide on the path of conversion.[13] Such office required holiness in the minister, ordination alone being insufficient. This aspect of the relationship is brought out in Halitgar's admonition to confessors, quoted earlier, as well as in the fact that in the Eastern Churches it was the monks, irrespective of ordination, who heard confessions.

Two other aspects of the penitent-confessor relationship were gradually highlighted in medieval practice and scholastic theology. The first was the importance attached to the act of confessing in itself. The second was the requirement of the power to forgive in the minister or confessor. Insofar as these two considerations prevailed in the theology of the sacrament, holiness and the capacity to guide were acknowledged as advantageous but hardly necessary. In technical terms, the minister's qualities are described as accidental to the sacrament, functioning to the good of the sinner *ex opere operantis ministri*. A greater integration of personal interaction into the structure of the sacrament seems presently desirable. This has been done liturgically in the renewal of the rite effected subsequent to the Second Vatican Council. It also has to be done theologically, if the gain is to be consolidated.

A change in understanding can be more readily brought about if the juridical analogy can be modified. A proper interpretation of the teaching of the Council of Trent seems to make this possible. As one author notes:

The Council does not make its own any precise or rigid concept of judgment and judgmental structure. The dogmatic indication which results from a hermeneutic of the Tridentine text is the following: a judgmental structure can legitimately be used to unify the data of faith on the sacrament of Christian penance; but it is always a question of *that* judgmental structure which is compatible with the nature of the sacrament. It follows that the term *ad modum judicii* is much less exhaustive of the nature of the sacrament than it would appear to be at first sight. Rather than being taken as a term which explains its nature, it is one which is put into crisis by the penitential reality itself.[14]

These observations on the history of penance allow us to distinguish three different circumstances in which the sacramentalization of penance can develop. The first belongs to the necessary expulsion of certain sinners and their necessary purification if they are to be fully reconciled with the church. The second concerns the community's constant need to express its sin and its desire for forgiveness and conversion. The third belongs to the order of interpersonal relations on a one-to-one basis, through which the sinner seeks to approach God.

In their own way, these three realities must be made actual for the present time. They are present in some way as the basis for the revision of the rites of penance published several years ago. It is to an examination of their present meaning that we can now pass.

SINS AGAINST THE COMMUNITY

Today there is a great effort to rediscover the community aspect of sin and reconciliation. It is rightly remarked that all sin does injury to the church, and likewise that it is in and through the community that reconciliation with God is obtained. To note this, however, is not yet sufficient. The meaning of canonical penance and medieval codification of sins needs to be further probed.

The imposition of penance and rituals of forgiveness always concern more than the individual sinner. They are not merely ways whereby one can expiate for sin. They would seem to be better understood in the way they affect and reflect social structures and community ideal. As we have seen, the forgiveness of the sinner and reconciliation with the church were not strictly correlative: one could not be reconciled with the church unless one did the due penance. Even if in the course of time the regulations were not too stringently enforced, the existence of the norms had its importance. Some of the things which may at first sight seem flagrant casuistry are not really so. The question at issue is how to maintain community holiness, upholding common standards, without being unduly severe on the individual sinner.

The extreme case to be dwelt with is that of the unrepentant sinner, whom it is felt necessary to excommunicate. Grounds for such action were found in Paul (1 Cor 5:11) and John (2 Jn 10), who state it as a way of removing evil from the community. The prescriptions of early times sound severe to us. But they present one aspect of the matter, which has to be balanced against the readiness to forgive which was always available, even when full reconciliation was regrettably impossible.

Why should it be necessary for the sinner to do penance and be purified before being reintegrated into the community? Or why is it that there should arise the occasional need to bar someone perpetually from full membership, even if repentant? These questions seem to be answered best in the light of their corporate implications and significance.

A useful point of comparison may be the pollution and purification laws found in the Book of Leviticus. The fundamental anthropological structure of such laws is explained by Mary Douglas in her book *Purity and Danger*.

> Culture, in the sense of the public, standardised values of a community, mediates the experience of individuals. It provides in advance some basic categories, a positive pattern in which ideas and values are tidily ordered. And above all, it has authority, since each is induced to assent because of the assent of others. But its public character makes its categories more rigid. A private person may revise his patterns of assumptions or not. It is a private matter. But cultural categories are public matters. They cannot so easily be subject to revision. Yet they cannot neglect the challenge of aberrant forms. Any given system of classification must give rise to anomalies, and any given culture must confront events which seem to defy its assumptions. It

cannot ignore the anomalies which its scheme produces, except at the risk of forfeiting confidence.[15]

Professor Douglas lists several ways in which anomalies are publicly dealt with in a group, not all of them relevant to our present question. The one way of counteracting the bad effect of what goes against the acknowledged public order which interests us here is its classification as impure. Contact with the impure is forbidden to other members. The person infected by impurity is to be purified by appropriate rituals before being allowed back into the group. These rituals have the effect of strengthening and affirming community purpose and order.

The laws of Leviticus mentioned above have to do with the holiness of the community as it reflects the holiness of God. For the Jewish community, holiness was akin to completeness and order, since it was thought that the holiness of God shone forth in the design and wonders of creation. What does not harmonize with order was considered counter to the holiness of God and consequently of the people. Hence there arose the need for laws of impurity and purification. One of the principal areas in which these laws applied was that of food, and about these prescriptions we can usefully listen to Professor Douglas' comment:

> Moses wanted the children of Israel to keep the commandments of God constantly before their eyes . . . the dietary laws would have been like signs which at every turn inspired meditation on the oneness, purity and completeness of God. By rules of avoidance holiness was given physical expression in every encounter with the animal kingdom and at every meal. Observance of the dietary rules would thus have been a meaningful part of the great liturgical act of recognition and worship which culminated in the sacrifice of the Temple.[16]

When we turn from such laws and ideas of holiness to the New Testament, we are dealing with an order of things in which they have been greatly spiritualized. Ritual impurity was practically eliminated from the church, though it crept in again in some forms in later times. Despite this spiritualization, something of the same pattern for the preservation of holiness remains. The greatest abomination for the New Testament community was the sinner who failed to keep the law of holiness of the Spirit. This abomination of sin had to be excluded from the church, and the sinner was not to be readmitted unless ritually purified by the stages and rites of the order of penitents. These were thought to reverse harm done by sin through their stress on the purification from sin which is the gift of God, and through their subjection of the sinner to the recognition of lowliness. In this way the entire community, and not only the repentant sinner, was saved from sin and its evil consequences.

There was the problem of listing sins that merited excommunication, and those that needed canonical penance. This was a question of deciding which sins were in total disaccord with the holiness of Christ's church. A similar problem can be detected in the various prescriptions of the *Libri Penitentiales*. These latter may have in some degree supplied for the inadequacies of confessors, but they are more properly considered as norms for community welfare. The anomalies which disrupt the holiness of the church are graded by the type of expiation which they require. It is the offense against public order which is uppermost in the rulings, not the extent of the individual's malice, though some reference to this occasionally slips in, as when a distinction is made between intentional and unintentional homicide. On the whole, however, emphasis is on the reparation of an offended order of things. A clear analysis of sinful acts and their intentionality appears only in scholastic treatises on sin and penance.

The consideration is not merely ecclesiastical, or a concern about the inner life of the church. Both canonical penance and penitential books can be better understood when related to questions of social order. The crimes most deserving of punishment were those affecting the church's relation to public order, whether this was a counterbalance to other values or a support of public ideals through a system of divine ordinance.

Some examples ought to clarify this relationship. At the time that the church was obliged to find her place in the Roman empire as a recognized religion, orthodoxy in the faith and virginity as a state of life were matters of high concern. The prescriptions of canonical penance alone would tell us this, even if we had no other evidence.[17] Given the other evi-

226 SIN, SICKNESS, DEATH

dence, we understand even better the canonical prescriptions on these two scores. Faith had to be strongly upheld by orthodox statement and profession, since erring in this matter would affect both the integrity of the church and the unity of the civilized world. Virginity, on the other hand, was of prime importance to a church which in time of peace sought a sign of the *eschaton* to replace that of martyrdom.

From the penitential books we derive a thumb-nail sketch of medieval culture and of the church's part in maintaining public order. We see how she had to regulate her own life in face of the threats of false worship and superstition which came with the entry into her ranks of the northern, Visigothic and Celtic hordes. In the medieval context, this was a question of both religious and political unity. Another point on which the penitentials show much concern is that of sexual mores. This is hardly explicable only on the basis of scrupulousness about sex. It is more fully understood in light of the close link between sexual order and public order. The quality of life in society, public relations, and economic systems are all affected by how people behave in the domain of sex.[18]

If this communitary explanation of the expiation of sins is correct, then there are a number of questions which arise for our own current attitudes and practices. In the liberal approach to morals which leaves so much to the conscience of the individual, we may forget the importance which it has for the community to establish standards of holiness and to redress anomalies ritually. Not that we can advocate a return to the norms of the fourth or fifth centuries, for it is a contemporary condition which the church now faces, and the evils of the times are different. At present we might well wonder about the Gospel values held by Christians or about the values of their witness to Christ, if the church practices an easy tolerance of, or offers a facile reconciliation to the racist, the extortioner, the building speculator, or in short to any person who lives on another's wound. It is the church's own reality, her values, and her witness, which are at stake.

It may well be that in our present age the needs of community holiness and witness are not to be met by sanctions against public sinners. Solidarity in the common evil may well be such that nothing less is required than a prophetic word addressed to the entire Christian community, as a corporate body. It is this need which underscores the need for community expressions of penance, conversion, and reconciliation. This is an approach which has been fostered by the recent renewal of the rites of penance, and we shall now turn our attention to this form of celebration in the life of the church.

EXPRESSIONS OF COMMUNITY PENANCE

It is not enough to expel the old leaven and take action against the most striking of offenses. In other ways also, the church seeks to invigorate her quest for constant repentance and reconciliation. Fasting, vigil, deeds of mercy, pilgrimage (to take but some examples) all belong to community penance. Every symbolic form, it can be said, in which Christians express their sense of sin and their desire for reconciliation in the Spirit belongs to the sacramentalization of penance.

Today, the church's felt need to sacramentalize these realities has taken on the particular form of communal celebrations of penance. This seems an appropriate way for Christians to re-examine the nature of sin, and their own involvement in sinful ways. It is admitted that in the past theology and catechesis on sin have been somewhat wayward and the expectations of salvation devious. A renewal in the spirit of the Scriptures through liturgical use of its symbols of evil and redemption seems singularly beneficial and meaningful.

The elements of penance brought to the fore in community celebration are those which were all too easily missed in the exclusive practice of private confession. They can be listed under two headings: (1) a better appreciation of the nature of the act of confession itself, when it is placed in a more complete context; (2) a use of symbolic language suited to the relation that exists between moral judgment and faith commitment.

What it means to confess sin is elucidated by the relation to God's word and to the church assembly which are inescapable in a community celebration. The word of faith calls to repentance and proclaims pardon. It is a word which issues forth from God and is given shape in the word of the church. God promises pardon, and in making that promise calls upon people to admit sin and to start on the way of conversion. Indeed, it is this divine word entering into the heart which prompts a person to repentance. and gives a language wherein to express desires and hopes. The hope whereby one responds to the divine pardon can mean a fuller self-acceptance in the knowledge that one is beloved of God, and a quiet integration of one's past, delivered from the infection of despair. What it means to be able (internally and externally) to confess one's sins is well expressed in the words of the dying priest in Bernanos' novel, *A Diary of a Country Priest*:

> Well, it's all over now. The strange mistrust I had of myself, of my own being, has flown, I believe for ever. That conflict is done. I cannot understand it anymore. I am reconciled to myself, to the poor, poor shell of myself. How easy it is to hate oneself? True grace is to forget. Yet if pride could die in us, the supreme grace would be to love oneself in all simplicity—as one would love any one of those who themselves have suffered and loved in Christ.[19]

The *confessio peccatorum* is also a *confessio laudis*, the confession of sins a confession of faith and praise. It is the type of praise so well expressed by Saint Paul, when he says: "Where sin increased, grace abounded all the more, so that, as sin reigned in death, grace also might reign through righteousness to eternal life through Jesus Christ our Lord" (Rm 5:20-21).

The communal expression of penance also highlights the solidarity which ought to be acknowledged in confessing sin. This means solidarity in sin, solidarity in conversion, and solidarity in the consequences of conversion and repentance. Solidarity in sin consists not only in the fact that we hurt each other by our sins, and hurt too the body of Christ. It is found even more basically in the awareness that we are part of a sinful humanity, lost in evil unless delivered therefrom by the grace of God. It is in this sense that original sin, however understood, needs to be confessed if individual sins are to be rightly set in focus. Solidarity in conversion means interdependence, our need for support, for mutual good example, for prayer. But again this is not enough, for beyond such sharing there is the ultimate equation between humankind's salvation and its reconciliation into one in Christ.

Of the social consequences of solidarity in sin and in repentance, the Old Testament sets a good example. The accusations of the prophets against God's people often had to do with the suffering of the widow, the orphan, the poor and destitute. Whatever may be said about the much disputed question concerning the relation between Gospel and human development, it is equally clear in the New Testament that conversion to God in Christ means turning to those in need (e.g., Mt 25:31ff).

True, existential, and interiorized awareness of sin requires symbolic language. It is through symbol that one is best equipped to confront the reality of evil, to hope for redemption, and to express the transcendent ground of the true Christian moral development. Symbolic language, in its various modes, establishes in living fashion the connection between faith and moral choice.[20]

To rediscover something of the biblical imagery and narrative of the reign of sin, or of the sin of the world, is to become aware anew of the corporate quality of our condition. It is true that the sinner's first consciousness of sin touches on what affects one personally. It is felt as what deprives one of well-being and ideal self-image. At the very most, one may be in some way conscious of adding to the sins of the world. The appropriation of biblical imagery allows the person to experience that sin is participation in the sinfulness of humanity. It drives home the fact that no individual person or community can be saved unless the world is saved, and that the person has to carry not only one's individual sin but the sin of the world. The way of redemption is that of the one for the many, the just for the sinner. He who is without sin is made sin for the sake of the brethren. Hence, it is not enough for a Christian community to avoid compromise with sin. As sacrament of reconciliation in Christ, it attains its full measure only when it takes account of the truth that it is of its nature to be made sin so that humankind can be freed from sin (2 Cor 5:21).

A Christian morality truly grounded in biblical symbol and narrative is grounded thereby in faith and hope. It is not a morality of ethical imperatives, but one having its roots in the desire of the infinite and looking forward in eschatological perspective. This is not to deny that ethical responsibility is necessary, nor to gainsay the need to probe in conscience the response to earthly and human values. What is implied is that all such probing has to be done in the perspective of infinitude and hope, a hope which in the face of earthly destruction and ethical failure still reaches out towards that infinitude which is the sea of love. The Christian and the Christian community are engaged in a constant ongoing conversion, which eventually leads to total abandonment to the Father in Christ.[21]

The new rites of penance allow for those occasions when community celebration concludes with general absolution,[22] as well as for other celebrations distinct from the sacrament in the strict sense of the term.[23] Since there is a sacramental structure of assembly, words, and prayer present also in these latter celebrations, the distinction made by the *Ordo* ought not to be hardened into a separation. These celebrations can also suitably close with a prayer for the Spirit which reconciles us to one another, to all people, to the earth on which we live, and to God.

Happily, the sacramental form given in the new ritual does not depend entirely on the juridical analogy of absolution. Though it concludes with the words of absolution, it is more properly a prayer for the grace of the Spirit.

> God, the Father of mercies, through the death and resurrection of his Son has reconciled the world to himself and sent the Holy Spirit among us for the forgiveness of sins: through the ministry of the Church may God give you pardon and peace, and I absolve you, etc.[24]

This prayer is appropriately accompanied by a laying on of hands, either individual or collective. The ceremony should not be seen merely as a convenient way to give the grace of the sacrament to more people. It is more truly an expression of the solidarity in the Spirit of which we have already spoken. The rubrics of the new ritual may not be completely free of juridical preoccupations and could certainly be read with a juridical mind. This reading is not imposed, and while not undermining the importance of person-to-person confession, communities and pastors who appreciate sacramental expression will know how to make broad use of the concession "on occasional circumstances" to give general absolution to a number of penitents, without previous individual confession. The procedures outlined in no. 35 of the rite, and the sacramental prayer in its new form, will make it possible to go beyond the juridical and individual need to a fuller sacramental awareness of what it means to be a community of reconciliation in Jesus Christ.

Within this community framework, there is a lasting significance to person-to-person confession. It is this which I would now like to examine.

PERSON-TO-PERSON CONFESSION

This is the form of the sacrament which in recent centuries is more generally spoken of as the sacrament of confession. For various reasons it has fallen on bad days. To be healthily and helpfully revived, the human context in which it takes place requires attention. The very fact that it is a confession to Christ exacts a genuine person-to-person encounter between confessor and penitent.

In the eleventh century Lanfranc of Canterbury spoke of the sacrament of personal confession as the mystery of the fusion of two consciences before God.

> The Lord in his person declared that confession is a threefold sacrament: it is a figure of baptism, it is one conscience formed out of two, and it is the sacrament of God and man united in the same judgment . . . Two consciences are fused into one, the conscience of him who confesses is fused into that of him to whom he confesses, and that of him who judges into that of him who is judged. The Son of God besought this unity of his Father when he said: That they may be one in us, as you Father in me and I in thee (Jn 17:21).[25]

Medieval and scholastic theology as a whole had a strong sense of the need to confess to another person, and of the personal dimension of this part of the sacrament of reconciliation. While the principle of confession to bishop or presbyter remains, particularly in the case of grave sin, the importance given to the act of confessing was thought to be such that in the absence of either of these it was advised to confess to a deacon, cleric, or lay person. Indeed, according to the evidence gathered together by A. Teetaert, confession to lay persons was quite common around the twelfth century.[26] The practice was rooted both in the felt need to confess in order to rid oneself of the sin (a kind of exorcism whereby the evil is ejected through the word),[27] and in the persuasion that there is value in another person's mediation.

In fidelity to a tradition which often appealed to the authority of the Venerable Bede, Thomas Aquinas refers to this custom as a "quasi-sacrament." He distinguishes two cases, one of the confession of mortal sin, the other that of daily faults or venial sin. The first is advocated in the absence of a priest, and its efficacy is attributed to the *votum sacramenti*. Aquinas writes: . . . *in necessitate etiam laicus vicem sacerdotis supplet, ut ei confessio fieri potest.*[28] Also: *Confessio laico ex desiderio sacerdotis facta sacramentalis est quoddamodo: quamvis non sit sacramentum perfectum. quia deest id quod est ex parte sacerdotis.*[29]

As distinct from this, confession of venial sin to a lay person stands on its own merits as a kind of sacrament and may be usefully practiced without restriction: *Non oportet quod venialia aliquis sacerdoti confiteatur quia ipsa confessio laico facta sacramentale quoddam est (quamvis non sit sacramentum perfectum) et ex caritate procedens.*[30]

The ground of such discourse is the need to go to God through the mediation of another person, capable of sharing one's conscience and living the mystery of reconciliation in communion before the Trinity. The sacramental reality is this oneness of two persons in faith and penance. It is an effective way of conversion and growth in grace. This awareness of the sacrament of communion with another person has to be rediscovered if the practice of individual confession is to be kept and renewed. This will doubtless lead to a greater use of confession to lay persons, and so at first sight it may seem a threat to the ministry of priests and to the requirements of order in the church. It need not be so, if there is simultaneously an ongoing development in the renewal of ministry. The particularities of confession to an ordained minister may themselves be better appreciated within the context of the sacrament of the other person and the recognized possibility of confession made to lay persons.

What takes place in this personal mediation is reflected in

the symbols which express the relationship to God of the penitent sinner. Awareness of sin is consciousness of alienation. Initially, it means a shattering of one's self-image. It leaves a feeling of dissatisfaction, loss of confidence in the ability to be of worth or to be an effective person. Divine judgment is the symbol of the negative feeling on the part of the sinner who feels excluded from God's grace and God's companionship and who feels judged to be unworthy.[31] To confess one's sins to another is a way to express that feeling. The sense of shame, of fear, of broken self-image, of being judged, become more tangible in the face of the one to whom the confession is made. The confessor's role is not to deny the sin or the lack of love involved. It is not to convince the penitent that despite such feelings one is still worthy in the sight of God. The purpose is rather to convey the positive realization of mercy and forgiveness, the sense of the gratuity of God's love and of the gratuitousness of the gift of conversion. This mercy, forgiveness, and gratuitousness are shared between the penitent and the penitent's mentor or friend in Christ. At one level, it is sacramentalized as something which the confessor is able to give according to the measure of one's own communion with God. At a second level, it is sacramentalized as that which both together hold in complete bounty through the grace of God. It takes time to interiorize this truth and the good confessor will not expect the same response from everybody. One can ask only that step forward which is within the power of the sinner who stands at any given time in a relationship with God.

The merging of two consciences and its sacramental confession can sometimes be achieved between lay persons. There are indeed circumstances when this may be more advantageous than confession to a priest. This is so, for example, when an individual is psychologically unable to open mind and heart to the fullness of the mystery of ecclesial communion. Thus a child's confession to parents is likely to have more meaning than confession to a priest. Normally speaking, a child cannot grasp the meaning of the priest's role in the community since this is outside a child's grasp.

As can easily be seen, the role of the priest is not determined in virtue of the power which he possesses. The analogy of judgment and of power to absolve need to be completed by other analogies, if the meaning of confessing to a priest is to be further clarified. His role in confession is an aspect and a part of his role in the community. What he signifies as ordained minister for the mystery of the church, he conveys to the penitent who comes to confess sin. Confession to the priest, and reception from him of the signs of forgiveness, allows an appropriation of ecclesial communion, in an acceptance of the full conditions of apostolicity, unity, and catholicity. In more simple terms, the personal contact with the priest fosters in the penitent a fuller awareness of ecclesial communion, and can make of individual confession a sharing in the mystery of communion.

It has been suggested that confession of sins once a year might be the general standard for a Christian person.[32] There is no need to set down norms of this sort, but the suggestion does bring home that when done in a serious manner and within the context of ecclesial awareness and celebration, individual confession does not have to be very frequent. When time is given to the exchange necessary for person-to-person confession, and it is integrated into the context of community liturgical celebrations, it becomes an occasion for genuine renewal in a person's life. Frequency is not the norm, but authenticity.

NAMING SIN: LANGUAGE OF CONFESSION

The need for a conversion and an expression particular to our age has been indicated in the foregoing. How then can the language of confession bring the church and its members through this conversion? How does its employment of the forms that appeal to the creative imagination bring an awareness of sin and a hope of purification? We can ask what is the particularly Christian perspective within which confession and conversion take place. Then we can ask what kind of experience this relates. In the cultural crisis to which sacramental practice is now subject, retrieval of the symbolic is imperative.

The peculiarly Christian perspective within which confession and forgiveness take place is discerned from the New

Testament and the Christian tradition. It is that of mercy rather than judgment, of a Father who calls to onenes with himself in the Spirit rather than to the reward of a happy life. In other words, the characteristics of confession and conversion in Christian horizon will be appropriated by appropriating the Father-Son relationship. This is a call and a future hope, rather than something given from the beginning. Sin is to distance oneself from that relationship or to refuse the call. All evil is the consequence of trying to come to terms with existence on a basis other than this. The "necessary evil" is the fact that people have to explore and discover for themselves that no other mode of being in the world is consonant with the tension between finite and infinite.

Already in the story of Adam and Eve we see the experience of alienation at the root of existence. This whole experience, as described by Paul Ricoeur, can be summarized in the symbols of stain, missing the mark and guilt (i.e., the attitude before a tribunal of justice of one who has to accept responsibility for what goes wrong).[33] It is easy to stay at this last stage and to try to repair sin at this level. It is not enough, however, to ask for pardon from a tribunal, but one has to go beyond such an attitude to ask to be taken into the Father's house, in virtue of the superabundance of grace. It is not that guilt has to be removed, but that the powers of the Spirit are to be unleashed. It is true that we are responsible for our own actions, but if we try to calculate the degree and seek justification by works we are under the bondage of the Law. In that case, either the sense of guilt will always remain, or there arises a false self-righteousness, resting on the wrong assumption that human works can bridge the gap between finite and infinite. The dynamism of the Spirit released, the hope to which it gives rise may be appropriated. This calls for an extraordinary death to oneself as "responsible," as also to the image of the Father as one whose benignity gives us our head. Our freedom is to lose it.

The horizon set, the language of confession emerges as a response to the way in which the call to conversion is put. Confession is a response, not a beginning. Its terms and images are properly dictated by the call. As an example of the manifold ways in which the Gospel states the call to conversion, we can examine the parables, the Beatitudes, and the Law as three complementary forms.

Cosmic and oneiric symbols relate the human to the sacred, the *mysterium fascinans et tremendum* of sharing in the divine. Poetic narrative and myth give a vision whereby these symbols are brought into the domain of human life. But the confession of sin is about behavior, about the faith and ethical response to the divine call in daily living. It is to this need that the threefold call mentioned corresponds.

It is only recently that the full force of the parable as literary and proclamatory device has been appreciated. Its advantage is to combine the extraordinary and the ordinary. As extended metaphor, it shows how the relations and doings of ordinary life are changed once they are allowed to partake of the extraordinary. The question put by the parable asks what happens when relations with God and others are put on a footing which is determined by the Gospel of Jesus Christ.

> Those fictions [parables] redescribe ordinary existence to show how authentic existence itself may occur: a life lived totally in and by the event, the gift of faith and faith alone. In reading the parables, we may suddenly find our imagination conceiving the possibility that, after all, it may yet be possible to live as if in the presence of a God whose love knows no limits. We find our sensitivities alert to the possibility that the mystics may indeed have found that this God can be loved in return without restriction . . . we may also find that such "a way" does not ask us to leave this world for some "greater" supernatural realm (but) . . . provide the basic orientation to our lives.[34]

The parables do not give concrete moral norms, governing particular situations, as once they were thought to do, at the risk of being allegorized. Instead, they are concerned with the type of relations which people live when they stand in face of God. They depict a relation which belongs to the everyday world, but which, present in that world, change everything. The Beatitudes, or passages such as the Sermon on the Mount, are more explicit about the values which are proclaimed as part of the liberating message of the Gospel. These, therefore, come next in the call to conversion and in examination of conscience. Through the parables they have been set in the context of response to a loving and merciful God. Proclaimed as essential to the Gospel, they remind us that unless we enter into the experience of living by the values which underpin the Gospel of liberation, we have no ground on which to stand, no experience out of which to hope in God as Father. In other words, God can be known only by those who live by the wisdom inherent in the ethical values proclaimed in the Beatitudes.

While the Decalogue has been much abused as a formula for the examination of conscience, it cannot be discarded on that account. The ten commandments have indeed often been analyzed as points for the examination of personal or private life. Properly interpreted, they are a social code, and so an impulse to an examination of the way in which we meet our social responsibilities. Placed in the context of the Covenant, the ten commandments and all other prescriptions of the Law appear as the outflow of the two great commandments of the love of God and of neighbor. Because they have to do with the inherent unity of a people and its place among other nations, when offered in a Christian context they are an instigation to examine the social and even political consequences of the covenant renewed in Christ. These differ from age to age, but the need to think on them does not disappear.

Thus the interrelation between religious, moral, and intellectual conversion is set. The religious horizon is fixed by the parables ("the kingdom of God is like unto . . .") which typify the relations appearing in the kingdom. Moral questions concern the values by which we live, and these are given in the Beatitudes or similar passages of the Scriptures. Thought is required to know how social life is to be correlated, what systems work, what demands are made, if these values are to be respected. The Law questions us as to whether we do not live by another "wisdom," or effectively pursue in social life another order of things, despite the values which we profess.

Sin is to refuse the call of the parables to encounter the God who thus enters our living experience. It is to take up values other than those of the kingdom, or to allow oneself to be mislead in social matters according to a plan devised on purely practical and not on "covenant" grounds. In confessing sin, we address God in hope, accepting the values of the kingdom, and allowing for their effect on every realm of existence.

238 SIN, SICKNESS, DEATH

It is the religious horizon which is in the final analysis de-
terminative, and even changes the questions of the moral and
social order. Through the appropriation of this horizon, one
may move from an order in which externals dominate to an
order of interiority, where communion and not community (as
social oneness) is what counts.

This is the mode of being in the world which is revealed in
the call to conversion and the responding language of confession. It situates humans in the world as beings open to the
transcendent, by the way of the threefold conversion in the
way of conceiving and appropriating reality. The world in
which we live becomes for us the place of God's revelation,
the event of a religious experience of hope.

The archaic symbols of stain, deviation, and guilt occur continually in the language used to express offense against moral
norms. In recent times they were used to bring attention primarily to sexual disorders and to conduct which the church
disavowed. The shift of Catholic conscience (to speak here
only of it) is marked by the ways in which these symbols are
now being used of other types of actions. One can note, for example, how words like "pollution" are used to speak of social
disorder or of the effects of technological progress on the environment. In the United States, to take another example, the remembrance of the war in Vietnam has become a symbol of a
deviation in direction that continues to threaten the country
even years after the end of that conflict. The sins of fatalism,
individualism, greed, ambition, and exploitation constitute the
guilt of a new generation, rather than those of sexual behavior.

A process of renaming sin is going on, though for the time
being it is hesitant and without clear focus. It can go with
some irresponsibility regarding sexual activity, which in face
of increased concern with the social and the public realm
tends to get pushed into what is called the order of private
morality. The answer to this, however, is not to focus anew on
sexual sins, but to direct the formation of a communal conscience about social evil and at the same time to bring to light
the communal and cultural implications of sexual behavior.
None of this can be brought about by a heavy emphasis on integral confession to a priest. It requires a concentration of
many ministries and activities, some addressed to the individ-

ual, some to the community. The multiple function of the confession of sins can be retrieved by separating it, and guidance in making it, from a narrow binding to sacramental practice. There are ancient traditions and there are traditions other than the Western Catholic from which much can be learned in this regard. The formation of a communal conscience can be served by education, and in a very important way by emerging forms of communal celebrations and penance, where too the Western Catholic tradition can learn from others. Though opened up by the new Order of Penance, their development requires a broad retrieval of penitential traditions in a new ecclesial and cultural setting.

Notes

1. *Ordo Paenitentiae* no. 6.
2. Capital sins were not always identical in number, though the number seven came to prevail.
3. *De celanda confessione libellus*, PL 120:627.
4. Halitgar of Cambrai, "Instruction to Confessors," cited by Cyrille Vogel, *Le Pécheur et la pénitence au moyen âge* (Paris: Cerf, 1969) 51-52.
5. E.g., C. Vogel and R. Elze, *Le Pontifical Romano-Germanique du dixième siècle*, vol. 2 (Città del Vaticano: Biblioteca Vaticana, 1968) 234-245.
6. E.g., Leonardo Boff, "The Sacrament of Marriage," *Concilium* 87 (1973) 25.
7. Karl Rahner, "What Is a Sacrament?", *Worship* 47 (1972) 282.
8. Louis Lieger, "Dimension personelle et dimension communautaire de la pénitence en Orient," *La Maison-Dieu* 90 (1967) 158-188; James Quinn, "The Lord's Supper and the Forgiveness of Sin," *Worship* 42 (1968) 281-291; Jean-Marie Tillard, "L'Eucharistie, purification de l'église pérégrinante," *Nouvelle revue théologique* 84 (1962) 449-475, 579-597; J.-M. Tillard, "Pénitence et eucharistie," *La Maison-Dieu* 90 (1967) 105-126.
9. See Victor Turner, "Passages, Margins, and Poverty: Religious Symbols of Communitas," *Worship* 46 (1972) 390-412, 482-494.
10. Cyrille Vogel, *Le Pécheur et la pénitence dans l'église ancienne* (Paris: Cerf, 1966) and *Le Pécheur et la pénitence au moyen âge* (Paris: Cerf, 1969); Herbert Vorgrimler, *Busse und Krankensalbung* (Freiburg im-Breisgau: Herder, 1978).
11. Vogel in the first of the two works cited (pp.15-17, 47-49) notes

the fluctuations in practice, often occasioned by the impossibility of keeping to the severity of the general norms.

12. Origen, cited by Paul Palmer, *Sources of Christian Theology: Sacraments and Forgiveness* (Westminster, MD, 1961) 35.

13. Ibid. 38.

14. G. Moioli, "Il Nuovo 'Ordo Paenitentiae' nella storia della prassi penitenziale christiana e della sua teologia," *Rivista Liturgica* 62 (1975) 66, note 27.

15. Mary Douglas, *Purity and Danger* (London: Routledge & Kegan Paul, 1970) 38-39.

16. Ibid. 57.

17. On the object of canonical Penance, see Palmer, *Sources* 375-385.

18. We may be somewhat surprised to note the presence of what can only be described as ritual impurities, e.g., punishment for eating the scabs off one's wound, or eating animals killed by the violence of nature. We can only suspect that these too must reflect an anomaly in the order of things which was considered ideal.

19. Georges Bernanos, *The Diary of a Country Priest* (New York, 1954) 230.

20. On fear, sin, and love, see Paul Ricoeur, *The Symbolism of Evil* (Boston: Beacon, 1969) 63-70.

21. See Paul Ricoeur, "Guilt, Ethics and Religion," in *The Conflict of Interpretations* (Evanston: Northwestern University Press, 1974) 425-439.

22. *Ordo Paenitentiae*, nn.31-35.

23. Ibid., nn.36-37.

24. Ibid., n.55.

25. Lanfranc of Canterbury, *De celanda confessione*, PL 150:626-627: *Tria esse sacramenta confessionis Dominus in sua persona declaravit: figuram baptismi, unam conscientiam de duobus, Deum et hominem in eodem judicio . . . Duae conscientiae in unam transeunt, confitentis scilicet in ejus cui confitetur, et judicantis in ejusdem qui judicatur. Hance unitatem imprecatur Filius Dei apud Patrem: Ut et ipsi in nobis, inquiens, unum sint, sicut tu Pater in me, et ego in te (Joann. XVII, 21).*

26. Amedee Teetaert, *La Confession aux laïcs dans l'église latine depuis le VIIIe au XIVe siècle* (Paris: Gabalda, 1926) 486-496.

27. Sometimes the desire to confess was so great that confession was made to animals or inanimate objects: thus the knight going out to battle confessed to his horse or to his sword. See Vogel, *Le Pécheur et la pénitence au moyen âge* 31.

28. *Summa Theologica*, Suppl. 8, 2, c.: "In case of necessity, even a layperson can take the place of a priest, so that confession can be made to him."

29. Ibid., ad 1m.: "Confession made to a layperson, out of the desire to confess to a priest, is in some way sacramental: although it is not a perfect sacrament, because it is lacking that which is required on the part of the priest."

30. Ibid., Suppl 8, 3, c.: "It is not necessary to confess venial sins to a priest because the confession made to a layperson is in some way sacramental (although it is not a perfect sacrament) and it is motivated by charity."

31. See Paul Ricoeur, "The Demythization of Accusation" and "Interpretation of the Myth of Punishment" in *The Conflict of Interpretations* 335-153, 354-377.

32. See Jean-Marie Tillard, "The Bread and Cup of Reconciliation," *Concilium* 61 (1971) 54.

33. P. Ricoeur, *The Symbolism of Evil* 3-34.

34. David Tracy, *A Blessed Rage for Order* (New York: Seabury, 1975) 134. Tracy makes use of the work of the scripture scholars Norman Perrin, Dominic Crossan, and Dan O. Via.

14
Let the Sick Call

ERNEST BECKER PLACED THE GREAT ILL OF OUR PRESENT WESTERN age in its inability to accept human mortality.[1] In a world where illness and death are institutionalized in forms which deprive them of their power over society only to place all their weight on the individual, the Christian way of expressing sickness' creativity is a countersign of no mean purpose. To date, however, the theological ministry has not fully coped with the change of wording from "extreme unction" to "anointing of the sick," and all that is thereby implied for the ode to immortality which is the sacrament of the sick.

It is indeed to be granted that theology is ancillary, not the driving force of change. Religious experience is mediated through language which is imaginative and symbolic. Theology mediates, in Bernard Lonergan's words, between the religion and the culture, or reflects upon the place in the culture of religious tradition, in its old and new unfoldings.[2] Hence, theology must disavow any pretension that it is able on its own to remedy the meaningless, or in this case, to give us a good celebration of the sacrament of the sick. If out of a religious past, in a new culture, we are to speak a healing word, it is the poet and songster who will proclaim it. The theologian will be their minister, by reflecting on what is happening.

Studying the sacrament of the sick offers the chance to come to grips, on a particular problem, with much that is now put forward by those who write on hermeneutics or on theological

243

method. Perhaps it is because it has to do with an exemplary case of so-called "limit experience" that it offers such a challenge in a rather unique way.[3] Within the limits, then, of theological enterprise, there are three things that can be considered in this chapter. (1) One can ask what is involved in examining a tradition such as that embedded in the history and literature of the sacrament of the sick. (2) On the basis of the reading of this tradition and with the help of contemporary phenomenology and psychology, one can attempt a phenomenology of sickness and sacramental healing, and of their relationship to one another. (3) The possibilities of theological discourse about the meaning and reality of the sacrament and what is signifies can then be presented.

EXAMINING THE TRADITION

Before deciding on the meaning of a particular tradition, the systematic theologian does feel obligated to know as much of it as possible. Yet, when it comes to giving an interpretation of the tradition as a unit, a selective process is noticeable. One does not give the same importance to all the texts and currents of expression, but gives some value over others.

In the case of the sacraments, that which has often been most valued in tradition is not always that which is most valuable. It has been too readily approached as a "history of ideas,"[4] and with insufficient attention to the kind of langauge in which meaning has been expressed. As pointed out by Paul Ricoeur and others, a phenomenology of symbols and imaginative discourse ought to be post-critical. On the other hand, no examination of a tradition which is insensitive to the forms of language can bring forth a capacity for imaginative discourse today. The form of language is in effect vital to meaning. To come in touch with any sacramental tradition we need to pay great attention to that aspect.

This means that the study of tradition is governed by four niceties. First of all, every text is aesthetically received, listened to for its own particular resonance. Reading back into history, there will be excruciatingly brilliant expressions of Christian hope, but there will also be puny wailings of self-pity. We dare not value both kinds of text equally. Second, every piece is related to the whole complex symbol system. Third, some use can be made of sciences such as psychology and anthropology to enlighten the intended, or unintended but actual, sense of a text. Fourth, the interpretation involves the interpreter and depends in part on how far the meanings and images in the text evoke an answering imagination.

Fundamental theologians may discuss the criteria operative in selecting texts. It is also possible not to focus primarily on ideas, nor on philology, nor even on the rules of rhetoric, but on a keener sensitivity to language, aware that the clue to the ontological potency of the tradition lies somewhere in this sensitivity. This being so, there are some rules which serve inquiry into the tradition of the sacrament of the sick. These can be listed as follows.

1. There is a difference between types of text, and all human discourse is not conceptual. There are the biblical narratives relevant to the topic, as well as the prayers and moral exhortations found in the Scriptures. There are the liturgical texts wherein humans address God in prayer, as well as the use of the Scriptures within the framework of the liturgy, with the consequences this implies for the meaning given to them. There are the legends and the pratices of popular religiosity, which offer hope to those who start life feeling ill-begotten. Nor can one neglect the theologians, some of whom are conceptualists but others of whom belong to a more authentic intellectual tradition. An awareness of the implications of different types of language of expression is needed to glean the meanings offered in these sources.

2. The reader needs to be purified to have eyes bright enough to see what is being said, with the result that reading is never finished.[5] The more clear-sighted the reading becomes, the more one finds oneself going back on some texts, while consigning others to those shelves in the library which gather the dross of centuries.

3. Each text expresses a world, and it is with that world that one needs to come in touch. While we note the milieu, the social environment, the psychological forces at work upon the author, in the end "what is to be interpreted in a text is a proposed world, a world that I might inhabit and wherein I might

project my ownmost possibilities."[6] It is a question of the new possibilities of being-in-the-world which are opened up within everyday reality through the text.

Now, some of these worlds are going to be monstrously disappointing, by no means a response to the capacities that one has come to sense in oneself and others. One must have enough faith in God not to confuse the description of a puny world, however orthodox and Christian in its vocabulary, with a divine revelation or with an authentic tradition of religious expression.

It is not always easy to explain how and why to make this sort of distinction, so perhaps it is best illustrated by an example. The example is a comparison between the prayer for the blessing of oil in the *Apostolic Tradition* of Hippolytus[7] and the form for the anointing of the sick in the *Rituale Romanum* of 1614.[8] Of the former, it has been pointed out that it did not stay for long in any liturgical family; indeed, it has even been suggested that there was a confusion between two kinds of oil, that for baptism and that for the sick, and that the reference to the anointing of prophets, kings, and priests belongs more properly to the former.[9] Despite this, within the context of the care of the ill it strikes one as far more powerful than the well-accredited form of the Roman ritual. In other words, the *status* of the latter may be greater, but its significance is less. Why is it that in effect it conveys so little? Probably, because there is little power of imagination and suggestion in the discourse. It narrows down the meaning of the sacrament to a forgiveness of sins, and very prosaically attributes the sins to the different faculties. The blessing in the *Apostolic Tradition*, on the other hand, makes of the oil a "tensive" symbol, enlightening the manifold possibilities of relating the state of sickness to the sacrament of baptism, to an Old Testament tradition of anointings, and finally to the mystery of the Anointed One, who is Jesus Christ.

4. The reader's own eschatological perspective plays a big part in the appropriation of worlds discovered in texts. This has both its negating and its affirmative moments, which will be found in the tradition on sickness as elsewhere. The moment of negation occurs in what it is said shall *not be*: the sick shall not be deemed useless, the sick shall not be chided for

guilt because of sickness, the sick shall not be alien to the healthy. The affirmative moment occurs in whatever gives a positive measure to illness and allows for hope.

5. The world of popular religiosity is a hard one to enter for any "savant" or theologian, and so it has been largely neglected by theologians.[10] It is also less well documented, this being in the nature of things where it is concerned. Yet it is a world to be known, and it has its own form of classic expression. Francis of Assisi belonged in that world, and his canticle of creatures is without doubt a most striking song for a sick man. No less fascinating is his desire to "die naked on the naked earth." Mother Teresa of Calcutta's thoughts about the sick also belong in this category, it is probably fair to say. Going back in time, one cannot escape the feeling that the peasant's wish to have blessed oil on hand for major and minor ills is as significant as the presbyter's sacred mumblings recorded in rituals and sacramentaries.

6. In the course of research one needs take proper account of the dogmas which the magisterium has propounded on the theme, without being confined by these (deceptively) clear statements.[11] They enunciate some aspects of the experience of illness which belong within the ambit of anointing and sacrament, such as the experience of guilt, the need for comfort, the forgiveness of sin, the reality of bodily healing, and the strengthening of faith. These are important, but on how they can be meaningfully put together the magisterium says little.

In all the work involved in examining a tradition, there is the importance of the functions of research, interpretation, history, and dialectics outlined by Bernard Lonergan.[12] However, in practice, while distinct, the operations are not easily separated, and this is why the above "rules" can help to take cognizance in a judicious way of the tradition on the sacrament.

PHENOMENOLOGY OF SICKNESS AND HEALING

The liturgical heritage relative to the meaning of the sacrament of the sick includes prayers for the blessing of oil, the ceremony of the anointing, the Masses appropriate to the occasion, and the ecclesiastical office *de infirmis*.[13] In all this, there are some points which stand out and give an impression of what is expected in the sacrament of the sick.

1. Sickness is apparently experienced as a state of guilt and sinfulness. The sick person has not the force needed to combat the powers of evil or to adhere to God. Thus the prayer book of Serapion prays that the oil "may become a means of removing every disease and every sickness, of warding off every demon, of putting to flight every unclean spirit, of keeping at a distance every evil spirit, of banishing all fever, all chill, and all weariness; a means of grace and goodness and the remission of sins; a medicament of life and salvation, unto health and soundness of soul and body and spirit, unto perfect well-being."[14]

2. One of the hardships of illness is that the sick person is withdrawn from the bosom of the community, and can no longer take part in its worship. Hence the constant prayers that the person be restored to health. The person may thereby be restored to the church, and once again offer praise and thanksgiving to God at the altar.[15]

3. The entire community is affected by the withdrawal of the sick person, must face this rupture and alienation, and take cognizance of the enigma of human infirmity and mortality. Jordi Pinell describes the office *de infirmis* in the Mozarabic liturgy as a meditation on the mystery of human evil and a prayer for the health and salvation which can come only from God.[16]

4. The object of the prayers, if not remission of sins, is often the request for health in mind and body, one being hardly envisaged without the other. Historians have remarked that pastors and preachers were anxious to counter a tendency to have resort in sickness to witches and sorcerers and so promoted a wider use of blessed oil.[17] People apparently felt that in illness they were subject to occult powers.

5. As indicated in number 2 above, what is expected from God as the culminating blessing, is that the person be restored to the church and to participate in its worship.

6. The healing process is expressed in three ways: (a) the healing virtue of oil, and its power in the hands of God or of the church to cleanse from sin and to restore strength of mind and body; (b) the comfort which is guaranteed through the

prayer of faith, and the forgiveness which goes with it; (c) the play on the word "anointing" which takes in a relation to the prophets, priests, and kings of the Old Testament, to the baptism which the sick person has received earlier in life, and finally to the Anointed in the Spirit, who is Jesus Christ.

The first two ways of describing the healing virtue of the sacrament are found in the prayer of Serapion quoted above, or in this prayer quoted by Paul Palmer: ". . . that the unclean spirit may not remain hidden in thee, nor in thy members, nor in thy organs, nor in any joint of thy members; rather, through the workings of this mystery, may there dwell in thee the power of Christ, all-high, and of the Holy Spirit."[18] The third way is expressed in this same prayer, when it goes on to ask that "through this ointment of consecrated oil and our prayer, cured and warmed by the Holy Spirit may thou merit to receive thy former and better health." It is of course also found in the mention of the prophets, priests, and kings in the *Apostolic Tradition* and later in the *Gelasian Sacramentary*.[19]

All this suggests that in the sacrament of the sick what is at stake is the sacramentality of sickness itself, or perhaps it would be better to say, the mystery which is revealed in the sick person who lives through this experience. In other words, the accent is not on healing, nor on forgiving, nor on preparing for death. It is on the sick person, who through this experience discovers God in a particular way and reveals this to the community. All the other factors enter in, but they are related to this as an organizing center.

To suggest that the core of the sacrament of the sick is the sacramentality of sickness itself, is to take up a particular notion of sacramentality. The sacramental meaning inherent in Christian liturgy is not something added on to nature of human experience. It is drawn out of this; it gives an orientation to the sacramental potentiality which is one with corporeal nature and the human person's presence in this world as an integral part of it.

As individual and as interpersonal beings, humans work out their destiny in relation to the things of this world. They try to do so in terms of an explicit or implicit finality, a finality which needs always to be more and more explicated, but in such a way that the gamut of relations which make up one's life are gathered together and unified in a meaningful way. The sacramentality of experience appears most sharply when one's being-to-the-world is put in crisis in such a way that the question of ultimacy is inescapable. It is thus connected with "limit-experience." The nature of this crisis can be expressed through the images which one possesses through being in the material world. These may be the greater cosmic images of sun, moon, water, mother earth, tempest, etc., or they may belong to the simpler things of life, wherein Augustine pleased to see the specific delight of Christian sacrament. There are but four elements, he said, to Christian sacrament: bread, water, wine, oil.[20] We can, of course, point to a uniting of the two, of the cosmic image and the everyday action, such as eating and drinking, washing, soothing. It is in relation to one's place on the earth and one's place in the human community, that a person suffers crisis, and so it is fitting that the nature of the crisis be expressed through the images and actions which evoke that presence. But it is also through a world which includes such images that the hope through which the crisis may be resolved is spoken.

We can better understand this sacramentality if we take note that a classical instance of passage is discernible in the images and projections of the liturgical action. According to van Gennep's description, passage includes crisis, withdrawal, and return.[21] These three moments occur in illness. There is a moment of crisis and exclusion, when the sick person is taken by illness from the community and forcefully excluded from its worship. This is followed by a moment of withdrawal, when one contends with the forces of evil, but is given strength to renew faith, is purified from sin, and restored to the necessary health of mind and body. Eventually, there is the third phase, coming back to the worship of God at the altars of the church.

This schema of reference is all the more plausible when phenomenological accounts of illness as a transition or passage are taken into account.[22] Illness is indeed a withdrawal, a forced withdrawal, wherein, whether or not it is unto death, one has premonitions of mortality. The sick person senses an alienation from society, with all the feelings of guilt this carries with it. Since it calls the ultimate reality of life into question, it can be counted among the privileged moments of existence. One can howl and rage at it, or whimper in helplessness, or cry out in the despair of hope, like the psalmist whose prayer prefigured the hope of Christ (Psalm 22). It afflicts not only the sick, but their associates as well, since for them also it is a withdrawal of the vigor of life, a disruption of family and of labor, something abnormal to be normalized.

What is the true nature of the return of a sick person to one's companions? Does it necessarily have to mean a return to the full vigor of health and activity? The understanding we are given of sickness and of the psychology of the sick suggests that a return is possible without the recovery of bodily health. The psychology of the sick person can make it possible to resume a fuller human sharing with family and friends, and an interest in the human enterprise which is disrupted at the onslaught of illness. On the side of the healthy, they can move from the unease which is felt in the presence of the ill to their inclusion, even in state of illness, in their continuing life. They have a healing function, which is to support and strengthen, but they must also receive, learning of the sick whatever they communicate to them of the reality and mystery of life.

When we put this in a Christian context, we can see how the sacrament is centered around the sickness and the sick person as the symbol of Christ and of the passage through weakness and death to life. The healing which is offered by Christ is the capacity to share suffering in the hope of resurrection. The sick person is not only the patient who receives the sacrament, but also the agent who professes faith and gives *martyrion*. Return to worship is not necessarily that of a healthy person. More importantly, it is the incorporation into the worship of the church of the sick person's faith and witness. Whether this sense of things was intended by rituals and actors in the past is not precisely the question. It is this meaning that stands "in front of" the texts.[23] It is in keeping with the ancient tradition which made of the eucharist the last of the sacraments of the sick, the final moment of the mystery of the sick person's sharing in the worship of the Body of Christ.

Focusing upon the meaning and symbolism of illness and not upon cure from it, nor even upon strengthening to support it, we can better grasp the harmony of the scriptural images, as well as of the liturgical celebration.[24] The scriptural images are most meaningful in that perspective: the confusion of Job before God when he dares to complain, the sense of guilt attached to being sick, the abandonment of the psalmist into the hands of God, the healing power of Christ which brings faith in the resurrection and salvation,[25] the anointing of the sick person to be one with the Anointed of Yahweh.

The sacramental action derives its meaning from the same organizing center. The premonitions of mortality demand strength which is psychosomatic, for in their face one must still affirm hope in life; the sense of guilt requires the experience of a merciful forgiveness; the taboo of ostracization yields before the presence of the elders and those who surround the sick bed.

Time is necessary to complete the passage, and the sacramentality of sickness is not confined to any one moment. Forced down into the depths, taken unwillingly into the realm of *sheol*, "not going down gentle," the sick must withdraw to meet the dark powers arraigned against them. In the silence, they can hear the voice of God and the Spirit who cries "Abba." How many times one will need to be anointed before this dark passage is complete, how can we possibly guess? The last stage of the passage is the sick person's own testament, the hope to which one gives expression and which marks the exit from the tunnel into light. The community is called upon to stay with the sick through the journey, not intruding but gently corroborating, slowly initiating them into the myths and stories of sickness, death, and healing, so that they will dodge nothing of the darkness and yet be sustained by the light of Christ which beckons.

That illness can terminate in hope, with or without cure, is itself a conquest of guilt and sin. The link between sin and illness is not at all something which keeps the ill away from God. Illness is a human condition in which God is glorified, for the sick become a symbol of Christ who gives his life for others. There is a reconciliation with God and with the church, because there is a reconciliation with one's own human condition, a healing of the feeling of being a person divided, a spirit incapacitated by the weakness of the body. The psychosomatic nature of the uplifting is a question which the theologian perhaps prefers to leave to the medical experts. The theologian is content to profess belief in the unity of mind and matter, and in the redemption God has promised in such a way that Tertullian could exclaim: *adeo caro salutis est cardo*, the flesh is the hinge of salvation.

POSSIBILITY OF METAPHYSICAL DISCOURSE

Past attempts to give a systematic explanation of the sacrament of the sick have been couched to a great extent in terms which speak of causality and effect. This very easily gives the impression of a world in which the person is the passive recipient of many external agencies, including the devil, the minister, ritual, and God. What is needed now is a metaphysical discourse which unearths the realities of being on the basis of the interiority of the subject. Raising the metaphysical question on that basis is more likely to facilitate a discovery of the ontological possibilities opened up by imaginative speech and act.

We need to understand better what is meant by metaphor and other types of imaginative language which break the forms of reality to suggest new ones. Metaphor and image are not merely a matter of comparison and illustration, as a weak use of the words might suggest. The force of metaphor, for example, is aptly described by David Tracy as "a new non-dictionary meaning (which) emerges from the 'twist' which occurs when certain unlikely terms are allowed to interact."[26] Much imaginative speech has this purpose of bringing together what at first brush appear as unlikely companions. On our present theme, the question which interests us is the potency disclosed through the images, symbols, and metaphors used to describe the realities of sickness. What does it mean that those whose condition forces on them intimations of mortality should be offered intimations of immortality, inseparable from this condition? How can one be configured to Christ both as sufferer and healer? How can one in weakened condition, and because of that very condition, be a witness and a prophet to the church? How can a return to worship be requested without any heed to the likelihood of ever setting foot in church again? How can a substance such as oil have so many meanings and powers?

If the words are taken literally, they either have to be naive or an appeal to the miraculous. It is not over-surprising that many will take them more or less in this latter sense, so that even sober theologians try to find explanations for likely bodily healings. This is the fault of the hearer rather than of the language itself. It is only when we allow for the metaphorical character of what is said that we can discern something of its power to express and transform being.

The appropriate metaphysical discourse will turn to the operations of interiority involved in entering into and overcoming the crisis of illness. It looks to the states of being which result therefrom, and to the relationship to object which is part of the operation and of the ensuing state.

The operations, as indicated in our phenomenology, are those inherent to crisis, withdrawal, and return; the paradigm of passage remains helpful when we turn to metaphysical discourse. There are the feelings involved, the values entertained, the adequacy of these values as they are understood and measured against experience, and the choice and commitment which are made, consequent on the entertainment of such values.

Feeling is the vehicle through which values and models of meaning are mediated. In the moment of crisis, what dominate are dissolution of feelings and questioning of the content and adequacy of the value system by which one has lived, with all its presuppositions of meaning. The object to which the feelings are related are, broadly speaking, family, earth, society, and God, under whatever name, implicit or explicit, the Divine may travel. The aspect under which these objects are experienced and viewed is that of the sharing of life, in whatever are conceived to be its most meaningful components. The state of being which results on such upheaval of one's world is that of being in crisis. This implies a questioning of the ground of being or of the ultimate reality and meaning of existence. Is existence participatory, or is the world a populace of centrifugal and dissolving existences?

The time of withdrawal allows for reflection upon the meanings and values of the Christian symbol system. Nonbeing and being enter into conflict. The feelings to be coped with, as they are indicated in the tradition which we have examined, are guilt, alienation, despair. They are countered by forgiveness, communion, hope. A basic image is that of the Son, sufferer and healer. That includes the tension of metaphor, bringing together the two apparently contradictory roles of patient and healer. Other images are joined to this: that of oil as healing, the anointing of the sick person as prophet and the anointed of God.

If one accepts the side of things suggested by guilt and its attendant feelings, one is on the side of non-being. This is a non-being experienced as the result of operational incapacities and the sundering of relationships. It is not possible for the sick person to take a part in the activity of healthy people, to be independent, to bring about a return to health. There is pure negativity here, if one wallows in such feelings. There is, however, also a reality of finitude to which consent is exacted, and which has to be integrated into the positive possibilities of the situation. In his book on the sacrament, C. Ortemann suggests that in relation to the material world a reunificiation of the subject is required which takes in four aspects of existence: reconciliation with one's own body, restoration to a sense of solidarity with the material world, integration of finitude and mortality, integration of the temporality of life.[27]

The perspective within which this reunification takes place is that of eschatological hope. In other words, the new relationships with self, the new sense of identity, the new relationship with the finite world and with time and history, comes about through the ultimate relationship with the Father, who is the object of ultimate hope. Into his hands, along with the Son, the sick person is invited to commit the self, so as to share in the Son's act of redemption. It is the integration of this perspective, the viewing of one's life in this new way, which permits the final stage of sacramental realization, namely, the return to worship. This is imaged in the eucharistic communion of the sick person, in the presence of the community. The operations here involved are consent and hope and love. Community is affirmed, in the Spirit of Christ, in the hope of the Father, for the redemptive "recapitulation"[28] of all reality.

What has been said thus far is that we are best able to understand the meaning of the sacrament of the sick when we take this to coincide with the meaning of sickness. To do this, we can pursue a metaphysics based on interiority rather than on causality. What is then seen to start as a negative experience becomes a sharing in the fullness of Being.

Something more can be said about how this revelation of Being comes about. However rooted in subjectivity our categories may be, a revelation of being and Being is about God. What can metaphysics grounded in subjectivity say to us about that? To answer the question, we have to take full account of the iconoclastic or "agnostic" element in Christianity. It is in the center of human consciousness that the revelation of Being takes place, namely, as symbols make known to one the modalities of one's participation in Being. What is found there is to a great extent negation and the surrender of self to the darkness, and nowhere is this experienced more than in sickness. Rather then than pass from the subject, its operations and relations, to a metaphysics of God which involves the Divine in change and process as Process Theology does, we might stay with Aquinas' injunction that it is easier to say what God is not than to say what God is.[29]

We are familiar with the Heideggerian axiom that the affirmation of God is philosophically impossible and that concern with the truth of Being is the poet's. What the poet sees is the negation of being and the readiness for death which is required for authentic existence. Simultaneously, and on the basis of this negation, the poet can give words to the possibility which derives from the negation of the limitation of being in actual existence.

In one of his essays, Paul Ricoeur remarks that ontology is impossible as long as we have failed to hear the Logos. To hear the Logos, we must live through the death of religion.[30] Here too, we are confronted with the demands of negation. Finally, in the list of "authorities," there is Bernard Lonergan's dictum that the grasp of meaning allows us to shed the empirical residue of time and space.

Now the symbols of transcendence are a word which removes from time and space, that is to say, from measuring out minutes and inches, to introduce us to the eternal and the one (negations of plurality in measurement of being's possession of room to expand). They "create a void" around event or thing, and reveal the "non-being" (empirical residue!) of our existence. This is our "being for death," experienced in sin, sickness, finitude, temporality, all the negative situations and the negative in all situations.

Inherent to the memory which symbols bring is this negation. We are brought back to the origin of personal existence and of all things, to the nothingness from which springs the possibility of all being, to the negation of limited being which is the requirement for the fullness of Being. It is the memory of "negation as possibility" which is the hope of the future, not the sort of memory which takes complacency in details (nostalgia). In other words, it is a memory of "eschatological being," which is the negation of what has been or is, in the hope of what is to be.

In Christian symbols, this sense of Being intuited through negation is expressed in the awareness of the Father as wholly Other, experienced by the Son in his abandonment. In other words, the *via negationis* of Christianity reaches its climax in the symbol of the Father as totally other, to whom the Son's self-surrender is imperative. The fullness of Being which occurs in that relation is symbolized in the Holy Spirit, in whom the Father and Son are united. In the anointing of the sick there is an anointing in the Spirit. This configures the patient to the Son and asks for abandonment to the Father, or, in other words, the denial of being, which is at the same time a share in the fullness of Being. To have reached that point is to have entered into "a silent and all-absorbing self-surrender to response to God's gift of his love."[31] There, metaphysical language has no more to say.

Metaphysically, it is easier to explain the negations involved in Love, more difficult to explain what Love is. But that is not to say there is no Love. Rather, it is to remain, at least sometimes (!), silent about what we experience only in part, but hope for in full.

Notes

1. Ernest Becker, *The Denial of Death* (New York: Collier Macmillan, 1973).
2. Bernard Lonergan, *Philosophy of God and Theology* (London: Darton, Longmann & Todd, 1973) 22, 33-34.

3. For a discussion of "limit-experience" in relation to religious discourse, see Langdon Gilkey, *Naming the Whirlwind: The Renewal of God Language* (Indianapolis: Bobbs-Merrill, 1969) 247-413. In developing the theme as I try to do here, I am following up the possibilities suggested by Lonergan, Tracy, Ricoeur, and others who are influenced by their methods.

4. See Ray L. Hart, *Unfinished Man and the Imagination* (New York: Herder and Herder, 1968) 275-281.

5. See Bernard Lonergan, *Method in Theology* (London: Darton, Longmann & Todd, 1972) 161: "The major texts, the classics, in religion, letters, philosophy, theology, not only are beyond the initial horizon of their interpreters but also may demand an intellectual, moral, religious conversion of the interpreter over and above the broadening of his horizon. In this case the interpreter's initial knowledge of the object is just inadequate. He will come to know it only in so far as he pushes the self-correcting process of learning to a revolution in his own outlook. He can succeed in acquiring that habitual understanding of an author that spontaneously finds his wavelength and locks on to it, only after he has effected a radical change in himself."

6. Paul Ricoeur, "The Hermeneutical Function of Distanciation," *Philosophy Today* 27 (1973) 140.

7. See G. Dix, ed., *The Apostolic Tradition of St. Hippolytus of Rome* (London: SPCK, 1968) 10.

8. Titulus V, Caput II.

9. The reference appears again in the blessing of the oil in the *Sacramentarium Gelasianum*, ed., L. Mohlberg, (Rome: Herder, 1960), no. 382. See Pierre Jounel, "La Consécration du chrême et la bénédiction des saintes huiles," *La Maison-Dieu* 112 (1972) 80.

10. On the relation between "religion populaire" and "religion savante," see Raoul Manselli, *La Religion populaire au Moyen Age* (Paris: J. Vrin, 1975) 16-24.

11. Discussions on the documents are not lacking; see the bibliography in G. Gozzelino, *L'Unzione degli Infermi* (Torino: Marietti, 1976) 193-194.

12. B. Lonergan, *Method in Theology* 127-133.

13. For an ample bibliography, see Gozzelino, *L'Unzione* 190-192.

14. English translation in Paul Palmer, *Sources of Christian Theology: Sacraments and Forgiveness* (Westminster, MD: Newman, 1961) 279.

15. E.g., C. Vogel and R. Elze, *Le Pontifical Romano-Germanique du dixième siècle* (Città del Vaticano, 1963), CXXXIX, nn.15, 18, 21, 26.

16. Jordi Pinell, "The Votive Office of the Sick in the Spanish

Rite," in *Temple of the Holy Spirit: Sickness and Death of the Christian in the Liturgy* (New York: Pueblo, 1983) 191-238.

17. See Adrien Nocent, "Sickness and Death in the Gelasian Sacramentary," in *Temple of the Holy Spirit* 175-190.

18. Palmer, *Sources* 295. Following H.B. Porter, Palmer attributes the rite to the ninth century.

19. See above, notes 7, 9.

20. See Frederick van der Meer, *Augustine the Bishop* (New York: Sheed & Ward, 1962) 13-16.

21. Arnold van Gennep, *The Rites of Passage* (Chicago: University of Chicago Press, 1975). John S. Dunne, *Time and Myth* (Notre Dame: University of Notre Dame Press, 1973) finds the elements of passage in any complete human story.

22. Elizabeth Kübler-Ross, *On Death and Dying* (New York: Macmillan, 1970), shows the stages in the behavior of the dying patient from denial to acceptance. Something of this progression is present in every serious illness.

23. In the sense in which Ricoeur, "The Hermeneutical Function," speaks of this.

24. See Gozzelino, *L'Unzione* 12-60, 116-136.

25. I am thinking of the miracle stories, which are eschatological in intent and ask for faith in Jesus as Savior in this sense.

26. David Tracy, *A Blessed Rage for Order* (New York: Seabury, 1975) 128. Ricoeur's work on metaphor is most important: see "Creativity in Language: Word, Polysemy, Metaphor," *Philosophy Today* 17 (1973) 105-112, and *La Metaphore vive* (Paris: Seuil, 1975), particularly the study "Metaphore et discussion philosophique" 325-399.

27. Claude Ortemann, *Le Sacrement des malades* (Lyon: Chalet, 1971).

28. I take the word *recapitulatio* in the meaning in which it is usually associated with Irenaeus of Lyons.

29. I do not deny the opportuneness of such attempts. I only want to underline another aspect of the matter.

30. Paul Ricoeur, "Religion, Atheism and Faith," in *The Conflict of Interpretations* (Evanston: Northwestern University Press, 1974) 440-467.

31. Lonergan, *Method in Theology* 273.

15

The Funeral Rites for a Suicide and Liturgical Developments

A PRIEST HAD THROWN HIMSELF ON THE TRACK IN FRONT OF AN ON-coming train, to the shock of all who knew him and of those who heard the reports. Never had the diocese seen such a large gathering of people and clergy for a funeral. There was a great sense of tragedy because of the loss of a man admired by all and because of the way in which he had ended his life. The bishop presided at the liturgy and preached the homily. He read a passage from the dead man's diary, revealing that he had for some time contemplated this action. For personal reasons he had found life untenable. The bishop passed no judgment. He asked the people to enter into the anguish of the deceased's mind and to feel the sorrow that enveloped his closing days. He reminded the parents of the man that they should hold in memory all the good that their son had done and assured them of the support and affection of the clergy of the diocese. To sustain the community's hope, he reiterated the belief in the lordship of Jesus Christ over life and death.[1]

Such a scene would have been unthinkable thirty years ago. The priest would have been buried hugger mugger, the circumstances of his death covered over by the veil of uninformed gossip. Today, the event cannot be seen as an isolated

261

one, for it is no longer unusual to give Christian burial to those who have ended their own lives, sometimes even in circumstances more clearly premeditated than in the story narrated. Some Catholics may offer moral justification for suicide in certain situations. More are probably still affronted and disturbed by it. Yet, while a few may still be scandalized by the Christian burial of a suicide, many are unwilling to pass judgment on the deceased person and deem it fitting to commend such a one to God's mercy.

CANON LAW

The canon law of 1917 forbade a Christian burial, or a Mass of suffrage, to all who ended their lives by their own hands. Suicides were explicitly listed in the canons among those to whom ecclesiastical burial was to be denied. They belonged with apostates, heretics, schismatics, Masons, the excommunicated, those who died in a duel, and those who had asked for their bodies to be cremated. The list ended with a catch-all phrase about not burying public sinners and avoiding scandal.[2] In the new code of 1983 this canon remains in substance, but the list of those to whom ecclesiastical burial is to be refused has been changed on several counts, reflecting changed attitudes. Particularly noteworthy is the omission of all mention of duelists and suicides.[3] While omission of the former may be only due to a sense of anachronism, the omission of suicides seemingly reflects an unwillingness to presume judgment upon such persons. This, of course, does not indicate moral justification of the act of suicide, but is more likely to express haziness about the psychological state and motivations of suicides.

THE MEANING OF CHRISTIAN BURIAL

To see the implications of giving ecclesiastical burial to suicides more clearly, it is necessary to look at the meaning of the Catholic funeral liturgy. This has in fact undergone considerable modification since the Second Vatican Council.

Before the liturgical revision prompted by that council, Christian burial was celebrated as an act of suffrage and absolution, having taken on this perspective in the Middle Ages.[4] Ecclesiastical authority exercised much the same power over the souls of the dead that it had exercised over them during life. The absolution over the coffin paralleled the absolution of the confessional. The priest's application of Christ's merits and satisfactions through the Mass to the souls of the deceased was understood to be an exercise of ecclesiastical power, extending even beyond the grave. Theologians were wont to argue whether offering Mass for the dead (as for the living) had an efficacy comparable to the *ex opere operato* efficacy of the sacraments, or whether it was to be understood as a plea in Christ's name to God's mercy, but few doubted the power of the priest to apply Mass for the deceased in his capacity as minister of the church.[5] The use of this power and authority required that the church's minister pass some judgment on the life and death of the deceased, just as the exercise of the power of absolution in the confessional could not be used without making somne judgment on the sinner's worthiness.

The attitudes thus expressed in the funeral liturgy reflect a rather secure vision of the cosmos, in which knowledge about after-life could be based on knowledge about this world. As a person's participation in the sacraments of the church could be based on a distinction between grace, mortal sin, and venial sin, so the church's ministerial relation to someone after death was bound to the threefold distinction between heaven, hell, and purgatory. The church was sure of the harmony between God's judgments and its own, relying much on the promise: "Whatsoever you bind on earth shall be bound in heaven. Whatsoever you loose on earth shall be loosed in heaven."

Morality had the same security, and whatever excluded a person completely from the church's sacraments during life excluded that person from ecclesiastical burial. Heretics, schismatics, and apostates were never supposed to set foot in church, alive or dead. The attempt on one's own life, if unsuccessful, did not carry the penalty of excommunication, but it was considered serious enough to debar a person from any ecclesiastical office for life, inclusive of deposition if one were already a cleric.[6] When the attempt succeeded, the church judged the person unable to be helped any further by its ministry. To pronounce absolution over the coffin, or to apply the merits of the Mass to such a person would have belied the church's securities.

THE NEW FUNERAL RITE

The new funeral rite, which was composed after the Second Vatican Council as a part of an integral liturgical reform, centers in the hope of the resurrection and is intended not only for the needs of the deceased but also for the consolation of the bereaved.[7] The absolution pronounced over the coffin has disappeared, to be replaced by a final commendation of the departed to God. Of this commendation it is said:

> This rite is not to be understood as a purification of the dead—which is effected rather by the eucharistic sacrifice—but as the last farewell with which the Christian community honors one of its members before the body is buried.[8]

In the prayer for the rite the minister asks for a merciful divine judgment and the forgiveness of the sins of the deceased, as well as for a part in the final resurrection of the dead.[9] In those parts of the world where an unordained minister presides at funerals, this rite and prayer are still included in the burial service.

Rather than being expressive of totally new attitudes towards death and after-life, and towards the church's relation to the dead, the introduction of this commendation into the funeral liturgy reflects attitudes in the process of change. Like much else in the new liturgy, it is not without ambiguity. On the one hand, there is a clear intention of removing any suggestion that the church is giving absolution to the dead person, and in that sense pronouncing judgment in God's name. Similarly, the focus of the church's hope is on the communion of all in the final resurrection rather than on obtaining a speedy release of the dead from purgatory. On the other hand, however, the insertion about the eucharistic sacrifice retains some of the old belief in the power of priests to affect the lot of the dead, by obtaining their purification from sin. However, this is now combined with an abstinence from any semblance of pronouncing judgment on the dead, and this is what is most important in the change from the old liturgy to the new. In other words, as far as the burial of suicides is concerned, celebrating a Christian liturgy in their memory implies no judgment on the morality of suicide, either negative or positive, but simply constitutes an act whereby the church commends them to God's mercy.

THE ABODE OF THE DEAD

From what has been said, it seems clear enough that the issue of suicide's moral justification or reprobation is not at stake in giving Christian burial to one whose life has ended in this way. The extent of lucidity and responsibility with which a person commits suicide differs greatly from case to case, but all who were members of the church during life can now be buried with Christian rites. It would seem, however, that these rites need to be celebrated with flexibility, and with recognition of the ambiguities inherent in the situation.

One of the complaints that has been made of the revised funeral liturgy is that it seems to be almost too presumptuous of the resurrection of the dead. In the effort to eliminate the lugubrious images of purgatory and judgment associated with the old rite, those who composed the new rite seem to have acted on the assumption that the dead person immediately reaches final participation in Christ's resurrection. The liturgy is suffused with an air of joy that is seldom muted, so that little room is left for the doubts and anxieties of the bereaved.

Culturally, this seems far from present attitudes towards death. The tendency in the western world to camouflage death, to gloss over its reality and finality, has often been commented upon. This is but the counterside of uncertainty about what it leads to, an uncertainty shared by Catholics. We are far from possessing the sure knowledge of after-life that was common in an earlier age.

In the early church the martyrs could be assigned their immediate place in God's joy because of their witness to Christ given in their own deaths. The manifestly evil could be assigned a place in the lower regions of the universe. All other deceased persons were afforded lodging in a place of rest where they were to await the final resurrection. Some further struggles with Satan, beyond the grave, were envisaged before they could attain their rest, and the remembrance of the dead in the liturgy was believed to assist them in these struggles.[10] In the Middle Ages two things happened to this vision. First of all, not only martyrs but all the dead were deemed to have immediate access to the beatific vision, the resurrection at the end of time being reduced in importance. Second, the place of waiting was turned into a place of purgation. Thus the bereaved who had reason to fear for their dead, because of the incongruities of their lives, could be relieved of their anxieties by the belief in purgatory.

This easy cosmology no longer seems to hold, with the result that fears and anxieties risk being suppressed by the all too ready and facile hope of paschal joy. We could compare earlier and present positions on after-life by comparing a person charting a course by a map on which all regions are clearly marked with a person trying to find a way out of a maze. In a maze there are false trails, deceptive indications, routes leading back to the starting-point. The person looking for the way out knows that there is one, but has to approach all avenues in order to find it. That is the game of being in the maze, and as different routes are tried out, markings need to be made in order to recall each experiment. The person who succumbs to frustration and terror, and fails to keep account of experiment, is lost.

If the liturgy of the dead is to accept some of the prevailing attitudes of doubts about after-life, without losing faith in Christ's pasch, the question is whether it can be charted by a disjunctive rather than by a locative map.[11] The medieval map was locative. That is to say, the ritual and symbol of celebration could place each person, living or dead, on a clear map, in a properly assigned place, and the roads to the various places were clearly marked. All fear and ambiguity could be overcome in this universe by reason of the way in which the church assigned people their places on this map, presuming this to represent God's attitude as well.

The disjunctive map would be more like the maze. Though

some order is assumed, wherever a person is placed on the map there is no clearly discernible road to follow. The rites and symbols of a liturgy charted by such a map would not presume to resolve all ambiguities and uncertainties. They would rather set up a play between the incongruities and highlight the tensions in the vision of the universe. The acceptance of the unknowability of God would be as much its faith as recourse to the knowable. It would accept that finding the way to the exit would bring us into the mercy and love of God, while recognizing that humanity's journeys were searches for that mercy and love. The bereaved would remember how the dead had struggled with the issues of life and death, had sought love and fought with despondency, and they would commend these struggles to God in Christ. There would be a sense that the living and the dead continue to search and struggle together, in the communion of a common hope in which all are involved in searching out the unknowable ways of God and of divine mercy and judgment.

It is within this perspective that in the case of a suicide a congregation can carry out the instruction "to consider the deceased and the circumstances of his life and death and be concerned also for the sorrow of the relatives and their Christian needs."[12] Rather than focusing on Christ's resurrection, or on resurrection in Christ, the funeral liturgy on such an occasion serves to recall the death of Jesus Christ and his struggle with the forces of death, throughout his ministry and at the point of his own consummation. The solidarity of Christ with the human race in its struggle is more likely to touch the hearts of the bereaved than words about our solidarity with him in paschal joy. Indeed, it is only out of the memory of Christ's solidarity with human strife that hope can be born whenever the ambiguities and tensions of life's meaning are as prominent as they are in the story of a suicide.

CONCLUSION

We are living in a Christian age when the church is more prone than at earlier times to recognize the limits on its own insights, sayings, and judgments, This affects many areas of church life. In turning to dogma, its definitive nature has to be combined with its reversibility, however paradoxical that may seem. In acclaiming the Lord's sacramental presence in the church, the negativity of absence has to be embraced along with the comforts of presence. In making judgments in the sacrament of penance, ministers and congregations are aware that there may not always be perfect correspondence between binding on earth and binding in heaven. In other words, whatever the occasion, while much is revealed in symbol, much is also veiled and congregations are learning to live with the uncertainty involved.

In fact, rather than creating doubt and confusion, this ecclesial uncertainty builds a firmness in faith on the foundation of the image of Jesus Christ as God's compassion. In the remembrance of his solidarity with the human race in strife and struggle, in facing the combat with death, there is the ground of hope. The funeral liturgy that is celebrated in the memory of a life that is ended in suicide is but a particularly poignant occasion whereon that ecclesial uncertainty finds its bearings through the commemoration of the solidarity of the body of Christ that was effected in Jesus' death.

Notes

1. For obvious reasons, name and place are not identified here. By way of contrast with the incident recounted, one is reminded of the story by the Irish writer, Frank O'Connor, "Act of Charity," wherein the parish priest has a doctor and undertaker falsify a death certificate when one of his curates commits suicide, so as to avoid the scandal of refusing ecclesiastical burial to a priest.

2. CIC 1240, par. 1.

3. *Codex Iuris Canonici auctoritate Ioannis Pauli PP. II promulgatus,* canon 1184.

4. On the history of the funeral liturgy, see Damien Sicard, *La Liturgie de la mort dans l'église latine des origines à la réforme carolingienne* (Münster: Aschendorf, 1978). For a comparison with the new liturgy, see Richard Rutherford, *The Death of a Christian: The Rite of Funerals* (New York: Pueblo, 1980).

5. On this theology, see Erwin Iserloh, "Der Wert der Messe in der Diskussion der Theologen vom Mittelalter bis zum 16. Jahrhundert," *Zeitschrift für katholischen Theologie* 83 (1961) 44-79.

6. CIC, canon 2350, par. 2.

7. *Ordo Exsequiarum* (Vatican City, 1969) nos. 1 and 18. In this article I am using the original *Editio Typica* rather than the rite as adapted to use in the United States, which has more local interest.

8. Ibid. no. 10. The English translation is taken from *The Rites of the Catholic Church*, vol. 1 (New York: Pueblo, 1976) 654. This precedes the adaptation of the rite in 1989.

9. OE no. 48. English translation, *The Rites* 678.

10. As a good example of these attitudes, see St. Augustine, *Confessions* Bk. IX, 13.

11. See Jonathan Z. Smith, "Map Is Not Territory," in *Map Is Not Territory: Studies in the History of Religion* (Leiden: Brill, 1978) 308f.: "These myths and rituals which belong to a locative map of the cosmos labor to overcome all the incongruity by assuming the interconnections to all things, the adequacy of symbolisation . . . and the power and possibility of repetition . . . The dimensions of incongruity . . . appear to belong to yet another map of the cosmos. These traditions are more closely akin to the joke in that they neither deny nor flee from disjunction, but allow the incongruous elements to stand. They suggest that symbolism, myth, ritual, repetition, transcendence are all incapable of overcoming disjunction. They seek, rather, to play between the incongruities and to provide occasion for thought."

12. OE no. 18.

CONCLUSION

16

People at Liturgy

THE CHANGES IN LITURGICAL TEXT AND CELEBRATION THAT WERE made possible by the decrees of the Second Vatican Council seemed to fulfill many of the aspirations of those who had been active in the preconciliar liturgical movement. At the same time, enacting these changes presented a considerable challenge to the church, universal and local. The chapters in this collection reflect the various questions that had to be faced as the nature of the challenge became more apparent. This conclusion represents both retrospect and prospect on my own work, as it has fitted into a current of liturgical studies.

REFORMS AND RETRIEVAL OF TRADITION

Three principles enunciated by the council were uppermost in determining the first phase of the reform, as they were also uppermost in the studies presented to guide and explain it.[1] First of all, the aim was to so order the rites that the active participation of the congregation would be encouraged to the greatest possible degree. Second, much was made of the need to restore the pristine structures and forms of church worship, since these had been grossly obscured by the accretions of over a thousand years, under the influence of elements in piety and church life that were not appreciative of the sacramental and symbolic, and accommodated sacramental pratice to peoples who did not know the tongue in which the liturgy was rendered. Third, great care was taken to foster simplicity of language and clarity of signs, so that the faithful could readily understand the meaning of rites and ceremonies. After the council, theology participated in promoting this kind of development. Its aim was to make known and understood the biblical foundations of liturgy and the content and purpose of the conciliar norms, as well as to give appropriate historical information on such matters as the rites of initiation and funeral liturgies, which were in the process of reform.

THE SYMBOLIC AND COMMUNITY

One of the things that had dogged the development of the Roman liturgy through a thousand years was that it had been subjected to many external changes that would render it attractive to common piety, without ever undergoing the kind of internal restructuring that would assimilate and educate the prevalent forms and expressions of this piety. Popular devotion flourished alongside the liturgy, often accompanying it, but was never truly integrated into it. In the prayer books and missals with which the laity were furnished up to the time of the council, there were often explanations of the parts of the Mass that owed more to the allegories on the Mass of the ninth- and tenth-century commentators than to its early history or inner structure. Not a few schoolchildren were brought up in the fifties thinking that when the priest washed his hands at the *lavabo* he was re-enacting the gesture of Pilate during the trial of Jesus.

Even the council did not seem to think much in terms of integrating piety and liturgy, contenting itself with the observation that popular devotions should be renewed in such a way that they could foster better participation in the liturgy.[2] The issue, however, of the relation between popular devotion and public worship had been raised in the decades immediately preceding the council, and there was considerable debate as to whether one could make a clear split between the official prayer and the prayers of the church's faithful.[3] One oft-cited example was the true nature of the difference between a common recitation of the rosary and a common recitation of the divine office. The official ruling repeated in documents that themselves were intended to foster liturgical growth was that liturgy comprised all that was contained in the officially approved liturgical books.[4] This was but a canonical answer to a theological and pastoral question. It was in line with much that had happened in earlier centuries when prayers such as the rosary or stations of the cross became the chief nourishment of the laity. The substitution of Paters and Aves for psalms had been a device whereby to give the laity ignorant of Latin a kind of marginal share in the liturgy. As popular piety was modelled on the piety of the mendicants, it was thought that the devout should be able to pray the office as the mendicants did. Failing that, the laity could adopt a suitable substitute. In effect, however, it needed to be asked, as it still needed to be asked in 1965, whether the church as a community of faithful could give proper expression to its participation in Christ's mystery in ways that were attuned both to tradition and to contemporary culture and popular needs.

When it became possible to think of the liturgy as an action of the community instead of as a priestly act attended by the laity, the implications of this question became more obvious. It involved in the first place the need to have a better grasp of how symbols and rites give expression to a sense of community and of how they transform experience and articulate the holy. This opened a new phase of inquiry. It is in this phase that attention to culture develops.

There is a marked difference between the studies that represent this phase of inquiry and those that accompanied the first phase of postconciliar change. Then it was usually asked what liturgical symbols and texts mean, and what diversity of symbolic expression may be found in different liturgical traditions. Good liturgy was somewhat behavioristically conceived as the communication of right thought and sentiment through the enactment of correct prayers and symbols. What later studies tackled was the perception that liturgy's growth is organic, as is true of all symbol systems. They employed more sophisticated means of investigating meaning, appealing to such tools as structuralism and to such sciences as sociology, anthropology, and psychology. These studies show the way in which meaning is given in context, and that by reason of different terms of reference the same ritual can be diversely understood and appropriated by different people. The presumption of some unqualified meaning and effect, issuing from a sacramental institution and tradition, is severely challenged by such awareness.

INTERPRETATION WITHIN LITURGY

There are three kinds of meaning that may be distinguished in the actual celebration of the liturgy. First, there is the meaning that the ritual has when it is taken as a text within a tradition, with a potential to be appropriated. There is, however, also the meaning that is given to the ritual by the participants when they employ it to refer to their own world of reference, one which may not be coterminous with the traditional sense of the ritual. This naturally affects the organic growth of the ritual and the ways in which it is passed on, to what moments of life it belongs, in which circumstances it is celebrated, and so on. One also has to make a further distinction, that between the meaning which may be given to the ritual by the official church representative and that which is given by the other participants.

This can be illustrated by looking at the role of the presider in a liturgy. For many participants, especially on such occasions as weddings and infant baptism, since the presider is a priest he is in their world of reference the guarantor of divine blessings and of protection against evil. As the chief actor in an official ritual of the church, he is on the other hand the official representative and agent of a power that determines the reality of the church as a social body. Many factors in the currently official law and ritual of the Roman Church identify this social power with the power of Christ. The symbols of blessing and divine power that belong within the Gospel's world of reference express a meaning that may be but poorly assimilated within the world of reference to which the other two meanings belong. Indeed, they may be partly stifled by the forms that have in the course of time been adopted to accommodate the official sense of the church or popular perceptions.

Within this context the concern with the pristine liturgy of the first years of the reform takes on a new perspective. The aim of such interest cannot be to restore this kind of celebration. Rather, it is to find a point of reference and a criterion of judgment whereby to assess the ongoing organic growth of the church's worship in its cultural setting.

CRITICAL REFLECTION

These issues surfaced already in treating such matters as the meaning given to the Scriptures in the course of celebration, the influence of popular piety on worship, the politics of liturgical change, or the structures of Christian initiation. A more self-conscious development of critical methodology was needed in order to overcome the gradual decline of good liturgical celebration in some places and in order to allow liturgy to be an integral part of new ecclesial developments through which Christian engagement in human existence was being newly expressed.

Religious sentiment and religious expression are highly ambiguous phenomena. The fact that they belong within the Christian populace or that they are sanctioned in liturgical publications is not guarantee against this ambiguity. Liturgical study has to learn from the methods and perceptions of critical hermeneutics and critical theory, if the apostolic tradition is to be given expression in new cultural situations. It is necessary to understand what has shaped liturgical development over the course of time, to recover and express what has been forgotten or suppressed, and to take account of the pluriformity of liturgical expression. It is common enough to speak now of the one faith and the many theologies. Similarly, one might speak of the one worship of God in which churches participate through a variety of liturgies. One can only write of liturgy as multicultural.

There are three parts to the kind of critical reflection here proposed. First, elements of critical theory need to be evolved that are appropriate to the study of liturgy and that make it possible to see the cultural and ideological factors that have influenced the shape of worship but are not identifiable with its core. Second, attention needs to be given to the connection that liturgy has with experience and praxis. Third, more has to be said about liturgy and culture, since the liturgical movement had scarcely begun to tackle the issues raised by the Vatican Council when it laid down the norms for the adaptation of liturgy to the temperament and traditions of peoples.[5]

CRITICAL THEORY AND LITURGY

Certain difficulties encountered in the course of liturgical renewal can only make those with a knowledge of history and of biblical symbolism suspicious. There is a sense that things ought to be other than they are. Though the new *Ordo Paenitentiae* enunciates the principle of the communal nature of the sacrament and gives texts for communal celebrations, one is hard put to find a congregation in which the community is the real locus of the experience of God's forgiveness. What has happened to penance and what is maintained in the new *Ordo* that prevents the retrieval of such an experience? The suspicion in face of this and other examples is that there are blocks in the life of the church as a society and institution that hinder growth.

Critical theorists are well aware of how much symbolic interaction is at the center of all social interaction and pursuit of common interest and values. They also point out, however, that symbolic interaction can actually reflect specific power systems and promote the ends of particular interest groups or secure the stability of society by establishing the dominance of a particular group or elite. What they then look for is the breakdown in symbolic interaction that prevents participation and interaction of subjects, giving rise instead to various forms of domination. Their interest is in a strategy that fosters the interaction between subjects in the pursuit of common values and common interests. To realize this, they see the importance of restoring effective symbolic interaction.

A number of theologians have applied this kind of thinking to elements of church institution, such as church structures and dogma, as well as to the church involvement in emancipatory praxis within society.[6] Its application to liturgy would seem to touch the heart of Christian community, since this is the place of symbolic expression and interaction where the church comes to be as a faith community. Liturgists will be interested in seeing what factors of church life in the course of centuries prevented the liturgy from expressing a community in which there is neither Jew nor Gentile, rich nor poor, male nor female. They will also want to ask what led to a symbolic expression which seemed to identify the kingdom of God with a system, and God's power with the clergy. The biblical images of hope that are emancipatory and that, if kept at the heart of liturgy would prevent this kind of identification, seem to have been ossified.

One of the things that this critical interest means for liturgy is that it will change the character of its memorial prayer, not of course by replacing Jesus Christ and his death, but in the way in which this mystery is remembered. No society that looks for emancipatory change will achieve it without taking the whole of its past into account. If it looks to the future because of the hope that is given in an originating event, it will not retrieve this without making sense in recollection of all that has happened in between. To the extent that it values its origins for the way in which it expressed the dignity and freedom of persons, it will be obliged to take mind of those who in between have been disallowed a part in the life of the society or who have suffered domination and oppression.

Writers of political theology speak of the need for anamnetic solidarity of the oppressed.[7] When the Christian community looks to the future in the hope of God's reign, it must perforce remember in Jesus Christ all the suffering and oppressed of the past, all those for whom the church has failed and still fails to take a prophetic stand or in whose oppression it has played a part.[8] It cannot do this without looking to its own liturgical structures, to the domination of clerical elements, to the absence of women in the ministry, and to the neglect of what is expressed in forms of popular piety.

As far as forms of liturgical prayer are concerned, more attention will have to be given to lament, where Old Testament paradigms may serve anew.[9] Recent studies on the origins of the eucharistic prayer include the *todah* as well as the *berakah* tradition.[10] While this is essentially a prayer of thanksgiving and supplication prompted by deeds remembered, it was shaped in part by lament and confession of sins. Looking to God's past wonders, the people of Israel also wanted to make sense in this remembrance of sufferings and infidelities. When calamity occurred, God had as it were to be named anew, even as the name revealed in the burning bush was recalled.

LITURGY AND PRAXIS

Such thoughts turn our attention to the link between liturgy and church praxis, or to the way in which liturgy relates to experience. The experience here intended is twofold. On the one hand, liturgy carries the power of symbolic expression to transform all experience by the formulation of meaning, by making out of the world which surrounds us a world of significance. On the other hand, the liturgical community will have special interest in the particular experience of those whose lives and action and prayer can be diagnostic for the whole church.

In the church there are not only individuals but whole communities that are deeply in touch with suffering, with the humanity that is threatened by oppression and absurdity, and yet within that experience are in touch through faith with the memory of Jesus in his death and with the belief that God does not abandon those who are in agony. Out of such living experience, these persons find ways of Christian engagement, of shaping community, and of prayer that are in contrast with much that goes on in the rest of the church. They can point to what is missing or at fault in the established ways. In other words, the church can find itself revealed in the mirror of such groups because of their faith and engagement.[11]

Liturgical development in this critical phase has to attend to such contrast realities. There are many instances that could be quoted. In the United States there are women's groups that convene for feminist liturgies in which voice is given to what has long been suppressed in the life of the church. This is not just a claim to right, but in the very best sense of the word it is affirmative action done in faith. One would hope for the eventual integration of this experience into the full life of the church. In a number of Third World countries, there are basic Christian communities in which people come to new ministerial structures and new kinds of prayer and symbolic action out of an experience of engagement in faith and hope with the poor and suffering. In places like the North of Ireland where populations are torn apart by religious differences, there are communities that are coming to an actual realization of what it means to integrate in one worship Catholic and Protestant traditions.

INCULTURATION

In writing of liturgical adaptation, Anscar Chupungco distinguishes between cultural adaptation or acculturation and inculturation. Acculturation he describes as the process "whereby cultural elements which are compatible with the Roman liturgy are incorporated into it either as substitutes or illustrations of euchological and ritual elements of the Roman rite."[12] Inculturation he describes as the process "whereby a pre-Christian ritual is endowed with Christian meaning."[13] That this twofold process continues to develop in liturgy is all the more necessary because it has much to do with the issue already raised of suppression in the tradition, of marginalization of groups and of suffering. Many of the poor and oppressed continue to find their most meaningful religious expression in the non-liturgical adaptation of traditions that are older than the advent of Christianity to their soil. Since these express the people's needs more deeply, they hold on to cultural traditions that have never been integrated into the church or society, but tend to be ignored or despised. One also notices that those groups who live by the hope of Jesus Christ in the midst of human suffering are often the groups that are most alert to the values of the cultures that have been trodden upon. Although greater attention is now given to acculturation and inculturation, the matter requires more persistent investigation and thought, in a way that links it to church praxis and experience.[14]

FUTURE PROJECTS

The analysis of the liturgical development with which I have tried to keep in touch carries within itself the seed of future projects. Historical studies will continue to be important. Every day research throws new light on historical questions. Paying attention to a diversity of forms and to the cultural aspects of past development allows us to see the ways in which the core Christian symbols and rites are at work and also the ways in which poor or ideological development can obscure or distort their meaning. We can introduce an element of dialectic into liturgical study which replaces the tendency to look for pure and univocal forms.

As the prayer of a people of faith, liturgy for its own development has to attend to non-liturgical prayer and to the prayer that is on the fringes of liturgy. Here it is that one sees how people strive to relate the memory of Jesus Christ to their lives, and from this we better understand what has to be integrated into worship. Not only do we find such prayer in the past, but we also find it in the present. Not only are there popular movements of devotion but there is also the prayer of those groups that, because of their involvement in human suffering and the courage of their faith and hope in the God of Jesus Christ, furnish the rest of the church with models of Christian engagement and with models of the prayer of remembrance.

I hope that the essays collected here may take their modest place in an intercultural collaborative effort, at the service of Christian believers and the Gospel of Christ.

Notes

1. Constitution on the Sacred Liturgy nos. 21-46.
2. Ibid. no. 13.
3. For the story of this discussion, see Salvatore Marsili, "La Liturgia, momento storico della salvezza," in *La Liturgia, Momento nella Storia della Salvessa* (Turin: Marietti, 1947) 137-156.
4. Sacra Congregatio Rituum, *Instructio de musica sacra et sacra liturgia ad mentem Litterarum Encyclicarum Pii Papae XII "Musicae Sacrae Disciplina" et "Mediator Dei"*, Chapter 1, 1 in AAS 50 (1958) 632.

5. Ibid. nos. 37-40.

6. For an overview of how theologians relate to critical theory, see Matthew Lamb, *Solidarity with Victims, Toward a Theology of Social Transformation* (New York: Crossroad, 1982) 61-99.

7. Ibid. 7-12.

8. In his article in *Concilium* 152 (1982) 56-65, "The Bread of the Eucharistic Celebration as a Sign of Justice in the Community" Enrique Dussel recalls the church's compromise with the conquerors who oppressed the Indian peoples of Brazil. This is but one example from many in history.

9. Claus Westerman, *Praise and Lament in the Psalms* (Atlanta: John Knox Press, 1981).

10. Cesare Giraudo, *La Struttura letteraria della preghiera eucaristica* (Rome: Biblical Institute Press, 1981).

11. See Chapter Six in Edward Schillebbeckx, *Ministry, Leadership in the Community of Jesus Christ* (New York, 1981).

12. Anscar Chupungco, *Cultural Adaptation of the Liturgy* (New York: Paulist Press, 1982) 81.

13. Ibid. 84. See Anscar Chupungco's articles in *Concilium*: "Filipino Culture and Christian Liturgy," *Concilium* 102 (1977) 62-71; "Liturgical Feasts and the Seasons of the Year," *Concilium* 142 (1982) 31-36.

14. This has been an interest in the editing of *Concilium* for some time. See particularly the volumes on *The Use of Hindu, Buddhist and Muslim Scriptures in the Liturgy* (never printed in English, no. 132 in other language editions), *Liturgy and Cultural Religious Traditions* (no. 102) (1977), *The Times of Celebration* (no. 142) (1981), *Liturgy: A Creative Tradition* (no. 162) (1983), *Blessing and Power* (no. 178) (1987), and *Music and the Experience of God* (no. 202) (1989).